The History of Civilization

Edited by C. K. OGDEN, M.A.

Ancient Persia
and Iranian Civilization

Ancient Persia
and Iranian Civilization

By

CLÉMENT HUART

NEW YORK

BARNES & NOBLE, PUBLISHERS

First published 1927
Reissued 1972
Published in the United States of America 1972
by Barnes & Noble, Publishers, New York, N.Y.

ISBN 0-389-04457-1

Translated by
M. R. DOBIE

Printed in Great Britain

CONTENTS

CONTENTS

PART THREE

THE SASSANIDS

LIST OF ILLUSTRATIONS

MAP

ILLUSTRATIONS IN THE TEXT

PLATES

FOREWORD

IRANIAN CIVILIZATION

THE series L'Évolution de l'humanité is based upon the idea, which is being more and more accepted, that there is a unity in the history of the groups of mankind. If it cannot be stated that all have one same origin (nor, indeed, can the contrary be affirmed), their solidarity, which is manifest to-day, is seen to be very ancient. However widely separated they might be, there were relations between them which were often close.

I do not think, interesting though the idea may be, that it would be in conformity with a truly scientific interpretation to place on the same footing, in a history of the " world ", every group which has inhabited the earth. It is with reference to the logical factor—the essential element, which is thoroughly explanatory— that all the matter of history should be arranged, as soon as one has a clear view of historical causality and all its articulations.

In conformity with this principle, after describing the great collective and in large part anonymous work which, in the course of prehistory, laid the foundations of human civilization, we have reviewed the great civilizations, differentiated from one another, which constituted the highroad of human progress ; we have seen the formation of the empires which sought to bring human resources together in combinations in which life became higher— but for a very limited number of individuals, for brilliance of " civilization " does not necessarily correspond to the happiness of the greatest number.

Before we continued our study of the Mediterranean world, namely, the countries and groups in which the special conditions of progress to which we have drawn attention came together, it was necessary to take a survey of the great masses of men which Rome left outside, on the fringe of her immense empire. One volume[1] was devoted to the Germans with whom she was in contact and conflict, who were soon to contribute to the downfall of the colossus. Other volumes[2] will deal with the peoples of the Far East who, though one cannot speak of isolation, developed in relative independence, and did not closely knit their history with that of the rest of mankind until late. But first we must call attention to an intermediate people, the Persians, whom we have already encountered ;[3] for it is not enough to have caught an occasional glimpse of them when reading of their relations with their Eastern neighbours or of drives to the West. We must define the part which they played ; if it was less brilliant than that of the Greeks or Romans, it was, all the same, considerable. That is what M. Huart has done in this book, with the authority of his great knowledge.

One has to make an effort to realize what was, as it were, the function of Iran in antiquity. To-day the country is off the great roads of the world ; once it was the connecting link between the Far East and the West ; it saw peoples migrating, and afterwards armies on the march, flowing over the high plateaus, between the Caspian Sea and the Gulf of Oman ; it was a highway and cross-roads of the peoples, where civilizations met.

---

[1] Hubert, *Germany and the Roman Empire*, in the History of Civilization.

[2] Granet, *Ancient China and Central Asia*, and Sylvain Lévi and Foucher, *India*, in this series.

[3] See Moret, *From Tribe to Empire*, pp. 353-4 ; Delaporte, *Mesopotamia*, pp. 264-5 ; Jardé, *The Formation of the Greek People*, pp. 199-201, 266 ff., 320-3, 335-6 ; and cf. Jouguet, *Macedonian Imperialism*, and Chapot, *The Roman Empire ;* all either published or to be published in this series.

The climate of Persia is as peculiar as its position—southern by latitude, but cool or cold by its height above the sea. The country is dominated by snowy peaks ; much of it is barren dessert ; but where watercourses bring fertility, before ending in salt lakes or vanishing in the sand, it offers delightful oases. In these favoured places, where cooling nights follow days of radiant light in a marvellously limpid atmosphere, " trees, plants, birds, the spring have the same look as in our own country."[1] It is the land of the rose and the nightingale, of perfumes and songs ; and its gardens have given their name to Paradise. The enchanted oasis explains all the voluptuous side of Iranian civilization, while the rugged mountains sent down into the plains men of clean morals and manly virtue.

In the course of this flow of peoples, bringing others in their wake, of the making and undoing of states of which we have read in earlier volumes, the land which enjoyed the very special conditions which I have mentioned received a population whose origin—we cannot speak of race[2]—was Aryan, and fairly close, from the linguistic point of view, to that of the people who occupied India. To the movements which took it on to the Iranian plateau and into the great Hindu peninsula " it is impossible to give a date, and we can barely follow their course ; but they probably came to an end between the XVth and XIIth centuries before our era, while their origin is lost in the night of time."[3] While the Semites of Asia and the Egyptians were struggling for the mastery, the invaders of Iran, divided into a great number of tribes, the chief

---

[1] See Loti, *Vers Ispahan*, pp. 4, 50, 106.

[2] See Pittard, *Race and History*, in this series, pp. 316, 360 ff. " When we think of the wide extent of the excavations undertaken in Persia, of the historic, aesthetic, and linguistic riches that resulted, we must profoundly regret that the ' anthropological material ' which would have thrown light on the ethnogeny of that ancient past did not have the luck to interest all the archæologists charged with these important researches " (pp. 362-3).

[3] J. de Morgan, *Les Premières Civilisations*, p. 314.

of which were the Medes and the Persians, absorbed or drove back the native populations. They were subjugated by their powerful Semitic neighbours, more advanced in material civilization than themselves ; but they subjugated these in their turn. They too became conquerors. Beyond the immense table-land rising abruptly from the Asiatic continent, which was their fortress, they extended their sway in every direction. They created an empire even vaster than those which had gone before, " the first of its size to be seen on earth."[1]

Under three successive dynasties, one of which was foreign, among changes of fortune born of its very ambition, this empire developed a composite civilization into which Egypt, Phœnicia, Assyria, Chaldea, and Greece—Asia, Africa, and Europe— introduced various elements ; yet it had a character of its own. It received much from outside ; but the collective individuality which we are discussing assimilated what it borrowed. Amid all this " reception " of different elements, its essential characteristics were maintained. Victorious or vanquished, and even after the period described in this volume, when the history of Persia was for the time being blended with that of the Arabs, Persia continued to be herself, and exercised influence in virtue of her inmost nature.[2]

In the history of the world Persia is a factor of real importance,[3] both because it has contributed towards the fusion of peoples,[4]

---

[1] P. 73.

[2] To understand Iranian life in the Islamic period, " it is simpler and more certain to start from inside than from outside " (J. Darmesteter, *Coup d'œil sur l'histoire de la Perse*, p. 37).

[3] On this importance see the reflexions of Sylvain Lévi (regarding India) in *Nouvelles Littéraires*, 14th March, 1925, and in *Revue de Paris*, 1st and 15th February, 1925, esp. p. 545.

[4] " Herodotos thought that he noticed (i. 135.1) that the Persians were very ready to model themselves on the manners of the peoples with whom they came into contact " (A. Reinach, *L'Hellénisation du monde antique*, p. 283).

and because it has added something of value, which I shall discuss, to the logical development of mankind.

In material civilization, in the arts, Persia was chiefly indebted to Mesopotamia. It underwent the influence of Assyria while it was subject to that country, and Assyria, as we know, was profoundly influenced by Chaldea ; Babylon created Oriental art. But Persia borrowed on all sides. " The ruins of Persepolis introduce us to a composite art, born of the royal fancy, which had gathered into an artificial, powerful unity every artistic form which had struck it in the provinces of Assyria, Egypt, and Asiatic Greece ; it was the caprice of an omnipotent dilettante with a love of size."[1]

Huge size and abundant colour, majesty and brilliance are the characteristics of all the art of the East.[2] But in art Persia had distinctive features. It loved colossal size, but it lightened it. The special feature of its architecture was the colonnade ; these columns, which it doubtless owed to Egypt, were made tall and slender, " in those ancient days when everyone aimed at massiveness and squat strength."[3] Persia was in love with colours, but it blended them harmoniously. It discovered an exquisite blue ; it captured its sky, as it did the perfume of its roses, for the delight of the senses.

The art of Persia was Oriental and it was Aryan ;[4] like that of Greece, to which it was indebted in sculpture, it displayed, to some extent, a sense of proportion and a love of order.[5] Its charm was to

---

[1] P. 89, quoting Darmesteter, op. cit., p. 18.

[2] See Foreword to Delaporte, *Mesopotamia*, in this series, pp. ix-x ; and P. Lorquet, *L'Art et l'histoire*, pp. 212, 220-7.

[3] Loti, op. cit., p. 133.

[4] " Persian art is already a first heralding of Europe " (L. Hourticq, *Encyclopédie des Beaux-arts*, vol. i, p. 119).

[5] On Greek influence, see A. Chapot, in *L'Hellénisation du monde antique*, pp. 278 ff.

affect the Arabs, and, through the Arabs, the Western art of the Middle Ages.

In morality and religion, much more than in the arts, the Iranians distinguished themselves from their Asiatic neighbours.

We only catch a glimpse of the process analogous to that which we have examined in an earlier volume[1]—the development from pastoral clans to fixed tribes, and from them to states—which created a powerful society in Iran. What we chiefly see in M. Huart's pages is the extension of the Medo-Persian kingdom, the formation of an empire—due in part to a formidable armament, and especially to the long pike, but even more to new principles. To leave the subject peoples their liberty, to tolerate their religion to administer them in a spirit which identified their welfare with that of the whole Empire, was a policy at once skilful and moral, utterly unlike the cold cruelty of the Assyrians.[2]

No doubt, Greater Mesopotamia had already been followed by Greater Egypt, which, for the first time in the history of the East, had set up a kind of beneficent protectorate in the place of " the brutal conquests, the thoughtless raids, the systematic massacres, the mass deportations, which to the Semites, nomadic or sedentary . . . had too often been the only way of treating vanquished peoples."[3] But the Egyptians had been gradually led, by geographical or economic motives, to extend their dominion. The case of Cyrus is different. Cyrus, of whom M. Huart gives us an arresting portrait, " is beyond dispute one of the greatest figures in history " ;[4] it seems that he had the " idea of genius " of organizing and unifying the world, and giving it a reign not only

---

[1] *From Tribe to Empire.*

[2] See *Mesopotamia*, pp. vii-viii.

[3] See *From Tribe to Empire*, p. 286 ; cf. pp. 358-9.

[4] See p. 43 below.

*of order, prosperity, and peace—the Peace of the Great King—
but of justice. And his successors inherited this inspiration in
greater or less degree.*

*The vast empire created by Cyrus, Cambyses, and Darius, that
other " administrator of genius,"[1] astonished and frightened the
free Hellenes ;[2] and yet, as a first attempt at an Aryan empire,
it served as a model to Alexander. What the Great King had
wished to do from East to West, Alexander attempted from West to
East. Through the pages of Xenophon, he followed Cyrus. " It
is known that he professed the highest esteem for this Persian,
idealized by an admirer of Agesilaos "[3] and had a genuine liking
for the Iranian nobility. The Persians came to him, astonished
and charmed. He wanted to blend the two elements. The Greek
city expanded to the dream of world-monarchy. It has been said
that " the history of Alexander is part of Persian history, its
normal continuation being the Hellenistic age."[4]*

*To understand the political wisdom and the moral bent of the
Iranians, one must go down to the original foundation of their
religious conceptions. It is above all in the domain of ideas that
the Iranians have left their mark on history. I say " the Iranians"
deliberately—the Persians and the Medes. It may have been that
the Persian was more active, the Mede more speculative ; the
Median tribe of the Magi played a great part in the evolution of*

---

[1] Darmesteter, op. cit., p. 17. On Persian administration, there are some very just remarks in Gobineau, *Essai sur l'inégalité des races humaines*, 3rd ed., vol. i, p. 547, and *Histoire des Perses*, vol. i, pt. iii.

[2] A. Jardé shows admirably that in the Persian Wars Greece defended, not civilization against barbarism, but individual liberty and reason against a humane but despotic kingship (*Formation of the Greek People*, pp. 266 ff.).

[3] A. Reinach, *L'Hellénisation du monde antique*, p. 205.

[4] S. Lévi, *Nouvelles littéraires*, 14th March, 1925. For this Græco-Oriental world, see Jouguet, *Macedonian Imperialism*, in this series ; A. Reinach and A. Chapot in *L'Hellénisation du monde antique*, pp. 201 ff., 277 ff. ; G. Radet, *Revue des Études anciennes*, vol. xxvii, 3.

Iran and of all mankind. However this may have been, the Persian armies were " the missionaries of a religious revolution "; they carried over the world, combined with a new conception of empire, a religion of higher quality—" the least pagan in the pagan world," as Renan says.[1] If the kings of Persia " tried to conduct war with moderation, and treated the conquered with mildness and benevolence, allowing them to keep their religion, their laws, and even their national chiefs," it was because " neither wars nor conquests could make them forget their religious law.".[2] " Full of wisdom," and endowed with every virtue in the eyes of the Greeks, of men like Æschylos, Plato, and Xenophon, Cyrus appeared to the Jews as the emissary of Jahveh. Now, he would never have become an " ideal figure " in Greek legend, and in the Deutero-Isaiah " almost an apocalyptic personage, a kind of pagan Messiah ",[3] if his historical conduct, the part played by Persia, and Iranian thought had not afforded a solid and wonderful basis on which imaginations should work.

It is hard to get back to the primitive beliefs of the Iranians, for the Avesta is a late compilation and, to a fairly great extent, " a Talmud, a book of casuistry and strict observation of the law ".[4] But they seem to have advanced beyond the nature-worship of which traces are preserved in the Gathas, the oldest portion of the Avesta. Many centuries before the Christian era, Zarathustra received a revelation from his god Ahura-Mazda ; and, whether a person of this name did or did not exist about 1100, this period saw the birth of " a purified worship, shorn of the blood-sacrifices which still soiled the altars of every Aryan people ".[5]

[1] *Études d'histoire religieuse*, p. 120.

[2] *Formation of the Greek People*, p. 267.

[3] See A. Causse, *Israël et la vision de l'humanité*, pp. 48-50.

[4] Renan, in J. de Morgan, op. cit., p. 318.

[5] S. Lévi, art. cit., *Revue de Paris*, 15th Feb., 1925, p. 801.

Zoroastrianism or Mazdaism went through changes of fortune. But the Achœmenids, from Darius onwards, and the Sassanids long after supported and protected it, and Ahura-Mazda (Ormuzd) held an ever higher place in the Iranian faith. If he was not the only god, he was the greatest of gods, as the King of Persia was the King of Kings,[1] and effaced the others. He was the sky ; he was light ; he was symbolized by fire ; but he had not, and could not have, an image. His will was for good, and men gained or lost merit according as they observed or disobeyed his law. " All the teaching of Mazdaism tends to produce . . . what a beautiful Zend formula calls humatem, hukhtem, huarestem, *' good thoughts, good words, good deeds '* (Yasna, 19, 45). *Whatever a man's condition may be—priest, warrior, farmer, or craftsman— this condition must be held by ' a pure man, whose thoughts, words, and deeds are pure '* (Ibid., 47)."[2]

The Iranians were well aware of the power of evil ; Angra-Mainyu (Ahriman), the principle of resistance, fights against the creative will, against the tendency to good. But Ahura-Mazda " directs and perfects the world which he has made," and the righteous are the " saviours ", who aid him in the accomplishment of his work.[3] Here we have a doctrine of progress, in righteousness and truth, a teleology which gives history its meaning and purpose.[4]

This victory of the god of goodness, of the beneficent principle, is the triumph of light. Victor Hugo appears as the heir of this

---

[1] " The heavenly kingdom has remained even in Christian tradition as a reproduction of the court of the King of Persia " (F. Cumont, quoted by R. Kreglinger in *La Religion d'Israël*, p. 248).

[2] L. Leblois, *Les Bibles*, bk. iv, vol. ii, 3, p. 773.

[3] See Causse, op. cit., pp. 33 ff. ; J. de Morgan, op. cit., pp. 318-19.

[4] It has been observed (S. Reinach, *Orpheus*, p. 97) that the Iranian pantheon has no goddesses ; it is an active, pure religion, which has no room for asceticism or for voluptuousness.

ancient and noble philosophy ; or rather, his genius recreated both the doctrine and the myth—

" Dieu n'a qu'un front : Lumière ! et n'a qu'un nom : Amour !"

But the rôle of the Persians in the history of human thought was not confined to the spreading of beliefs of their own.　Because they were in relations with so many peoples, and because they treated even the conquered well, they greatly contributed to the syncretic movement which prepared the way for the coming of the universal religions.　As early as the Achæmenian epoch, this movement " began to develop amply.　From the east to the west of the Empire, cults were blended and gods allied."[1]　This process became more marked under the Sassanids.　" Situated in the centre of the three great empires of the time, Constantinople, China, and India, the Sassanian Empire was to be for four centuries the point where the human mind exchanged ideas."[2]　From Mazdaism other religions broke off—the worship of Mithra,[3] the doctrine of Mani[4]—which propagated and at the same time contaminated Iranian thought.　This period of religious ferment has been and will be discussed in other volumes ; here it will be enough to lay stress upon this fact—Persia was of great account in the logical process which was to end in the conception of one God and one morality for all men, in the idea of humanity.

In the portion of history embraced by this volume the difficulties are considerable.　Writing only appeared late in Persia, and we only see the beginnings of Iran through the texts of foreign peoples or through the Avesta, which was compiled two or three centuries after Christ.　Even when we make use of the inscriptions and

---

[1] Causse, op. cit., p. 30.

[2] J. Darmesteter, op. cit., p. 31.

[3] A combination of Iranian and Semitic elements.

[4] " A dazzling combination of Zoroastrianism, Buddhism, and Christianity " (S. Lévi, art. cit., *Revue de Paris*, 1st Feb., 1925, p. 548).

objects excavated, the harvest is not what one could wish. So the author of this book unites with J. de Morgan, with A. Moret, with L. Delaporte, in calling on historians to take up the militant studies which unearth the buried past.

Nevertheless, so far as is possible, with extreme caution, M. Huart calls up the civilization of ancient Persia, in its different aspects. We had no work of the kind in France, and perhaps nothing of the kind could be found elsewhere. Our collaborator is not merely the student who deciphers the East ; he is the traveller who has seen it. By his work of synthesis he will have made a valuable contribution to the Persian studies in which a constellation of Frenchmen—Anquetil-Duperron, Sylvestre de Sacy, Eugène Burnouf, Stanislas Guyard, Barbier de Meynard, James Darmesteter—have left a brilliant record.

HENRI BERR.

ANCIENT PERSIA

INTRODUCTION

CHAPTER I

THE PHYSICAL CONFIGURATION OF PERSIA[1]

THE country which we commonly call Persia is a state
created at the end of the XVIIIth century by the Qajar
Dynasty, of Turkoman origin, which still reigns there to-day.
It includes only a part of what has, in the course of the ages,
been Iran—a term retained as its official appellation in the
Persian language. That name comprises, in addition to the
state enclosed within limits determined by treaties, a certain
number of provinces which have been detached from it by
historical events, such as Afghanistan, Baluchistan in the
south-east, the Pamir plateaus in the east, and Shirvan in the
north. There at the present day men speak, understand, and
write a literary language, Persian, by the side of which local
dialects have survived, chiefly in such regions as are removed
from the political influence of the central power, and constitute
separate states, like Afghanistan and Baluchistan, or in the
provinces formerly subject to Russia, like the Republic of
Adharbayjan, which enjoyed a brief independence and has
lost it again.

This vast land of Iran stretches, in Asia, from the summits
of the Zagros range in the west to the Sulayman Mountains in
the east ; it is bounded on the south by the Persian Gulf, and
on the north by Transcaucasia, the Caspian Sea, and the River
Oxus or Amu Darya as far as its source. Between the valleys
of the Tigris and Euphrates on one side and that of the Indus

---

[1] The Author has taken from Sir Percy Sykes' *History of Persia*, **XXVI**,
a certain number of details which are the more interesting since that historian
has himself explored the country with which he deals. [TR.]

1

on the other rises a huge plateau, trapezoidal in shape, surrounded on all sides by lofty chains of mountains. In the
north, the Alburz range (Hara-Berezaiti) detaches itself from
the mountains of Armenia to follow the southern shore of the
Caspian, its highest point being the volcanic mass of Damavand
(18,040 feet) ; by the Kuh-i-Baba, covered with eternal snow
(16,880 feet), it connects with the Hindu Kush (Paropamisus),
which ends in the Himalayas ; in the south are the mountains
of Kurdistan (Zagros), which turn eastwards, running parallel
to the coast of the Indian Ocean, almost to the mouth of the
Indus. This plateau is terminated in the east by the three
parallel chains of the Sulayman Mountains, running north and
south. It has an area of 1,004,000 square miles ; the larger
half, 637,000 square miles, forms the territory of the present
state of Persia. The plateau is very high, falling gently
towards the north. Kirman is at an altitude of 5,530 feet,
Shiraz at 5,100, Tihran at 4,142, Mashhad at 3,465, and Tabriz
at over 4,000 ; Isfahan and Yazd are at similar altitudes.
The centre of the plateau is taken up by a vast desert, a
depression considerably lower than the inhabited country
surrounding it, but still about 2,000 feet above the average
sea-level.

Geologically, the southern and eastern chains form a single
system, characterized by nummulitic limestone (Eocene
Tertiary) ; on Zagros granite is found in the neighbourhood of
Lake Urmiyah ; the mass of Alvand (11,283 feet) overhangs
Hamadan. In the north-western corner we find volcanic
masses, extinct volcanoes, like Sablan (15,787 feet), above
Ardabil.

The plateau is composed of valleys filled, to a considerable
height, with sedimentary deposit uniformly composed, in the
deeper strata, of a compact mixture of gravel, sand, and earth,
through which shafts and underground galleries can be dug
without sheeting. It would therefore appear that this plateau
was submerged before the Quaternary period.[1]

The climate of this region is extraordinarily dry ; the central
desert is the driest point on the globe ; the high mountains
stop the clouds. At Tihran and Mashhad only 9.30 inches of
rain fall yearly, there is still less at Isfahan and Jask, and
Bushire, by the sea, gets barely 11 inches. The clouds driven

[1] LIa, vol. ii, 3.

by the north wind are stopped by the Alburz, and very few cross it ; so Mazandaran and Gilan are well watered by abundant rains, and have magnificent forests to show, while the plateau extending from Tihran to Isfahan remains arid, and enjoys only a little rain in spring.

But the artificial irrigation of the country has been wonderfully developed from time immemorial. The springs are tapped in the mountains and the water from them is led to the cultivable land by subterranean channels now called *qanats*, an Arabic word which has supplanted the old Persian term *kariz*. At intervals of about a dozen yards large holes are dug in the ground, through which it is possible to enter the underground channel to clean it. These conduits are carefully kept up ; if they became blocked the villagers would have no water, and would be compelled to emigrate.[1]

The climate is continental, and goes through alternations of great cold and intense heat. In winter the thermometer sometimes falls below zero in the plains and more often in the mountains ; men and beasts die of cold when they are caught in the snowstorms. In the high districts the snow sometimes lasts four or five months and prevents farm work. On the other hand, the air is very pure and exhilarating. The heat of summer is tempered by the coolness of the nights ; therefore in this season the caravans prefer to travel by night. Since the towns are not very far from the mountains, the townspeople migrate to upland villages in the hot season, and so avoid the unpleasantness of the torrid heat.

The winds blow with remarkable uniformity either from the north-west or from the south-east, for the mountain ranges make a fairly narrow passage running just in that direction. The west winds which bring the storms from North America, after traversing the Mediterranean, reach the Asiatic continent at Syria, and cross it towards Persia and India, while those which come from the east start in the Indian Ocean and follow exactly the opposite route. In autumn and winter the north-west wind prevails ; in spring and summer, the south-east wind. In certain provinces there are regular winds of great force ;

---

[1] Polybius (x. 28. 3) relates that when the Persians conquered Asia they gave the inhabitants, for a period of five generations, the usufruct of all naturally arid land which should be fertilized by an artificial irrigation channel ; this was to be in payment of the work done to lead in the water.

the district where this phenomenon is most remarkable is Sijistan, where there is a wind called the " Wind of the Hundred and Twenty Days", which may attain a velocity of 72 miles an hour. The regularity and strength of this wind led to the invention of windmills of a special type. The Arab historian Mas'udi relates, in the *Meadows of Gold*,[1] that the Caliph Omar's assassin, called Abu Lu'lu'a by the Arabs, a Mazdean from Nahavand, had boasted of being able to build a windmill ; he must have seen them in the mountains of Zagros.

The great central desert is called Lut by the Persians of the south and Kavir by those of the north. The latter term more especially designates the broad tracts of water dried by the sun, which leave salt on the ground—what are called *sebkhas* in Algeria. In this desert are shifting sand-hills, which make it like the Sahara. It is difficult for caravans to cross it, and it is dangerous to be caught by a storm there ; between the muddy bottoms of the Kavir and the moving dunes the traveller has small chance of escaping with his life.

Between the Indus and the Tigris there is no navigable river except the Karun, and that does not really belong to the plateau of Iran, for it flows for the greater part of its course through the low-lying plains which to-day form the province of Arabistan, known in antiquity under the name of Susiana ; it is a district where the Iranians never dwelt. The Karun has often been mentioned in the Press, in virtue of its navigability, which makes it a possible way of penetration, leading fairly far into the territory of modern Persia (112 miles), but stopping at the first spurs of the Bakhtiyari Mountains.

The Zandah Rud flows from the same mountains, but in the opposite direction, northwards, watering the plain of Isfahan ; after passing under the famous bridges of that ancient capital it loses itself in the swamp called the Gav Khanah.

The Araxes in its lower course forms the boundary between Persia and what was Transcaucasia under the old Russian administration. The longest river in Persia is the Qizil Uzen, which becomes the Safid Rud after flowing through the Alburz mountains by deep valleys, and is the Amardus of the ancients ; its source is near Urmiyah, and its mouth is on the Caspian east of Rasht.

---

[1] **CLXIV**, vol. iv, p. 227.

The Tajand is better known under the name of Hari Rud, the " River of Herat ", and it waters the fertile valley descending northwards from that ancient city, which has belonged to Afghanistan since the middle of the XVIIIth century ; it has little water, and that unfit for drinking, save in flood-time. After picking up the Kashaf Rud, or " Tortoise River ", east of Mashhad, it loses itself in the sand, like the Murghab (properly Marg-ab, River of Marv).   On the east we find the Helmund (Etymander), which flows entirely through Afghan territory, and ends in a vast swamp, the lake of Zirrah, in Sijistan, between Persia and Afghanistan ; its banks are covered with ruined cities whose history has never been written.

The north-eastern boundary was once formed by the Oxus, which now flows entirely through Russian territory.   This river proceeds from the Pamir, makes a semi-circle round the city of Badakhshan, which has given its name to the balas ruby, and then flows north-westwards to fall in the Sea of Aral. Formerly, at an uncertain date, it used to fall into the Caspian, as did the Jaxartes, according to the statement of Herodotos. Strabo, quoting Aristobulos, who speaks of the navigability of the Oxus, declares that goods from India came down it to the Caspian, then went up the Cyrus (the present Kur), the river of Tiflis, and were finally carried overland to join the Euxine (the Black Sea).[1]   At the time of the expedition of Alexander the Great the Oxus still flowed into the Caspian ; then it changed its course, until 1220, when the Mongols, after the fall of Urganj, the capital of the state corresponding to the Khanate of Khivah, turned it, making it resume its old bed, which it kept for about three centuries ; then it again flowed in its present bed, and the British traveller Anthony Jenkinson, who visited Khivah and Bukhara in 1558, states that the Oxus fell into the "Lake of Kithay", which can only have been the Sea of Aral.   It was in the Mongol period, too, that the Oxus, which the Arabian geographers knew as the Jayhun, received the name of Amu Darya, and the Jaxartes, the Sayhun of the Arabs, that of Sir Darya.

A certain number of lakes, all salt, survive of the sea which covered this plateau in the days before it rose.   The west of Persia is remarkable for the three great lakes collected fairly close together in the mountains.   Political vicissitudes have

[1] Strabo, xi. 7. 3.

placed Lake Van in Turkish territory and Lake Gukchah in
Russian Armenia. The third and largest is Lake Urmiyah,
4,100 feet above sea-level, which is about 80 miles long, from
north to south, and 20 miles broad, from east to west. Its
water is salter than that of the Dead Sea and it is about 50 feet
deep.

South-east of Shiraz are the Darya-i-Mahalu, and, further
to the north-west, the lake of Niriz, cut in two by a promontory.
In the east, towards the Afghan border, we find the great lake
of Sijistan, called the Hamun (plain). Its level varies greatly
according to the season, for it is filled by the snows which cover
the mountains at whose feet the Helmund and its tributaries
spring, and the amount of the water depends on the melting
of the snow. In the winter months the whole area is dry; but
as a rule it is covered with water, which rapidly increases in
volume, so that it looks as if the whole country would be
submerged. In years of exceptional flood the surplus water
flows through a broad channel named the Shela into the
Gawd-i-Zirrah, the 'Hollow of Zirrah', a huge depression
measuring a hundred miles by thirty, into which the water
of the Helmund formerly flowed direct. In the spring of 1911,
the Shela was 200 yards wide and 30 feet deep, and flowed at
a rate of 4 miles an hour; this represents an enormous volume
of water.[1]

Another *hamun* of the same type is the Jaz Murian in
Kirman, into which the Rivers Bampur and Halil discharge
their waters.

The southern frontier is formed by the Persian Gulf, a branch
of the Indian Ocean, separating Persia from the Arabian
peninsula. The Persians, who once supplied the Caliphs with
sailors, and navigation with technical terms,[2] are no longer
navigators; the native ships which frequent the ports are all
Arabian. The Gulf is one of the hottest points on the earth,
surpassing even the Red Sea in this respect.

In the north Persia is bounded by the Caspian Sea, which
washes the provinces of Gilan, Mazandaran or Tabaristan, and
Astarabad. The sea is divided into three basins: the
northernmost is the shallowest, in consequence of the silt

---

[1] **XXVI**, vol. i, p. 26.
[2] G. Ferrand, " L'Élément persan dans les textes nautiques arabes des
XVe et XVIe siècles ", in the *Journal asiatique*, vol. cciv (1924), p. 257.

deposited by the Volga ; the middle basin is deeper ; the greatest depths are found in the south. The level has sunk steadily in historical times.

The vegetation of the plateau is everywhere poor and scanty ; it gives a general impression of aridity, and the yellow colour of the earth predominates. Few trees grow naturally, but they are vigorous in districts of artificial irrigation. Turf is unknown, except in a few swampy parts. In spring, for a very short time, the bushes are covered with flowers and the hills produce thousands of Alpine plants, but everything disappears at the first heat of summer. Along the rivers and in the irrigated regions the commonest tree is the poplar ; then come the aspen, plane, elm, ash, willow, and walnut ; pine and cypress are rare. The poplar supplies timber for construction, the plane is used for making doors, the elm is used for plough-handles, and the other trees give firewood. The cypress, acacia, and Turkestan elm (*Ulmus nitens*) serve for the adornment of gardens, in which lilac, jasmine, and red rose are popular ; one variety of this last flower, called *mahmudi*, is used for making attar of roses. Hawthorn and the Judas tree abound in the mountain valleys.

Fruit-trees are grown in extraordinary abundance, though on empirical methods, the peasants being destitute of any scientific knowledge. Pears, apples, quinces, apricots, black and white grapes, peaches, nectarines, cherries and black and white mulberries are found everywhere. Figs, pomegranates, almonds, and pistachios grow best in the hot districts ; there the date and orange are found, and the grape and melon are celebrated. In the mountains there grow rhubarb, mushrooms, manna (a resin yielded by the *Cotoneaster nummularia*), and tamarisks by the watercourses ; the thorny shrub eaten by camels supplies *turanjabin* or ' wet honey '. Caraway is the speciality of Kirman ; asafoetida grows abundantly in the Hindu Kush.

A certain number of plants acclimatized in Europe originally came from Persia. Pliny tells us that lucern (*Medicago sativa*) was introduced into Greece from Media by the expedition of Darius. Mazandaran was probably the original habitat of the vine. The peach (*Malum Persicum*), pomegranate, jasmine, lilac, and myrtle come from the same region. As for the rose, its very name, in the Indo-European languages no less than in

Aramaic and Arabic, indicates its provenance, for in all tongues it is derived from the Zend *varedha*, the 'plant' above all others.

Wild beasts are now rare ; the lion and tiger, which were frequently found in historical times, have almost entirely disappeared. The tiger still exists in the Caspian provinces, and Sir Percy Sykes[1] saw the body of a lion floating down the Karun. The bear (*Ursus Syriacus*) also is rare. On the other hand, there are quantities of wolves, leopards, hyenas, lynxes, wild cats, foxes, and jackals. In the forests of the Caspian provinces stag and roebuck are found, and the fallow deer inhabits the Zagros Mountains. The hills are full of wild sheep and ibex ; the boar, which the Moslems do not hunt, is found everywhere ; gazelles roam over the plains, and the wild ass is found near the marshes. The hare is scarce.

Media was the country where horse-breeding was done on a large scale, after *Equus Przewalski* had been domesticated ;[2] the Nisæan horses of Khurasan were known to the ancients ; to-day three breeds are distinguished—Arab, Turkoman, and Persian. Livestock is represented by our common ox, *Bos taurus* ; the zebu (*Bos Indicus*) is found in the northern provinces and Sijistan ; and in the former and in Susiana the buffalo is also reared. The sheep are of the fat-tailed kind, *Ovis aries steatopyga*, which is found all over the East. The camel has one hump (*Camelus dromedarius*) ; those of Baluchistan are renowned for their speed ; the two-humped camel, *Camelus Bactrianus*, is sometimes seen in the north, brought by caravans.

Birds of prey are numerous, eagles, hawks, vultures, above all the Persian vulture (*Gyps fulvus*) ; among these last one should distinguish the bearded vulture or lammergeyer, the *huma*, which played an important part in ancient Iranian mythology, for it was the protector of the kings ; the adjective *humayun* is derived from it, and means ' august '. Many other birds of our countries are found in Persia ; we need only

---

[1] **XXVI**, vol. i, p. 34.

[2] In Egypt, on the other hand, the horse, camel, and sheep do not appear on the monuments of the earliest Dynasties, but the horse becomes common from the time of the Hyksos onwards. Cf. **XVIII**, pp. 9, 323. A representation of Przewalski's horse will be found on an Elamite ivory plaque from Susa (Jéquier, **LXXXVII**, vol. vii, p. 26, fig. 15), which should be compared with an ornament engraved on a silver vase from Maikop, Kuban, S. Russia (Rostovtzeff, *Rev. archéol.*, 5th series, xii (1920), p. 27).

mention the nightingale, dear to the poets, who sang its mystic loves with the rose. The cock was unknown in ancient Egypt, and was only introduced there from Asia by the Persian conquest ; but we cannot infer from this historical fact that it originally came from Central Asia rather than from any other country.[1]

There are no mines being worked in Persia now, but this was not the case in the past. The Assyrian cuneiform inscriptions tell us that lapis lazuli came from Mount Damavand. Shah Abbas I tried to revive work in the mines, but the profits were small, on account of the cost of labour ; Tavernier speaks of the silver-mines of Karwan costing ten and yielding nine, and says that this had become a proverb. But there is still some activity in this field. Coal is extracted near Tihran and Mashhad, and copper in the Sabzavar district and at Qal'ah Zarah, on the eastern edge of the great desert. Petroleum probably exists from the Caucasus to the Persian Gulf, but few borings have been made up to the present. In 1907 successful borings were made 30 miles east of Shushtar, and this industry is being developed to-day.[2] Petroleum, and also rock-salt, are found on the island of Kishm. Red ochre is worked at Hurmuz and on Bu Musa and Halul in the Gulf, and sulphur is found east and west of Lingah. Turquoises are found at Nishapur, lapis lazuli and balas at Badakhshan, a transparent yellow marble at Yazd, and iron, lead, and copper in Adharbayjan.[3]

TRADE ROUTES

In the East roads are simply mule tracks, of various width, which have been more or less beaten hard by the hooves of pack-animals. But, like roads everywhere, they cross the mountains by the lowest passes, and, after serving commercial relations, they have been ways of invasion and have been used for the transport of troops in the case of military expeditions.[4] It is, therefore, of historical importance to know them.

[1] P. Lacau, *Comptes rendus de l'Académie des Inscriptions*, Sept.-Oct., 1920, p. 363.

[2] **XXVI**, vol. i, p. 38.

[3] F. Houssay, **X**, vol. xxvi, pp. 445 ff.

[4] " The great trade routes have always been, since the beginnings of civilization, the great military routes " (Lammens, " La Mecque à la veille de l'hégire ", in *Mélanges de l'Université St. Joseph*, vol. ix, p. 107, Beirut, 1924).

When the traveller, starting from the once civilized valley of the Tigris, wants to climb to the plateau of Media, his road first goes up the valley of the Diyala. To-day Bagdad is the point of departure; once it was Seleuceia, but the road is still the same; slow caravans and quick motor-cars go the same way. In the past the first station was Artemita, whose site is to be found in the present ruins of Kurustar, near Ba'quba and not far from Qizil Rubat; then one came to Chala, the capital of the district of Chalonitis, now Hulwan; from here the climb begins up the Zagros Mountains, which are called the Pusht-i-Kuh, or 'Mountain's Back'; then one left the Diyala and made for the upper valley of the Karkha, crossing the province of Cambadene, whose capital Baptana is either Kirmanshah or a site nearer the mountain of Bisutun (Behistun) famous for its rock carvings. One passed Concobar, the present Kanguvar, where remains of a temple of Artemis are to be seen, and from there reached Hamadan, the ancient Ecbatana. Here one was on the plateau, and various roads radiated from this point.

Hamadan was connected with Susiana by roads which, starting from Dizful at the foot of the Bakhtiyari Mountains, ran northwards to Khurramabad and Burujird.

From Bandar Abbas, which, till the end of the XVIth century, was called Gombroon, the road follows the plain as far as Darabjird, where there are still palm-trees; from there, two roads cross the mountains, the more northerly by Lake Bakhtigan, also called the Lake of Niriz, and the other by Fasa and the salt lake of Mahalu; both lead to Shiraz. Beyond that city, one enters the Pulvar valley, in which are the ruins of Persepolis, and so goes up to Yazdikhwast and Isfahan.

From Ray, the ancient Rhages, now superseded by Tihran, an easy road, almost entirely in the plain, runs to Adharbayjan by way of Qazvin. From this town a road branches off to the north and follows the valley of the Safid Rud, the 'White River', by Rudbar down to Lahijan in Gilan; the present road runs to Rasht, whence one can easily take ship at Enzali on the Caspian Sea.

Out of Khurasan a road runs from Mashhad to Nishapur, and along the southern foothills of the Alburz by Damghan and Samnan; from there, hill paths over the crest lead to the sea-level in Tabaristan.

Iran is separated from India by the Sulayman chains.   The route by which these have been, and still are, passed is that of the valley of the Kabul River, which bounds them on the north; there are three ways down to Peshawar on the Indus, but the shortest, most convenient, and most frequented is that over the Khaiber Pass.   Through this pass the conquerors of India came—Baber (whose name is more correctly pronounced Babur) the founder of the empire of the Grand Moguls, and Nadir Shah who delivered Persia from the Afghan yoke ; and this was the route taken by the British troops on their campaigns in Afghanistan.   From the plateau formed by this country one can cross the Hindu Kush and go by Bamiyan to Bactra (Balkh) in the upper valley of the Oxus ; there are six passes, but some of them can only be crossed on foot.[1]

These are the chief ways of access.   The country itself, which is almost wholly mountainous, is a network of tracks of the same kind, but these are hardly used except for local traffic, and are of no general interest.   The roads which are important to know are those leading into Persia which were taken by international trade before the discovery of the Cape of Good Hope, and were utilized by the armies of conquerors.

[1] CV, i, 5-119.

CHAPTER II

The Scripts of Persia

THE history of the decipherment, reading and interpretation of the various scripts used by the Persians in the course of their long evolution is one of the most interesting chapters in European learning, and one which is the most to its honour. We owe it to the marvellous penetration of several generations of scholars that we can now read the documents left by Iranian antiquity. When Champollion set out to decipher the Egyptian hieroglyphics, he had the trilingual inscription of Rosetta, the Greek part of which gave him a solid basis for interpretation ; but archæological research was defied by the cuneiform inscriptions, which offered no bilingual monuments, still less trilingual (it is only quite lately that the presence has been reported, in the British Museum collections, of Babylonian epigraphic texts accompanied by Greek versions). The existence of three different systems of writing, probably covering three special idioms, had been established, it is true, but where was one to commence the attack on these texts, formed solely of nails or wedges (hence the name ' cuneiform ') set in every position imaginable ? By methodical research the problem has been solved.

The Persians used three systems of writing in succession :

(i) The cuneiform script, used in the inscriptions of the Achæmenids ;

(ii) The Pahlavi writing of the inscriptions and coins of the Arsacids and of the commentaries on the Avesta ;

(iii) The Zend script, derived from the preceding, and used for transcribing the sounds of the so-called Zend language, in which the Avesta is written.

The Persian Cuneiform Script.—Various European travellers had reported the presence of inscriptions in this writing among the ruins of Persepolis, and had brought home copies. In 1622 the Roman Cavaliere Pietro della Valle had observed that the writing ran from left to right, as in our European languages. In 1765 the Danish traveller Karsten Niebuhr spent several days on the same site, and brought back better copies. He established that the inscriptions were drafted in three different alphabets, and that the first and simplest contained about 42 signs ; moreover, he confirmed beyond dispute that the writing ran from left to right. O. Tychsen identified the sign used to separate words. F. Münter supposed that the language in question was Zend, and tried, unsuccessfully, to read words, using the system of decipherment which is based on the frequency of the signs employed. Only in 1802 did Grotefend recognize in Niebuhr's Inscription B, at the beginning, a word x, and in G a word y, both followed by titles among which Münter had already identified that of ' king '. Now, in B there appeared, further on, a new word z, and in G the previous word x, again with the royal title. From this Grotefend concluded that x and y were names of kings, and that the former was the father of the latter. As for the father of x, he must be z, who had no royal title. Going through the names of the Achæmenids, Grotefend rejected Cyrus and Cambyses because he thought (wrongly) that these two names began with the same letter ; Artaxerxes was too long ; there remained Darius and Xerxes for x and y, and consequently z must be Hystaspes, who, indeed, did not hold kingly office. Thus he obtained three names in which he determined thirteen signs, four of which were rejected later as incorrect.

The great French Orientalist Silvestre de Sacy recognized the value of Grotefend's discovery and announced it to the learned world ; he had the better title to deal with the matter in that he had himself deciphered the Pahlavi inscriptions of the Sassanids. J. Saint-Martin correctly read the name of Vishtaspa instead of the modern form Gushtasp, and R. Rask determined the genitive plural in *anam*, and so the value of the signs representing m and n. P. Bopp could then read the title ' King of the Lands '.

In 1836 E. Burnouf, making use of the copies of inscriptions from the Alvand and Van, found among the papers of Schulz, who was murdered at Julamerk, discovered the name of Ahura-Mazda and a certain number of other signs, and established that the language of the inscriptions was different from that of the Avesta, although belonging to the same group. Lassen found that the consonants implicitly contained a short *a*, and that they had a different shape before *i* and *u*.

A great advance was made when, in 1837, Sir Henry Rawlinson was able to copy the greater part of the inscription of Bisutun (Behistun), but the mission in Afghanistan with which his country entrusted him interrupted these researches for a time. When he returned to Bagdad in 1843 he completed his copy of the inscription of Darius, and succeeded in determining the nature of the consonants implying the vowels *i* and *u*, a discovery which E. Hincks made independently at the same time. Finally, J. Oppert made up the whole alphabet, determining the value of certain signs which had remained uncertain.[1]

The Pahlavi Script.—This is derived from the Aramaic. Making use of the copies brought back by the travellers Flower (1667), Chardin, and Niebuhr, Silvestre de Sacy published in 1793 the results of his decipherment[2] of short trilingual inscriptions at Naqsh-i-Rustam and Naqsh-i-Rajab, written in Greek and in two Pahlavi dialects in different characters called Chaldæo-Pahlavi and Sassanian Pahlavi. Other inscriptions, found at Shapur and Taq-i-Bustan, are in this last-named alphabet. Finally, Haug made use of the knowledge of Pahlavi which he had acquired among the Parsees of Bombay to decipher the bilingual inscription found in a cave at Hajjiabad near Persepolis ; this is written in the two scripts mentioned above, and the two texts complement each other.[3] The document was drawn up to record an exhibition of bowmanship given by the king in the presence of the court—probably by Bahram II (276-293 A.D.).

Papyri found in the Fayyum, in Egypt, have preserved for us a script dating probably from the VIIIth century after Christ ; they are, therefore, the earliest specimens of Persian hand-writing.[4] Other examples of ancient writing are found

---

[1] F. H. Weissbach, **IX**, vol. ii, pp. 64-70.
[2] **CLXXV.**
[3] Haug, *Essay on Pahlavi*, pp. 45-65.
[4] Sachau, " Fragemente von Pahlavi-Papyri aus Ägypten ", in *Zeitschr. f. ägypt. Sprache*, 1878, pp. 114-16 ; P. Horn, " Zur Entzifferung der Pehlevi-Papyrus ", *Z.D.M.G.*, xliii, 50-2, 609-12, Leipzig, 1889.

in ten signatures of witnesses on a copper plaque given to the Syrian Church in Southern India, which are supposed to have been written in the IXth century,[1] and in four inscriptions of the XIth century, containing the names of Parsees who had visited the Buddhist caves of Salsette, near Bombay.[2] These inscriptions are only three centuries older than the date when the oldest Pahlavi manuscript preserved by the Parsees was written at Cambay (1323).

The Zend Script.—It is an error to call the language of the Avesta *Zend*, for this word, in tradition, designates the Pahlavi commentary on the sacred book of the Parsees ; it is only in obedience to inveterate custom that I use the term Zend for the script in which the manuscripts of the Avesta are written. Since the consonants and vowels of this language were more numerous than those of the Pahlavi, it was necessary, in order to transcribe them, to invent new characters, derived in great part from the alphabet which was used under the Sassanids.

THE DECIPHERMENT OF THE AVESTA

Thomas Hyde, a professor at Oxford University, was the first to try to discover the religion of the Magi, studying the Oriental manuscripts which were accessible to him, namely Arabic and Persian documents, for he had been unsuccessful in his attempt to read the few manuscripts of the Parsees preserved in the libraries of Great Britain. The result of his researches was a treatise on the religion of the Persians, in which he gives, with a translation, a fragment of the *Sad-dar*, the ' Hundred Gates ' (or chapters), a didactic poem in Persian verse on the principles of Mazdean theology.[3] Previously, an Anglican clergyman at Surat in India, Henry Lord, had reported the existence of manuscripts of the Avesta,[4] and so had Gabriel de Chinon and Chardin.

Anquetil-Duperron, who knew that new manuscripts had been brought to England, and had been able to see in Paris, in 1754, some pages of the Oxford manuscript containing the

---

[1] *Journ. of the Roy. Asiat. Soc.*, vii, p. 343 ; new series, iv, p. 388 ; Haug, *Essay*, pp. 80-1.
[2] West, in *Indian Antiquary*, ix, pp. 265-8, Bombay, 1880.
[3] *Historia religionis veterum Persarum*, Oxford, 1700.
[4] *The Religion of the Parsees*, 1630.

Vendidad-Sadah, was seized with enthusiasm, and resolved to go to India and there learn the language in which the Avesta was written. He was not rich ; he enlisted as a private soldier in the French East India Company's service, sailed on the 7th February, 1755, and landed on the 10th August of the same year at Pondicherry. After many adventures, he reached Surat in 1758 and stayed there until 1761. There he took lessons from the *dastur* Darab, and, on his return to France, published the first translation of the Avesta into a European language (1771).

In spite of the imperfections of this first attempt at translation, done under the inspiration of his teacher Darab, whose knowledge of Pahlavi, and still more of Zend, was indifferent, it gave the impetus to a series of researches which are still being pursued at this day. Kleuker translated Anquetil-Duperron's work into German, and improved it by researches of his own.[1] The Danish philologist Rask travelled in Persia and India from 1819 to 1822, brought back to the library of the University of Copenhagen the oldest and best manuscripts which we possess, and established the true relations existing between Zend and Sanskrit.[2]

Eugéne Burnouf was the first to undertake the methodical decipherment of the sacred book. Going back to sources, and using the manuscripts brought to Paris by Anquetil, he tried to establish an absolutely certain text by comparing the different versions, and to explain it, taking the Sanskrit translation of Neryosangh as a basis. He brought the grammatical facts together and tried to form a lexicology.[3]

The publication of the text of the Avesta by the Dane Westergaard (1852-1854), and that of the *Vendidad* (1853), the *Visperad*, and the *Yasna*, with the Pahlavi translation (1898), by Spiegel in Vienna, led this latter to produce a German translation. James Darmesteter, a French scholar, taking up the work of Anquetil-Duperron and Burnouf, issued, first in English and then in French, the latest translation of the Avesta, for which he used, first, the traditional interpretation, and, secondly, the resources offered by comparative philology

---

[1] *Zend-Avesta, Zoroasters lebendiges Wort*, Riga, 1776-7.
[2] *Om Zends prøget og Zendavestas ælde og ægthed*, Copenhagen, 1826. German translation by Von den Hagen : *Über das Alter und die Echtheit*, etc., Berlin, 1826.
[3] *Commentaire sur le Yaçna*, vol. i, Paris, 1833-5.

and chiefly Vedic Sanskrit. In this way he combined the two explanations which had come to light in the course of the XIXth century, that which was based on the traditions of the Parsees themselves, and that which sought to explain difficult words by Sanskrit analogies, preference, however, being given to the former.

SCRIPTS OF CENTRAL ASIA

The archæological missions which have in these latter years explored and studied Chinese Turkestan have brought back documents which throw quite a new light on the political and economic relations of the Persia of the early Middle Ages with the Far East. This is the work of Sir Aurel Stein in England, Messrs. Grünwedel and von Le Coq in Germany, and M. Pelliot in France, and chiefly of the last-named. They have brought to our knowledge some new Indo-European languages, Sogdian and Tukharian, the latter of which has two varieties. The surprising thing is that these tongues are allied to the European group rather than to the Indo-Iranian group. Sogdian, in particular, was in the Middle Ages " the instrument of an advanced civilization and the international language of all Central Asia ".[1]

Sogdian Writing.—As early as 1890 fragments of manuscripts in writings of India, brought from Central Asia, had aroused the curiosity of students and shown that interesting discoveries might be made among the ruins found in those almost desert regions. In 1900 Sir Aurel Stein left India for Chinese Turkestan and found the oldest Persian text of which we know, written in Hebrew characters. Two years later Messrs. Grünwedel and Huth, sent on a mission by the German Government, discovered, in the region of Turfan, Turkish and Pahlavi documents (for the first time, these latter contained no ideograms), among which Herr F. W. K. Müller, in the course of deciphering them, found a new Indo-European language, to which Herr Andreas gave the name of Sogdian, from the province of Sogdiana, which is now the region of Samarqand ; it was written in Manichæan characters. A second German expedition, that of Herr von Le Coq, brought

[1] E. Benveniste, in *Bulletin de la Société de linguistique*, xxiv, no. 74 (1924), p. 40.

from the neighbourhood of Turfan fragments of the Gospels in the Sogdian language and Syriac writing. Lastly, in 1907, Herr Grünwedel, who had stayed at Turfan, got wind of the existence of a walled-up cave at Tung-hwang, where a quantity of Chinese and other documents had been stacked ; in the same cave M. Paul Pelliot's French mission managed to obtain documents, now in the Bibliothéque Nationale, among which Robert Gauthiot deciphered Buddhist texts in the Sogdian tongue.

Sir Aurel Stein's second expedition yielded more texts. While exploring the fortifications built by the Chinese to bar the way against incursions of nomads, they found, in a watch-tower, documents on cloth and paper, folded like letters and covered with Aramaic characters in which Gauthiot recognized Sogdian. Now, these old fortifications were abandoned as early as the first century of our era ; this gives a date for the documents.

We have, therefore, two successive stages in the development of this script—the letters discovered by Sir Aurel Stein, which date from the beginning of our era, and the Buddhist texts, written between the VIIth and IXth centuries.

What is the origin of this alphabet ? Aramaic, certainly, but, as in the case of Uighur, which it greatly resembles, we must refuse to see in it Estrangelo or Archaic Syriac. Its many resemblances to the Pahlavi of the inscriptions take us to Palmyrene and the Aramaic of the papyri, which seem to have given birth to the various Pahlavi types. In the first stage which we have just determined, Early Sogdian, the letters are not linked together in a regular way, whereas in the second, that of the Buddhist documents, they are so connected, therein resembling the Syriac and Arabic scripts. This alphabet afterwards became Uighur, being applied to the Turkish language, and from this sprang the Mongolian and Manchu, which are still used by these two peoples.

The Sogdian language, transcribed by this alphabet, descends from Indo-European through Northern Iranian ; at the present day the only tongue corresponding to it is the Yaghnobi spoken in the upper valley of the Zarafshan and Ossetic, an Iranian dialect of the Caucasus.[1]

---

[1] **CXLVIIIa**, pp. x ff, 5, 25.

Manichæan Writing.—The religion of Mani, as we shall see later, became very popular in Central Asia. It brought with it, for the transcription of the sacred books of its founder, a writing derived from the Aramaic, which was used for transliterating texts in Pahlavi or Turkish. Fragments of these texts have been brought to Europe by the various missions mentioned above, and deciphered and studied by Salemann and Radlov in Russia and F. W. K. Müller and von Le Coq in Germany.

THE IRANIAN LANGUAGES

The languages spoken, either in the course of history or at the present day, on the Iranian plateau form, with those of Northern India, a branch of the Indo-Iranian group of the Aryan or Indo-European tongues. Those which were written in the past, to which epigraphic or manuscript documents bear witness, are : (i) the Old Persian of the Achæmenian cuneiform inscriptions ; (ii) Zend, the language of the Avesta ; (iii) the Pahlavi of the Sassanian inscriptions, the commentaries on the Avesta, and the documents found at Turfan in Central Asia.

Old Persian is an Indo-European language of archaic appearance, allied to the Sanskrit of the Vedas. It was very probably the speech of the Persians about Darius, if not of the king himself ; it was the language of the court and nobility, but not of the public services ; the offices doubtless used Aramaic. For the Persians had satraps and generals, but no scribes, or subordinate office staff, for the administration of the vast empire founded by Cyrus. They had to depend on a personnel which was already there, " the elements of which they found at their disposal in Babylonia ".[1] It was probably these civil servants who took over from the cuneiform script the thirty-six characters which form the elements of Persian writing, keeping however, a few ideograms, which are not much used on the whole.

Zend is a sister-language of Old Persian, of which the *Gathas* have preserved the most ancient form.

[1] **LXXIXa,** pp. 4, 13, 19.

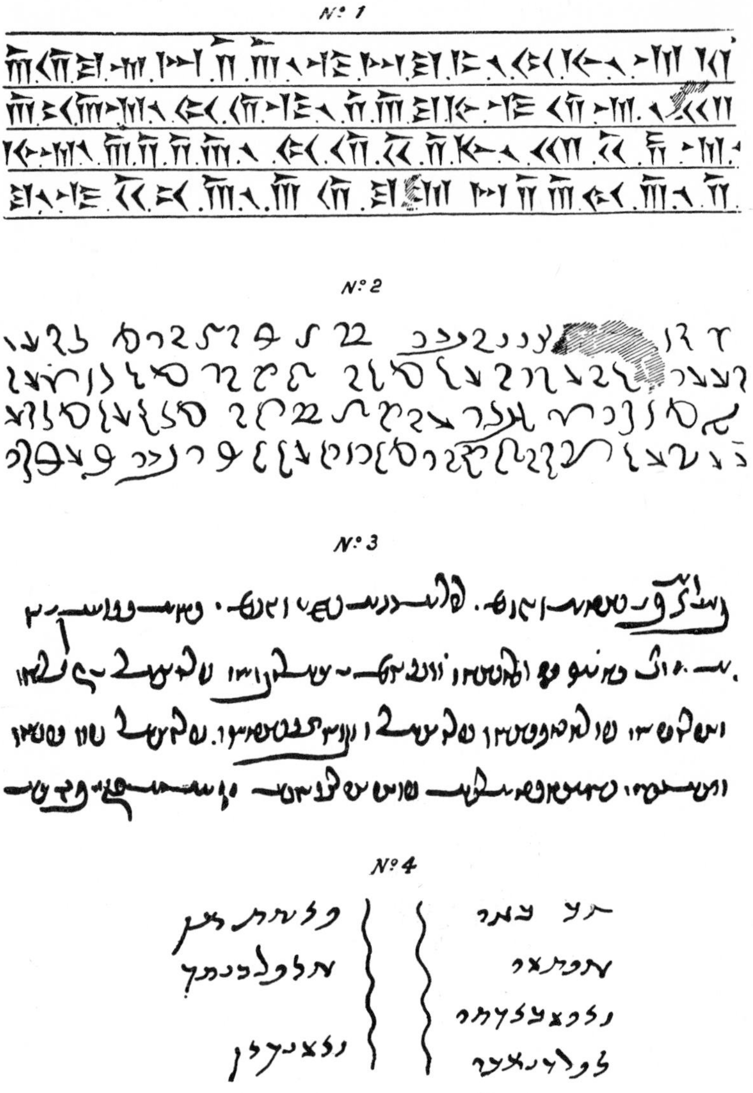

Nº 1

Nº 2

Nº 3

Nº 4

Fig. 1. The Scripts of Persia

1. Persian cuneiform script.
2. Pahlavi writing of the inscriptions.
3. Zend script.
4. Early Sogdian script.

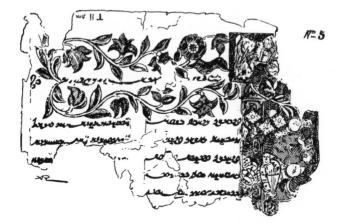

Fig. 1. THE SCRIPTS OF PERSIA

5-6. Manichæan scripts.   7. Modern Sogdian script.

Pahlavi is not exactly descended from Old Persian, but, like it, it represents a speech of Persis.[1] The reading of it was for long complicated by the presence of many ideograms, about a thousand, which are the Aramaic equivalents for corresponding Persian expressions; but the texts found in Central Asia do not have these ideograms, for which the contemporary reader must assuredly have substituted the equivalent Persian word. Modern Persian is the direct descendant of Pahlavi.

The languages spoken at the present day are :

(i) The literary language, Persian, spoken by the educated classes not only in modern Persia, but also in Afghanistan. From the creation of the empire of the Grand Moguls at the beginning of the XVIth century down to the suppression of the commercial function of the British East India Company in 1833, it was the learned written language of India. It is spoken by the people in the big cities of the present Iran.

(ii) Afghan, spoken by the aborigines of Afghanistan. It is called Pushtu in the south and Pukhtu in the north.

(iii) Baluchi, spoken by the natives of Baluchistan, where it has a rival in Brahui, an Indian language.

(iv) The Kurdish of the mountains of Kurdistan, which is divided into several dialects. Since the frontier between Persia and the former Ottoman Empire, now the Turkish republic of Angora, follows the crests of the hills and the watershed, Kurdish is divided between these two states. The Bakhtiyaris and Lurs do not like being regarded as Kurds, but, since the dialects spoken in these two groups are closely related to Kurdish, it is natural to include them under this generic appellation from the linguistic point of view.

(v) Minor dialects distributed sporadically over the plateau of Iran—those of the Pamir (Sarikoli, Shighni, Wakhi, Ishkashami, Sanglichi, Munji or Munjani, and Yidgah), including Yaghnobi, the last surviving remnant of Sogdian ; those of the shores of the Caspian (Mazandarani, Gileki, Talij, Tat, Samnani) ; and those of the centre (Kashi, Gabri, Nayin, Natanz, and Siwendi).

(vi) Ossetic, spoken by an Iranian people which lives in the mountains, valleys, and passes of the middle Caucasus, having

---

[1] A. Meillet, " Notes iraniennes ", in *Mém. de la Soc. de linguistique*, xxii (1921), pp. 222-3.

the district of Kasbek, the highest summit of the chain, on the east, and extending westwards in the neighbouring hills. These people seem to be the descendants of the Sarmatians and the Scythians of Pontus, and were known in the Middle Ages under the name of Alans.

The Jews speak and write a Judæo-Persian, influenced by the various localities. In Bukhara, for instance, their speech has been affected by the Persian spoken by the Tajiks, a people of Iranian origin.

PART ONE

THE MEDES AND THE ACHÆMENIDS

CHAPTER I

The Iranians on the Plateau of Media. Campaigns of
the Assyrians

PREHISTORIC Persia has been studied by J. de Morgan,[1]
but no light has yet been thrown on the invasion of the
plateau of Media by the Iranians from the North. Settlements
are found on the southern slope of the Damavand massif in
Mazandaran and in the Lar valley near Muhammadabad, and
prehistoric remains in the silt of the torrential Ab-i-Parduma,
recalling the crudest types of the European Quaternary period.
Neolithic workshops have been discovered in the Pusht-i-Kuh
(the Kassite country) and at Tepe Gulam in Luristan. Bronze
Age tombs and a dolmen have been found at Kraveh-Kadeh,
in the mountains above Lenkoran on the Caspian. At an
undetermined but certainly very ancient epoch Elam or Susiana
was inhabited by Negritoes.[2]

The cuneiform inscriptions of the Assyrian king Tiglath-
pileser I, a great warrior, about 1115-1100 B.C., tell us of the
expeditions which he undertook to extend his sway. He
attacked the Moschians, north of Commagene, and then the
mountains of Armenia, where he was confronted by
impenetrable forests ; he went as far as Lake Van.[3]

Not until the expedition of Shalmaneser III in 837, nearly
three centuries later, do we find mention of the Parsua, in the
mountains of Kurdistan, between the sources of the Zab and
the Diyala, a district in which twenty-seven princes reigned
over as many states, and the Amadai, that is, the Medes, who

---

[1] **LXXXII, LXXXIV, LXXXV.**
[2] **LXXXIII, XX,** vol. iv, pp. 3, 7, 17, 118, 161.
[3] Delaporte, *Mesopotamia*, in this series, pp. 246-7 of the English.

inhabited the plain ; so these peoples appear for the first time.[1]

Both peoples spoke an Indo-European language ; for this fact we have the evidence of Strabo, who tells us that the Medes, Persians, Bactrians, and Sogdians spoke one same language with slight variations.[2] They were not autochthonous, even so far as this term has a meaning in the case of primitive peoples which we see moving from one place to another, in the remotest antiquity known to us, and even in prehistoric times. They were immigrants from the vast, almost desert tracts, which the ancients knew under the name of Scythia, and perhaps from the part of that enormous territory which corresponds to the present Southern Russia. The memory of these movements has been preserved in the Avesta, which speaks vaguely of a lost country, a kind of earthly Paradise called Airyanem-Vaejo. Driven from their original habitat by the cold, the Aryans came to Sogdiana (Bukhara and Samarqand) and Margiana (Marv), whence they were compelled by an invasion of locusts and hostile tribes to move further south, to Balkh and then into Khurasan, whence they spread into Persia.[3]

Is it possible to determine the approximate time of this migration ? In 1100 the Medes were not yet established in the country which was called, after them, Media. Moreover, the Hittites had constituted in Asia Minor an empire which fought against the Assyrians and the Egyptians.[4] The Medes only appear on the scene long after these first invaders. We can hardly give a date earlier than the first millennium to their intrusion on to the high plateaus, which were at that time inhabited by a population whose racial origin is unknown to us. This population was either driven back into the hills or assimilated by the invaders.

The Medes were divided into six tribes, whose names Herodotos has preserved for us—Busæ, Paretaceni, Struchates,

---

[1] XVII, p. 453.

[2] Strabo, xv. 724.

[3] **CV**, vol. i, pp. 211, 683.   Cf. Avesta, *Vendidad*, 1, 6 ff, and *Bundahish*, cc, 25, 30.   The latter places this country north of Adharbayjan, the Arran of the Middle Ages, the modern Qarabagh.

[4] Herodotos (i. 72) knows of a tribe which had advanced as far as the Halys. This was the Hittites, or Kheta, whom the ancients called Leuco-syrians or White Syrians. Recent discoveries at Boghaz-Keui (Pteria) have shown that one, at least, of the languages of their inscriptions was Indo-European.

Arizanti, Budii, and Magi.[1] They were a pastoral people, possessing horses, oxen, sheep, goats, and trained watch-dogs. They travelled in waggons with wheels and axles rudely cut from tree-trunks. The family was based on patriarchal authority and polygamy, and brides were carried off by main force—that is, they practised exogamy. They were acquainted with gold, electrum (a compound of gold and silver, which they could not separate), and bronze. Their art was confined to very simple decoration. When they were established in the country they took to agriculture, but they remained divided into independent clans, which were, however, able to combine in time of danger.

When Shalmaneser III made his first expedition against Namri (Kurdistan), in 844, the Assyrian king found a country which had long been under Babylonian influence, under a king with the Semitic name of Marduk-Mudammik. The latter fled into the mountains ; his treasures were seized and his people made captive ; and a king of Kassite origin, named Ianzu, was chosen to reign over the devastated country. This Ianzu revolted seven years later ; he escaped into the forests, but was finally taken and led into Nineveh in triumph.

Under the successor of Shalmaneser III, Shamshi-Adad IV (824-812), the Medes are mentioned once more, as being conquered and paying tribute. It would seem that their country was well populated, for it has many cities, great numbers of prisoners are brought in, and the horses and cattle taken are reckoned in thousands. Adad-nirari III, the son of the foregoing, led seven expeditions into Media in 810 and the following years, without making much headway.

In 744 Tiglath-pileser III, who had ascended the throne on 13th April, 745, invaded the country, where, like his predecessors, he found the clans disunited, and attacked them one after another. From this campaign he brought back sixty thousand prisoners and enormous numbers of oxen, sheep, mules, and dromedaries, which he led in triumph to his capital Calah. One of his generals advanced as far as the foot of Bikni, the ' Crystal Mountain ', Mount Damavand, which the conquerors regarded as the extreme northern limit of the world. This excursion decided the succes; of the campaign, and the chieftains of the country hastened to pay homage. Later,

[1] Hdt., i. 101.

in 737, the whole of Media was ravaged, doubtless in consequence of a revolt ; the furthest valleys and the most rugged mountains were scoured, and a throng of captives took the road to the plains.

Fifteen years later, in 722, Sargon II took Samaria and carried off the people of the Kingdom of Israel, as is narrated in the Second Book of Kings (xvii, 6). The Israelites were distributed between Calah, the capital of Assyria at the time, the banks of the Khabur, and the cities of the Medes. Some years after this historic event, in 715, the same king, in the course of a campaign against the Mannai, who inhabited Adharbayjan south of Lake Urmiyah and were related to the Medes, captured one of their chiefs, named Dayaukku, and, contrary to the inveterate custom, spared his life and sent him and his family into exile at Hamath in Syria. Now, this name Dayaukku is the same as that of the founder of the Median empire, which the Greeks have transmitted to us in the form Deioces ; but the similarity of name does not prove that it was the same man. Once more the suzerainty of Assyria was recognized for a time, and twenty-two chieftains of Medic tribes took the oath of allegiance.

In the reign of Esarhaddon, Sennacherib's son, about 674, the armies of Assyria made their way beyond Damavand to the salt desert, a country rich in lapis lazuli, which they had never reached before. This is sufficient evidence that the statements in the inscriptions of Tiglath-pileser I, mentioned above, had exaggerated greatly. Esarhaddon captured two kings, Sidirparna and Eparna, and took them to Assyria, with their subjects, their two-humped camels, and their trained horses. Other kings accompanied him to Nineveh and appealed for his protection, bringing gifts of lapis lazuli and horses.

CHAPTER II

The Empire of the Medes

DEIOCES

HERODOTOS tells us that Deioces, son of Phraortes, had such a name for his sense of justice that the people of his village, and then the members of his tribe, all submitted disputed cases to him. Seeing that he was growing powerful, Deioces let it be known that he could not spend all his time at the expense of his own affairs, and gave over this activity, whereupon thefts and disorders began once more. Then the Medes resolved to set up a king, and for that office they chose Deioces.[1]

The first act of the new king was to surround himself with a powerful bodyguard ; his second was to make himself a capital. For this he chose the town of Hamadan, which the Greeks called Ecbatana. He did not found it, for it is mentioned under the name of Amadana in the inscription of Tiglath-pileser I, but he gave it new glory, increasing the population. The name Hangmatana means ' Meeting-place ' and seems to indicate that the clans, formerly scattered, gathered there in a more concentrated fashion. The new city was built on the model of the cities of the plain. It stood on the hill now called Musalla, to the east of the present town. The walls, seven in number, were concentric, and increased in height inwards, so that the innermost rose above all the rest. The king's palace, which held his treasures, stood inside the seventh wall, which had gilded battlements, whereas those of the other walls were painted in bright colours, like the Birs Nimrud.[2] Among the Babylonians these colours symbolized the sun, moon, and planets, but among the Medes they were merely artistic imitation. This old palace must have survived a long time, for we find a description of it in Polybius (x, 24).

Deioces also instituted a court etiquette, probably copied

---

[1] Hdt., i. 96-8.   [2] Hdt., i. 98-9.

from Assyrian usages ; no one might see the king face to face, and petitions had to be carried to him by messengers. This rule and many others were intended to inspire fear and reverence, by making access to the sovereign difficult.[1]

During his reign of fifty-three years (708-655) Deioces had time to work for the unification of the Medes, hitherto dispersed, in a single nation. He was fortunate enough to escape the attention of the Assyrians, if he is not the same as the Dayaukku of the cuneiform texts, for Sennacherib was too busy fighting Babylon and Elam or Susiana to give thought to the high and difficult mountains of Kurdistan, and the only expedition which menaced Media was that which was conducted against Ellipi, that is, the district of Kirmanshah. The rest of the country kept quiet and paid its tribute regularly, so that the Assyrians had no cause to intervene.

PHRAORTES

Deioces was succeeded by his son Phraortes (Fravartish), who bore the same name as his grandfather. He carried on his father's policy, that is, the maintenance of good relations with Assyria, where Assurbanipal was on the throne,[2] by the regular payment of tribute, and the conquest and absorption of the tribes of the same stock established on the plateau. In this way the Medes came to take possession of the parts inhabited by the kindred Persians. Emboldened by these successes, they tried to shake off the yoke, and attacked the Assyrians ; but those veteran troops, which had finally subdued Elam, which were well disciplined and had grown old in their arms, were too much for the impetuous Medes. The latter were utterly defeated, Phraortes was killed, after a reign of twenty-two years (655-633),[3] and the greater part of the army was wiped out.

CYAXARES

Then Cyaxares (Huvakhshatara), an able administrator and a successful general, ascended the throne. The defeat which

---

[1] Cf. Behistun inscription, ii, l. 14 ; **LXXVI**, p. 105.

[2] Assurbanipal, after taking and burning Babylon in 648, had attacked Elam and then Susa, and had dethroned the last Elamite sovereign, Khumban-Khaldash. Elam was depopulated and struck off the list of nations and its territory was annexed to Assyria in 645. **XI.**

[3] Hdt., i. 102.

had cost his predecessor his life taught him that levies raised by feudal chiefs were no match for regular troops, and he resolved to form an army on the Assyrian model. He had an infantry armed with the bow, the sword, and one or two javelins a man. His cavalry was more numerous than the enemy's, thanks to the horse-breeding practised by the Medes ; his troopers, armed with the bow, were trained from childhood to shoot from all positions, both charging and retiring—tactics which were always practised by the Medo-Persian cavalry, and sometimes defeated the Roman legion.

Cyaxares trained his troops for war by stubbornly resisting the Assyrians ; this delaying policy at last brought his opportunity, and his army triumphed over the generals of Assurbanipal ; Assyria was invaded and Nineveh besieged.

It was only a blockade, an echo of which comes down to us through the prophet Nahum (iii. 2-3). Cyaxares might possibly have succeeded in taking the town by famine, when he was urgently recalled to his country by the invasions of the Scythians.[1] These peoples had crossed the Caucasus by the Darband Pass and had invaded Adharbayjan ; the Median king went to meet them north of Lake Urmiyah, and was defeated and compelled to accept the terms of the conqueror (633). The Scythians ravaged the whole country ; there were no forts to resist this devastating torrent which reached to the Mediterranean and was witnessed by Jeremiah (vi. 23). The terror was brought to an end by a ruse of Cyaxares, who invited Madyes, the King of the Scythians, and his chief officers to a banquet, at which he made them drunk and had them put to death.[2] Deprived of their leaders, the Scythians were attacked and, in spite of a desperate resistance, were finally driven out about 615, after an occupation which had lasted twenty-eight years.

Assurbanipal had died about 625, and under his successor Saracus the governor of Babylon, Nabopolassar, assumed the title of king. He first marched against unknown invaders who were coming up the Tigris and Euphrates from the mouths, but then called the Medes to his help, and was joined by Cyaxares. Nineveh was besieged, and, when the Assyrian

---

[1] Hdt., i. 103-4 ; Trogus Pompeius, in Justin, **II, 3** ; Jordanes, *De Origine Getarum*, 6.

[2] Hdt., i. 105.

king saw that all resistance was impossible, he kindled a pyre and perished in the flames with his family. The capital was taken in 606, and razed to the ground ; nothing remained of it save ruins. The other cities and the sanctuaries of the gods who had not assisted Nabopolassar were treated in the same way, as the cylinder of Nabonidus expressly states.[1]

Henceforward the Medes held sway over a great part of Nearer Asia. Nebuchadnezzar, the son and successor of Nabopolassar, concluded an alliance with them and married Cyaxares' daughter, Amytis. While the Babylonians kept the plains for themselves, the Medes held the plateau of Iran, to which they joined Armenia, the sources of the Tigris, and Cappadocia, where they found ancient Aryan invaders established, kinsmen of their own. The conquest of these regions was all the easier because they had been ravaged by the Cimmerians and Scythians, and since then had been in a state of anarchy which deprived them of all power of resistance. The Medes only stopped at the Halys (Qizil Irmaq), where they found themselves face to face with the warlike and powerful kingdom of Lydia, under the government of Alyattes of the Mermnad dynasty.

A curious legend relates the alleged cause of the breach between Media and Lydia. Cyaxares had taken into his service a band of Scythians as huntsmen, and had entrusted certain young nobles to them for instruction. One day, when these huntsmen came home empty-handed, the king insulted them ; in revenge, they killed one of the young nobles, cut him up, and served him to the king as a dish ; then they fled to Alyattes, who refused to give them up. War broke out. The Medes, though more numerous than the Lydians, had no troops to compare with the Greek hoplites or the famous Lydian cavalry. For six years hostilities went on without gain on either side ; in the seventh year an eclipse of the sun, which Thales of Miletos had predicted (28th May, 585), so frightened the two armies that they decided to lay down their arms ; negotiations followed ; and Babylonia, acting as arbiter, fixed the Halys as the boundary between the two states.

[1] Col. ii, ll. 2-41.

ASTYAGES

In the following year Cyaxares died (584). He must have been an energetic, powerful personality, and a remarkable organizer, to give Media an army which, after being defeated by the Assyrians and the Scythians, gained the upper hand over both, drove out the latter, took Nineveh, and conquered half Asia Minor. Herodotos says that he made separate corps of the bowmen and cavalry, who had previously fought all together. He was succeeded by Astyages (Ishtuvegu), who had a long and wholly peaceful reign. The court of the king, modelled on Assyrian manners, was a centre of brilliant luxury, with its swarms of courtiers in their red and purple robes and their golden chains and collars. Hunting was the chief amusement, in the open country or in closed parks. But the people must have had cause for discontent, for, when the Persians attacked the kingdom, the king's subjects deserted him and went over to the enemy. Thus the empire of the Medes fell, in 550, without much difficulty, beneath the blows of Cyrus.

CHAPTER III

THE PERSIANS. CYRUS

THE Persians, like the Medes, were divided into tribes—the Pasargadæ, Maraphii, Maspii, Panthialæi, Derusiæi, and Germanii, all agriculturists, and the Dai, Mardi, Dropici and Sagartii, who had remained nomads.[1] The Pasargadæ were the most important, and the Hakhamanish were a clan of this tribe.

Susa, the capital of Susiana or Elam, in the plain at the foot of the mountains, was at that time under the rule of a dynasty which had supplanted the native Anshanite kings. This was the clan Hakhamanish, out of which the Greeks created the eponymous king Achæmenes. It was an Aryan family which, in consequence of events unknown to history, had come down from the mountains of the Parsua and had settled in the midst of a population of wholly different origin, the Cossæans or Anshanites, who may have been related, by their speech, to the Georgians of Transcaucasia. The Hakhamanish had brought with them the people from which they had come, the Persians. There had already been three successive kings of this race, Chishpish (Teispes), Kurash, and Kambujiya, mentioned on the cylinders of Nabonidus. Kurash II, whom we call Cyrus (Greek Kyros),[2] succeeded these in 558,[3] and, by his sudden, astounding conquests, created an immense empire,

---

[1] Ten tribes in all (Hdt., i. 125). Xenophon (*Anab.*, i. 2. 5) mentions twelve ; two new tribes may have been formed in the course of the centuries.

[2] Κῦρος (Æsch., *Pers.*, 768), where the υ is long. The Persians said that this name meant "sun", and accordingly connected it with the Zend *hvare* ; but this may be merely popular etymology. If it is an Anshanite name, it means "shepherd" (Sayce, *The Ancient Empires of the East*, p. 69, n. 3), which would be a curious name for a king.

[3] Herodotos states (i, 214) that Cyrus reigned twenty-nine years, whereas Ctesias, followed by Deinon and Trogus Pompeius, says thirty years. Nabonidus places the capture of Ecbatana in the sixth year of his reign (Schrader, *Die Nabonid-Cyrus-Chronik, Keilschriftl. Bibliothek*, vol. iii, part 2, pp. 128-31), i.e., in 550; so it was in the eighth year of his reign that Cyrus vanquished Astyages. See also Hagen, "Keilschrifturkunden zur Geschichte des Königs Cyrus", in *Beiträge zur Assyriologie*, vol. ii, pp. 218-19, 236.

such as had not been seen before, stretching from the Hellespont
to the borders of India. We have little information about
Cyrus, and some of it is contradictory, but he must have been a
great military and organizing genius, to subjugate so many
peoples and to bequeath to his successors a state which it
took an Alexander to overthrow, two and a half centuries later.

What were the Persians doing in their mountains before the
clan Hakhamanish, taking advantage of some favourable
circumstance unknown to us, detached itself from the tribe
of the Pasargadæ and founded a new kingdom on the ruins
of the Elamite empire ? The Assyrian monarch who caused
the black obelisk to be engraved in the IXth century boasts
of having made twenty-seven Persian princes tributary to
himself. From then onwards the Parsua remained subject to
the kingdom of Nineveh, under Belochus (second half of the
IXth century), under Sargon-Shalmaneser (731-713), and under
Esarhaddon (667). Escaping from the domination of the
Semites, they passed under that of the Medes, their kinsmen,
who were already more civilized. Was this new domination
the occasion which the Achæmenids seized to leave their homes
and make themselves a principality in the hot district of
Susiana ? We may suppose this, but cannot be certain.

Our sole authority for this period is Herodotos, who only
gives us legends ; but these seem nearer to historical truth
than the stories of Ctesias. Astyages dreamed that there
flowed from his daughter Mandane a torrent which not only
filled his capital but covered all Asia. Fearing to marry her
to a noble Mede, who might fulfil this dream, he gave her to
a Persian of good family but quiet temper, whom he regarded
as inferior to a Mede of even modest condition. This was
Cambyses, a historic name, which we have seen in its original
form, Kambujiya, in the list of the kings of Susa. They must
have been poor kinglets, if Astyages deemed them lower than
the middle classes of Media. In a second dream he saw a vine
rising from his daughter's body and covering the whole of Asia.
In terror he sent for Mandane, and when the child was born he
handed it to Harpagus, a man of his own family whom he could
altogether trust, with orders to kill it. Harpagus, unwilling
to do murder with his own hands, and anxious to provide for
the future and to forearm himself against the vengeance which
Mandane would certainly wreak on the murderer of her son

when she came to succeed her father, entrusted the child to
one of the king's shepherds, named Mithradates, with instructions to expose it in the wildest hills, where it would at once
die. The shepherd's wife, whose name was Spaco, ' Bitch '
(the only Medic word which the Greeks have transmitted to us),
had just given birth to a still-born child ; she persuaded her
husband to change it with Mandane's child, and to show the
body to Harpagus. Later, however, the child was recognized
by his grandfather Astyages, who was glad to find him alive.

It is said that Harpagus was cruelly punished. Astyages
had his son killed, and caused the flesh to be served to him at
the royal banquet, while the head, hands, and feet were offered
to him in a basket. Harpagus said nothing, but some years
later he entered into correspondence with Cyrus, who had been
sent home to his parents. He persuaded him to revolt (553),
won adherents for him among the Medes themselves, and became
the chief instrument in the fall of the empire of Astyages ; for
the king committed the incredible folly of entrusting to
Harpagus the army which was to fight the rebels, and Harpagus,
by arrangement with Cyrus, did not fight, thus satisfying his
justified hatred. Cyrus, after a first defeat, won the battle of
Pasargadæ, whereupon the troops of Astyages mutinied, put
their king under arrest, and delivered him to the victor (550).[1]
Astyages remained a prisoner in chains, but did not suffer
other ill-treatment.

This is how the annals of Nabonidus relate the fall of Media :
" As for Astyages, his troops revolted against him : he was
taken and delivered to Cyrus. Cyrus marched on Ecbatana,
the royal city ; the silver, the gold, the furniture, the riches
were looted ; the furniture and the riches were carried into the
land of Anshan ". There are no other details, but we know,
thanks to these documents, the date of the fall of Ecbatana
—550.[2]

---

[1] Latrille, "Der Nabonidcylinder", in *Zeitschr. für Keilforschung*, ii,
pp. 242-5 ; Peiser, in Schrader's *Keilinschriftl. Bibliothek*, vol. iii, part 2,
pp. 98-9 ; Pinches, *Trans. Soc. Bibl. Archæology*, vii (1880), pp. 130-76 ;
Proceed. Soc. Bibl. Arch., 1882-3, p. 7. According to Nic. Dam., it was at
this battle that Cyrus's father Kambujiya died from wounds. See **LIa**,
vol. i, p. 23, n. 3.

[2] Ctesias relates that Cyrus, after dethroning Astyages, married his
daughter Amytis. If this is true, as Eduard Meyer thinks (*Jewish Encyclope-
dia*, vol. iv, pp. 402 ff.), we must suppose that Cyrus, being Mandane's son,
married his own aunt. There is nothing improbable in this.

Fig. 2. CYRUS THE ACHÆMENID

In 549 Cyrus appears in the tablets with the title King of Anshan ; in 546 he has the title King of Persia. The local traditions preserved by the classical authors tell us that it took three battles to reduce Media, but that is all ; they say nothing of the way in which the conqueror's title was changed. It is possible that after the fall of Ecbatana the Medes asked him to be their king, and that he then changed the modest title of King of Anshan (Susiana) for that of King of Persia, Media being then attached to his hereditary domains.

With Nabonidus reigning in Babylon, the new king had no trouble from that side, but this was not the case with Lydia, where Crœsus (Kroisos)[1] had succeeded Alyattes. Crœsus further extended the conquests of his predecessor and annexed Miletos and the other Greek colonies of Ionia. In the east, in less than ten years, he extended his possessions to the left bank of the Halys ; so it would seem that the line fixed by the treaties had been lost by him or by Alyattes. The fall of Media and the great development of Persia, which came into history for the first time, were such as might well cause him concern. He had lost an ally. However, he had a trustworthy army and a magnificent cavalry, and he could count on Greek mercenaries and the support of Babylon and Egypt.[2] If, therefore, he resolved to take the offensive and to invade Cappadocia, it was because the new state caused him considerable alarm, and he wanted to fight it before it became stronger still.

It appears, from Diodorus Siculus, that an agent whom Crœsus had supplied with large sums to enlist Greek soldiers (he had made an alliance with Sparta) fled to Persia and disclosed to Cyrus the coalition by which he was threatened.[3] The new king decided to forestall Crœsus and to attack him before his allies arrived (546). There is something astonishing in his march over the mountains to Asia Minor. Having crossed the Tigris not far from Nineveh, he went through Mesopotamia, perhaps following the foot of the mountains which terminate it on the north. On entering Cappadocia, he sent to Crœsus offering to leave him his life and his kingdom, on condition that he swore to conduct himself as a loyal vassal. The King of Lydia refused, and the first encounter was a victory for him.

---

[1] Κροεσος on a vase in the Louvre, reproduced in **XVIII**, p. 619.
[2] Hdt., i. 82 ; Xen., *Cyrop.*, vi. 2. 10-11.
[3] Diod. Sic., ix. 32.

There followed a truce of three months ; then, on the resumption of hostilities, battle was engaged at Pteria (Boghaz-Keui), without decisive result. However, Cyrus did not think it advisable to resume it the next day, and Crœsus took advantage of the night to retire to Sardes, laying the country waste so as to prevent the Persians from advancing, and perhaps counting on the Babylonians to prevent any further action of Cyrus by threatening his rear. Nabonidus, however, accepted the peace offered to him, and the conqueror marched rapidly on Sardes.[1]

Crœsus, thinking that the winter snows would delay the Persian advance through the mountains, had disbanded part of his forces and put off the arrival of his allies until the spring. Surprised by his opponent's march, he prepared to face him, and sent his cavalry to the plain of the Hermus. Cyrus placed his camels in front of his troops,[2] and the smell of these animals terrified the horses of the Lydians and rendered them unmanageable. This may seem strange to travellers who have observed that in the East the horse is not in the least afraid of the camel and lives with it familiarly, but here it is a matter of habit, as with dogs and cats which live together ; the Lydian horses saw—and, still more, smelled—camels for the first time, and so were thrown into uncontrollable panic. Sir Percy Sykes has himself been witness to the terror of a young Australian horse he was riding, on seeing a camel for the first time.[3] The presence of camels in Cyrus's army seems to show that a large part of his forces consisted of Susians, who lead a nomadic life, like the Bedouins, in the barren plains between the mountains and the Shatt-al-Arab.

Secure in his capital, in a very strong position, Crœsus hoped to wait for the fine season and the help of his allies from Greece and Egypt. The Spartans were about to sail. But after fourteen days of the siege a Mardian soldier, Hyriades, inspired

---

[1] On the difficulty of reconciling Hdt's. account (i. 76-7) with that of Polyænus (*Strat.*, vii. 8), see Maspero's judicious remarks in **XVIII**, p. 616, n. 3.

[2] Hdt., i. 80 ; Xen., *Cyrop.*, vii. 1. 48 ; Polyæn., *Strat.*, vii. 6 ; Aelian, *H.A.*, iii. 7. Cf. Radet, *La Lydie et le monde grec*, p. 250, n. 3.

[3] It is chiefly the smell of the camel that frightens the horse, as is noted by a traveller who has recently explored Persia. "From time immemorial, on the roads of Asia, horses and camels have travelled side by side. But the horse has never been able to accustom itself to the smell emitted by this humped quadruped, and holds it in horror " (Claude Anet, *Feuilles persanes*, Paris, 1924, p. 79). Cf. Hdt., vii. 87.

by the reward offered by Cyrus to the first man who should
enter the city, observed a Lydian of the garrison, whose helmet
had fallen into the moat, climbing down at a place which from
a distance looked inaccessible, and returning the same way.[1]
With some of his comrades, the Mardian soldier went up the
way revealed by the rashness of the Lydian, surprised the
careless garrison, which trusted to the strength of the position,
and opened the gates to the besiegers.   So Sardes fell, in 546,
the very year which Cyrus had assumed the title of King of
Persia.   Crœsus climbed on to a pyre which he had had made,
meaning to die on it with his family ; but the Persians seem
to have arrived in time to put out the fire and save the king of
Lydia.   What Herodotos relates, beyond this fact, is merely
the echo of a legend.

The conquest of Lydia was followed by that of the Greek
colonies, but Cyrus left it to his subordinates to complete his
work.   His absence led to a revolt of the Lydians, who
besieged his general Tabalus in the citadel of Sardes.   It was
led by Pactyas, to whom Cyrus had entrusted the conquered
treasures.   The arrival of reinforcements under the Mede
Mazares made it possible to quell the insurrection, and Pactyas
fled to the Greeks.   The cities of Asia Minor were besieged and
taken, thanks to the skill in soldiering acquired by the Medo-
Persian troops in their contact with the Assyrians.   The
Ionians had acted very imprudently ; having refused to join
Cyrus, they had not stirred to help Crœsus ; they trusted in the
support of Sparta, which failed them.   The Spartans contented
themselves with sending an ambassador to threaten Cyrus with
hostile measures if he pursued his designs against the Greek
colonies ; the king thanked them for their good advice, but
added " Take care that I do not soon give you cause to prate,
not of the misfortunes of Ionia, but of your own ".   Emigration
followed ; the sea was free, and the Persians had no fleet ;
the Phocæans went and joined those of their fellow-citizens

---

[1] There are several accounts of this event ; see Schubert, *Geschichte der
Könige von Lydien*, p. 106, and Radet, *op. cit.*, pp. 251-3.   It is difficult
to place the Mardian people ; Alexander came across them and subdued
them after the fall of Persepolis ; they occupied the territory of the present
Mamaseni ; but he subdued other Mardi in the Alburz, about Mazandaran and
Gilan, and they are also found in the mountains between Bayazid and
Lake Van, and even in Hyrcania.   **CV**, vol. ii, pp. 528, 538 ; vol. iii, pp. 77,
159.   If they are the same as the Amardi, they must have lived on the River
Amardus (Safid Rud), as Droysen holds.   **CV**, vol. i, p. 75.

who, sixty years before, had founded Marseilles on the Ligurian coast.

We know almost nothing of the campaigns which Cyrus then undertook in the east. For five or six years, from 545 to 539, he was fighting unknown peoples dwelling between the Caspian and India. He took Balkh, and this led to the submission of Margiana (Marv) and Sogdiana (Samarqand) ; he advanced as far as the Jaxartes (Sir Darya), and there built forts which were still standing in Alexander's time, such as Cyropolis (Ura-Tubeh), commanding one of the chief fords of the river. He subdued the Sacæ, who had not yet settled in Sacastene, the modern Sijistan. He seems to have lost an army in the deserts of Gedrosia (Makran) ; nevertheless, this province henceforward formed part of his empire.[1]

There remained Babylon, whose ancient glory, recently revived by the help given to the Medes at the time of the taking of Nineveh, seemed to defend it against any rash attack. Nabonidus, the son of a priestess of Sin at Harran, was the tool of the priests, and spent his time in hunting for the cylinders of ancient sanctuaries and restoring the latter, raising heavy taxes to cover expenses. He partly alienated the priests when he introduced into Babylon the gods of Ur, Uruk, and Eridu ; he did not even enter his capital, although his presence was necessary, but caused his son Belshazzar to take his place. Cyrus thus became the protégé of Marduk, as he is called in the proclamation which the cuneiform texts have preserved for us. The conquest of the ancient city, aided by the supporters whom the Persians had within the walls, was easier than might have been expected, from the triple fortification which surrounded it and its immense resources. The march of the conqueror had been facilitated by the Babylonian Kubaru (Gobryas), the governor of the province between the Zab and the Diyala, who had joined his side and supplied recruits.[2]

Cyrus, in 539, began by diverting the water of the Euphrates when the river was low. He then advanced against Belshazzar's army, which had remained at Opis, and so was cut off from the capital, and defeated it without difficulty. Nabonidus, driven

---

[1] Nearchus, Frag. 23, in Müller, *Scriptores rerum Alexandri Magni*, p. 65, in connexion with the same disaster to Alexander's army on its return from India. **CV,** vol. ii, p. 541, n. 2.

[2] Delaporte, *Mesopotamia*, in this series, p. 59 of the English.

out of Sippar, fled, and Gobryas entered Babylon without a blow.[1] The temples were protected and looting was forbidden ; when the conqueror appeared in person he was acclaimed as a deliverer (27th October). Nabonidus surrendered voluntarily and was interned in Carmania (Kirman), where he lived till his death. Cyrus " took the hands of the god Bel-Marduk " (20th March, 538). This was his consecration as king of Babylon ; in this way he made it clear that he did not impose on anyone the religion of his family, or of his people, and still less that of the Median tribe of the Magi. He restored to the various cities the images of the gods which Nabonidus had removed to Babylon, and, in application of the same principle, he gave back to the Jews in their exile the gold and silver vessels from the Temple of Jerusalem which were found among the royal treasures.[2] He did even more for the Jews, for he allowed them to return to Palestine and to rebuild the Temple, which had been destroyed. The edict which he issued on this occasion, in the first year of his reign as king of Babylon, is a famous landmark in the history of mankind.

The great king's attitude to the exiles from Palestine has been explained in various ways. He is said to have acted thus in return for services rendered during the campaign, or in order to secure a body of devoted supporters not far from the frontier of Egypt, which he may well have wished to conquer, as indeed his successor did. These motives are perhaps insufficient, especially the second ; for few Jews gave up the positions which they had won by hard work in the countries to which the fortune of war had brought them, to return to the stony lands where their fathers had lived. It was only a small colony (42,360 souls) which followed Sheshbazzar, the son of King Jehoiachin and a descendant of David,[3] and set to work, at the end of seven months, to rebuild the Temple. Surrounded as they were by hostile tribes, remnants of the natives or exiles from elsewhere, it was only through the aid of the Persian governor that they were able to complete their work (536).

We do not know what were the last campaigns of Cyrus, nor how he died. We may suppose that he was recalled to the east

[1] " Without skirmish or battle," as the cylinder of Cyrus says, l. 17 ; cf. *Annals of Nabonidus*, col. iii, ll. 15-16.

[2] Enumerated in Ezra, i. 9-11.

[3] Ezra, i. 9-11 ; v. 14, 16. It is an incorrect transcription of Shamasha-baluzur (**XVIII**, p. 639, n. 1).

of his empire by an invasion of the nomads who would, for ages
to come, pour out of the steppes of Central Asia over the
more civilized countries of the south.   According to the account
of Herodotos,[1] he had offered marriage to Tomyris, the queen
of the Massagetæ, who lived beyond the Jaxartes, but, his
proposal having been rejected with scorn, he invaded her
country, defeated her advanced guard (which had surprised
the Persian camp almost without defence, but had lingered
there pillaging and, still more, drinking wine, to which they
were not accustomed), and captured her eldest son and heir
apparent, Spargapises, who committed suicide.   In a great
battle which then took place Cyrus was defeated and killed (528).
The queen, to avenge the death of her son, dipped the hero's
head in blood, crying, " I give you your fill of blood ".   But
the king's body did not remain in the hands of the enemy,
whether it was given back or taken, for it was carried to Pasargadæ and there buried in the tomb which now goes under the
name of Mashhad-i-Madar-i-Sulayman, ' the Mausoleum of
the Mother of Solomon '.   His coffin still existed in the time of
Alexander, and was seen there by Aristobulos.

According to Berosus,[2] it was during a war against the Dahæ
(Dai) of Parthia that Cyrus was killed; Ctesias[3] says that it was
while fighting, not the Massagetæ, but the Derbices, a people
east of the Caspian, whose king Amoræus was allied with the
Indians and had elephants in his army.

Cyrus is, beyond dispute, one of the greatest figures in history,
and only the scantiness of the evidence left us by antiquity has
prevented him from being a very conspicuous figure.   The idea
formed of him down to times not far from our own, based on the
classical authors, made him a legendary type like the
Charlemagne of the Mediæval romances.   To raise himself
from the rank of a petty king of Susiana to that of the founder
of the empire of the Achæmenids, he must have been a great
general and an admirable statesman ; he must have brought
into the East a new idea and principles of government unknown
before his time.   He reduced three great empires to subjection
and, even if he was aided by circumstances—a vague word which
stands for a whole number of situations which are little known

---

[1] Hdt., i. 204 ff.
[2] In Eusebius, *Chronicon*, p. 29 ; cf. **XXI**, p. 24.
[3] Frag. 29, §§6-7, in Müller, p. 47.

and insufficiently estimated—it is none the less true that the energy which he displayed destroyed for ever the three states known as the Median Empire, Lydia, and Babylonia.

A leader would be little without the value of his soldiers. Napoleon would not have been able to display all his genius if he had not had in his hand that wonderful instrument, the Army of the Revolution ; the Turkish armies, which certainly never had any great leaders, defeated the troops of the Holy Roman Empire and advanced as far as Vienna. What was this army, with which Cyrus conquered Nearer Asia ? We know nothing of it, but we may suppose, from what we know of the Achæmenids, that it was composed of feudal troops raised by chiefs of the tribes, among the inhabitants of the plain of Susiana, or among the hillmen like the Bahktiyaris of our own time. They were not a national army, but troops recruited and commanded by chieftains of their own nationality. The enamelled bricks of Susa show us two types in the Royal Bodyguard, one white, the other very dark, or even black. The first must have been Persians of the mountains ; the second, Susians who lived in the sun-baked plain. These soldiers were better organized than the troops of the other states. Their armament was without doubt better than that of the neighbouring peoples, and perhaps even than that of the Median and Lydian empires.

The favourite weapon was a long bow, in the handling of which they were past masters. Xenophon says[1] that the Cretan archers could not shoot so far as the Persians, although the former were trained in firing their arrows upwards a long distance. But the Persians had found in the Carduchi opponents who were able to maintain their independence[2] ; these had a bow nearly three cubits long, and arrows of nearly two cubits ; to shoot, they drew the bowstring downwards, setting the left foot against the bow, and could pierce shields and breast-plates.[3] The Persians also used slings, but their slingers, who shot large stones, were no match for the Rhodians, who used leaden bullets and sent them twice as far as the Persians.

The Royal Guard were armed with the bow, the universal weapon, and a long pike. Their proficiency with this latter arm may have given them the advantage over their contemporaries. The organization of the army had been commenced

---

[1] *Anab.*, iii. 3.   [2] *Ibid.*, iii. 5.   [3] *Ibid.*, iv. 2.

long before by Cyrus's predecessors on the throne of Susa, just as, in the XVIIth century, the Electors of Brandenburg prepared the Prussian army which served the designs of Frederick the Great. With this instrument, Cyrus had the courage to attempt a work of conquest, which must have seemed too great an undertaking to his predecessors, if they ever thought of it.

Moreover, Cyrus had an idea which was at once political and religious. Babylonia and Assyria, unable to get away from the fetishist idea attaching to the plastic images of the gods, used to carry off the gods of the conquered peoples as trophies,[1] making them form a kind of triumphal procession under their own national god. So far from carrying off these images, Cyrus restored them to the peoples whose palladia they were. He gave the statues of gods which he found in Babylon back to their lawful owners ; in the same spirit he returned the sacred vessels of the Hebrews. One can easily imagine the sentiment of gratitude felt by the peoples conquered by Babylon, on the news that their national gods were coming home. This idea of genius consolidated the power of the conqueror ; the Persian Empire was founded.

All this was new to the East—so new that, thanks to the publicity given it by the Jews, the name of Cyrus is still a household word among us.

---

[1] The Persians did not destroy the cities they conquered, and were content to reduce them to the condition of subjects, except in case of rebellion, whereas the Assyrians set out to raze walled cities and to transplant peoples. " I have given the cities to the flames, I have demolished them, I have destroyed them. I have made of them ruins and rubbish, I have laid on them the heavy yoke of my domination " (**XVII**, p. 281).

CHAPTER IV

THE ACHÆMENIDS

CAMBYSES

K AMBUJIYA was the eldest son of Cyrus and Cassandane. Already, in his father's lifetime, he had been associated with him as king of Babylon, and he was no doubt regent of the empire during the last campaign. He was cruel ; when one of the seven supreme judges was convicted of corruption, the new king ordered him to be flayed, and, moreover, had his seat covered with his skin, and commanded the judge's son, who was appointed to his office, to sit on this seat when he delivered justice. The younger brother of Cambyses, Bardiya, whom the classical authors call Smerdis,[1] had been entrusted with the government of the eastern provinces, Khwarizm (Khivah), Bactriana, Parthiene, and Carmania (Kirman). The new king's power was not at once recognized everywhere ; there were revolts among the peoples recently subdued, which it took four years to put down. Having ascended the throne in 529, it was not till 526 that he was able to think of continuing the enterprises interrupted by the death of his father, and to turn his eyes towards Egypt, the only civilized state in the Orient which the Persians had not yet encountered.

The presence of Bardiya was an obstacle to this undertaking, for he was popular, and it was to be feared that he would take advantage of the king's absence to try to seize the crown with the help of the army which he must have maintained in the provinces which he governed. Whether justified or not, this fear prevailed, and Cambyses secured his peace of mind by having his brother secretly murdered.[2]

---

[1] Ctesias calls him Tanyoxarces (*Persica*, §8) and Xenophon Tanaoxares (*Cyrop.*, viii. 7. 11). The similarity of these two names indicates another source than Herodotos. The name Bardiya is established by the Behistun inscription.

[2] Herodotos (iii. 30) believed that the assassination took place during the Egyptian expedition, but the Behistun inscription shows that it was before (H. Rawlinson, " Inscription of Darius on the Rock at Behistun," in *Records*

Amasis, the king of Egypt, saw the storm coming. The fall of Lydia and Babylonia were calculated to cause him lively concern, and he made preparations for defence, although internal troubles prevented him from giving his whole attention to the problem. He made alliances with the Greek islands, and particularly with Polycrates, tyrant of Samos, in order to obtain a fleet against that of the Phœnicians and Ionians, who were now subjects of Persia, but in this quarter he was sorely disappointed. Cambyses opened the campaign, and first marched on Gaza ; there he was joined by Phanes of Halicarnassos, who, with his fleet, had deserted the cause of Amasis. A treaty was concluded with the chiefs of the Bedouins, who collected thousands of camels laden with water-skins to await the army at different stages. Thus the Persians were able to cross the desert which extends from Palestine to Egypt.

By a crowning stroke of fortune Amasis, a gallant soldier and a capable administrator, died at this time, and was succeeded by his son, Psammetichus III, who was of a very inferior character. A battle took place before Pelusium ; the Egyptians were defeated, and Psammetichus, losing his head, sought safety in flight, instead of defending the passages of the canals, by which action he would at least have delayed the advance of the enemy (525). No obstacle now remained between Cambyses and Memphis, which, after resisting for a time, finally surrendered. The independence of Egypt was at an end. Psammetichus was taken prisoner, and executed on a charge of conspiracy. According to Ctesias, he was conveyed to Susa, where he died in prison. A Persian, named Aryandes, was appointed governor of the conquered country.

Cambyses, true to his father's policy, adopted the double cartouche, the ceremonial, and the royal costume of the Pharaohs. He went to Sais, and, in personal spite, burned the mummy of Amasis, but he showed great consideration to Ladice, the king's widow, sending her home to her parents.

---

of the Past, vol. i, p. 112 ; Oppert, Le Peuple et la langue des Mèdes, p. 117 ; Weissbach and Bang, Die altpersischen Keilinschriften, pp. 12-15). We need not accept the hypotheses of Beloch (Griechische Geschichte, vol. i, p. 345, n. 1), Rost (Untersuchungen zur altorientalischen Geschichte, pp. 107-9), and Winckler (Altorientalische Forschungen, vol. ii, pp. 138-40), who, contrary to the opinion of the ancient writers, suppose that the story of the False Smerdis was invented by Darius to further his policy.

Persian troops had taken up their quarters in the great temple of Neith, to the scandal of the pious, and had done damage there ; Cambyses caused the temple to be evacuated and the damage repaired. He even took instruction in the mysteries of the Egyptian religion.

Memphis appeared to him an excellent base of operations from which to effect the conquest of the West. There the supreme power was Carthage, whose possessions covered the shores of the western Mediterranean. Cyrene had surrendered voluntarily; the Persian king, despising the gift of 500 minas of silver sent him by Arcesilas III, distributed them as largess to his troops. He intended to reach Carthage by sea, but the Phœnicians, whose assistance was indispensable, refused to help him against their old colony.[1] So he had to go by land, that is, the Desert of Sahara. From Thebes he sent fifty thousand men to occupy the Oasis of Ammon, but after this army had passed the Great Oasis it was never heard of again. Probably, as the story went at the time, it was destroyed entirely in a sandstorm (524). In spite of the failure of this expedition, the Oasis of Ammon was later, at some date unknown, attached to the Empire, to which it paid tribute.[2]

Nubia appeared to offer an easier prey, for it was only necessary to go up the Nile, which offered a base for supplies. The kingdom of Napata had become independent of Egypt, but the northern part of the country, once flourishing, was ruined and almost a desert. Cambyses led the expeditionary force himself. The army seems to have gone up the Nile to Korosko, and then to have set out across the desert towards Napata, but food and water ran short when they had made only a quarter of the way, and they had to retire after many losses. However, the districts nearest Syene remained subject to the Empire, and in the time of Darius I we find Ethiopians, south of Egypt, included among the subjects of the Great King.

From his childhood Cambyses had suffered from epileptic fits. The failure of his expeditions against Nubia and the Oasis of Ammon greatly upset his mind. He went mad. On his return to Memphis with the remnants of his army, he found

---

[1] Cf. Gsell, *Histoire ancienne de l'Afrique du Nord,* 1913, vol. i, p. 418.
[2] Deinon, in Athenæus, ii. 74, p. 67.

the city holding holiday, for a new ox was being consecrated as Apis. Imagining that they were rejoicing over his defeat, he had the magistrates and priests put to death, and, sending for the sacred ox, stabbed it in the thigh with a dagger ; the beast died of the wound some days later. The people of his court did not escape his mad actions ; he killed his own sister Roxana, shot the son of Prexaspes, and caused twelve of the chief persons of his retinue to be buried alive. He ordered the execution of Crœsus, who had accompanied him, and then revoked the order, but put to death the officers who had not obeyed the order which he had himself revoked. He left Egypt in 522, and was crossing Syria, when he learned that his dominions were in revolt, the leader being a Magian, who bore a strong resemblance to his brother Bardiya and gave himself out as being that prince. The stay of Cambyses in Egypt had been fatal to the respect which the peoples owed to the royal majesty ; his absence had ruined him ; the Magian was proclaimed King of Persia. Cambyses made an effort to put down the rebellion, and then killed himself in despair. It is supposed that he took this course in consequence of some serious defection, but the only historical authority which we possess on this event, the inscription of Darius, which confirms the facts, is silent regarding the motives which brought them about. According to the legend which comes to us through Herodotos, the king was mounting his horse, when his dagger wounded him in the thigh, at the very place where he had stabbed the Apis ox, and this happened at an Agbatana in Syria, in fulfilment of a prophecy which had led him to suppose that he would die in Ecbatana.

The name of the Magian was Gaumata. In his character of Bardiya, the False Smerdis, he destroyed many temples in a few months,[1] made away with all who might know the fate of the true Bardiya, and proclaimed exemption from military service and from taxation for three years. He retired from public life as soon as possible, thereby surprising no one, for it was the usual etiquette, but he ordered the members of his family to break off all relations with one another, and

---

[1] By this we must understand temples of the conquered peoples, for the Persians had none. It was clearly religious fanaticism which drove him to this extreme action, which was a serious political mistake. Cf. Behistun inscription, col. 1, ll. 63-4 ; Weissbach and Bang, *Die altpersischen Keilinschriften*, pp. 14-15.

this attitude aroused the suspicion of the heads of the seven great noble families, who had the right of access to the sovereign at all times. They first made certain that Gaumata was not Bardiya, and instructed one of his wives, Phædymie, the daughter of the Persian chief Otanes, to ascertain discreetly whether his ears had been cut off, as had indeed been done, in execution of a penalty which was once very frequent in the East. Being sure of their facts, the conspirators[1] presented themselves at the gates of the fortress of Sikthauvatish or Sikayahuvati in Media, were admitted by the door-keepers without difficulty, broke past the eunuchs who forbade them access to the private apartments, and forthwith put Gaumata and his suite to death (521). They then hastened to the capital, roused the people, showed them the head of the impostor, and organized a massacre of his Magian supporters, the memory of which was celebrated by the Feast of the Magian-killing. This last detail proves that the Median tribe of the Magi had taken up the cause of the False Smerdis, probably in the hope of avenging the fall of Media and establishing a theocratic power.

The popular traditions with which Herodotos regales us make out that, in order to choose which of the heads of the seven great families should ascend the throne, it was agreed that he whose horse should neigh first at sunrise should be king. This is an example of divination by the horse, or hippomancy. The groom of Darius took his master's horse to the appointed place beforehand, and let him see a mare; so, next morning, when the horse recognized the spot, he started neighing joyfully. It was by this ruse, people said, that Darius won the crown.[2]

---

[1] The names of the conspirators are given in the Behistun inscription : Vindafarna (the Intaphernes of Herodotos) son of Vayaspara, Hutana (Otanes) son of Thukhra, Gaubaruva (Gobryas) son of Marduniya, Vidarna (Hydarnes) son of Bagabigna, Bagabukhsha (Megabyzus) son of Daduhya, and Ardumanish son of Vahuka. Except that Herodotos does not give the last, and Ctesias does not give the last two, the information of the Greek authors agrees with the inscription of Darius.

[2] This popular tradition (Hdt., iii. 68-87) throws doubt on the genealogy which Darius gives himself in the inscription ; if he was really descended from " Hakhamanish " (really the name of a clan) by a line parallel to that of Cyrus, he should not have needed divination by the horse to be chosen king, for, as next of kin to Cambyses, he was naturally his successor. According to the tradition, he was merely a noble of one of the seven privileged families. His father Hystaspes was still alive, and was Satrap of Hyrcania.

DARIUS I

He had to reconquer the Empire, for the provinces had revolted.

Elam was the first to try to shake off the yoke, at the instigation of Athrina, the son of Upadarma, the descendant of an ancient royal house which had been driven from the throne of Anshan by the Achæmenids. He was captured by

Fig. 3. Darius I

an expeditionary force sent to Susa, and led in chains to Darius, who put him to death. In Babylon Nidintu-Bel, who pretended to be the son of Nabonidus, assumed the name of Nebuchadnezzar III. The King of Persia placed himself at the head of his army, but could not cross the Tigris, which was held by a strong fleet, supported by a considerable army. After deceiving the enemy as to his intentions by a succession of feints, he managed to cross the river, and defeated the

Babylonians in two battles. Nidintu-Bel was compelled to take refuge in the city itself, which then had to be besieged.

Meanwhile, revolts were occurring on every hand. One Martiya, who came from a town in Persia named Kuganaka, took charge of the rising in Susiana, but the people of the country themselves seized him and put him to death. The Median army, quartered in the land of its origin, listened to the voice of Phraortes, who declared that he was Kshatrita, a descendant of Cyaxares, and proclaimed him king. Darius entrusted one of his subordinates, Vidarna, with the repression of these attempts at independence, and a battle was engaged, which seems to have been undecided, for the expeditionary force received orders to await the arrival of the king.

To Armenia Darius sent Dadarshish, himself an Armenian, to subdue the rebellious country. He won three battles without obtaining a decisive result, and was replaced by a Persian named Valaumiza, who was no more fortunate ; two battles were fought, without any more success, and the army had to be patient until Darius himself could join it.

The king had seen that the fall of Babylon was the solution of the whole problem, and would release the troops which surrounded the city. Herodotos tells of the self-sacrifice of Zopyrus, who mutilated himself and so won the confidence of the besieged.[1] The great city was taken after a blockade of nearly two years (521). Darius then proceeded to Media, and won a first battle against the rebel Phraortes, who fled to Ray and was there taken prisoner. The king caused his nose, ears, and tongue to be cut off, and his eyes put out, and kept him in this condition for a time at the court, where all might see him ; in the end he had him hanged from a gibbet in Hamadan, while his chief supporters were massacred in the citadel of that town.[2]

Sagartia, that is, the mountains about Arbela, now inhabited by the Kurds, also took up arms, at the call of Chitratakhma, who declared himself descended from Cyaxares. Against him Darius sent a Medo-Persian army under the command of Takhma-spada. Chitratakhma was defeated, was treated in the same way as Phraortes, and was finally hanged at Arbela.

---

[1] On this legend, of which Ctesias gives a different version, see the remarks of Maspero, **XVIII**, p. 680 ; Marquart, *Philologus*, suppl. vi. 626.

[2] Cf. Behistun inscription, col. i, ll. 64-8 ; Weissbach and Bang, *op. cit.*, pp. 18-21.

Further east, Parthiene and Hyrcania were reduced by Hystaspes, the king's father and governor of those regions. Margiana accepted the rule of a certain Frada ; Dadarshish, the satrap of Bactriana, was instructed to deal with the rebels, and brought them to their senses with one battle. Then a second False Bardiya, "son of Cyrus," declared himself king in Persia itself, and was followed by the Persian army stationed in the country. Darius placed Artavardiya at the head of a Medo-Persian force, which defeated Vahyazdata, as the pretender was named, in two battles. The pretender was

Fig. 4. REBELS LED BEFORE DARIUS

captured and hanged, with his principal adherents, in the town of Huvadaichaya in Parsis. But before he was defeated and taken the False Bardiya had sent an expedition to Arachosia which was governed by the satrap Vivana ; defeated in two encounters, this expedition and its leader took refuge in a castle, where they were taken and slain by Vivana.

In the meantime, Babylon revolted again at the call of an Armenian named Arakha, who also claimed to be Nebuchadnezzar, and took possession of the city ; but it was taken by Vindafarna, a Mede of the suite of Darius, and the rebels were executed.

So, in nineteen battles and seven years of fighting, Darius

and his generals overcame nine pretenders who had proclaimed themselves kings.   The unity of the empire founded by Cyrus and increased by Cambyses was thus re-established.   During these disorders, Orœtes, Satrap of Lydia, who had made away with Polycrates of Samos on the pretext that he was conspiring against the king, was himself slain by the devices of Bagæus, whom Darius had entrusted with the mission (about 519). The king visited Egypt in person, and set himself to win over the priests, who were still all-powerful, by benefactions of every kind (517).   The problem was to organize his vast empire.   Darius gave up the transportations in mass,[1] which had been the usual practice of the Assyrians, especially since the time of Tiglath-pileser III.   He divided the Empire into satrapies, or governments-general, taking care not to con-centrate all powers in the hands of one man, and so tempting him to dream of complete independence ;   beside the satrap he placed a military commander and a secretary of State who received orders from the court direct and kept an eye on each other.   In this way the king armed himself against the perpetual danger of seeing the governor of a distant province evade the orders of the central authority and pursue schemes of inde-pendence on his own account.[2]

Darius built a Royal Road from Sardes to Susa, of a length of about 1,500 miles, which a pedestrian would take three months to cover.   Leaving Sardes, it crossed Phrygia, reached the Halys near Pteria, the old capital of the Hittites, and then ran southwards over the mountains to the Euphrates at Samosata.   It crossed the Tigris at Nineveh, near Mosul ; then, after following the river for some way, like the present Mosul-Bagdad road, it went over Susiana to the capital.

At intervals there were post-stations, held by troops, and very good hostelries, and the mountain passes and fords were guarded by forts.   At the stations, horses were kept in readiness, and the couriers passed their orders on from one to another ;   this system of mounted posts was called *angareion* in the Persian language.[3]

The building of this road, especially in the difficult passes of the mountains of Asia Minor, naturally was of great

---

[1] He only effected them on rare occasions.
[2] See below, chap. v, " The Organization of the Achæmenid Empire."
[3] Hdt., v. 52 ; viii. 95.

convenience for the transport of troops to the west. It served a project of Darius which must now be considered.

The Empire seemed to have reached its natural limits : the Caspian, the Caucasus, and the Black Sea bounded it on the north ; in the west its shores were washed by the Mediterranean ; there could be no question of extending beyond Egypt, for the bitter memory of the expeditions of Cambyses into Nubia and to the Oasis of Ammon were too much alive in the king's mind for him to cast his eyes in that direction. The Persian Gulf opened a way for coasting vessels to the shores of India.[1] Arabia, defended by the desert, was impregnable. Why did Darius contemplate the conquest of Scythia ? Cyrus had already come into conflict with peoples inhabiting the present Turkestan, to his cost. This time it was Scythia in Europe, Southern Russia, inhabited by nomads of Aryan stock (but not Slavs), that Darius had in view. If his real object was a campaign against Greece, as is probable, since this was the ruling idea of Xerxes, who had doubtless inherited it from his father, we may suppose that he wished to conquer Scythia in order to protect himself against a flank attack during the expedition. It has, however, been observed that this was attaching far too much importance to these nomads, and that, if he had wished, instead of annexing Thrace and accepting the submission of Macedonia, he could equally well have moved southwards and attempted an attack on the Hellenic cities. It might rather be that the King of Persia, remembering the damage which had previously been done in Nearer Asia by the Scythian invasion, wished, by occupying their cradle, to put an end to their troublesome inroads.

Before sending out his army, Darius commanded the Satrap of Cappadocia, Ariaramnes, to make a raid on the north coast of the Black Sea and to bring back prisoners. Among these was Marsagetes, the brother of a local chieftain, whose information was of great importance (515).[2] Next year the army crossed

---

[1] About 512 Darius descended into the Punjab (Hapta-Hindu) and conquered extensive territory, which was made into a new satrapy, that of India, which is not mentioned in the Behistun inscription, but appears in the lists at Persepolis. At Peucela he built a fleet, which went down the Indus under the Greek admiral Scylax of Caryanda, and in less than thirty months sailed round the coasts of Gedrosia (Makran) and Arabia. Scylax wrote an account of the voyage, which has been lost, but was seen by Aristotle. Cf. Hdt., iv. 44 ; Arist., *Pol.*, viii. 13. 1.

[2] Ctes., *Pers.*, 16.

the Bosphorus, over which the Greek cities of Asia Minor had, at the king's command, made a bridge of boats, which was guarded by the Greek colonies in the neighbourhood. From there, crossing Thrace, where only one tribe, the Getæ, put up a resistance, the force reached the delta of the Danube, where a second bridge of boats had been built by the tyrants of the Ionian cities. Beyond lay the steppes, with mobile nomads avoiding all contact. For two months the Persian army made a military promenade in these barren solitudes. It lost men, suffered from disease, and had great difficulty in obtaining provisions, which had to be brought from the base, since the country yielded none and the Scythians had destroyed the fodder and filled up the wells.

Darius summoned the King of the Scythians to submit; the latter replied by a silent message, borne by a herald, which consisted of a bird, a mouse, a frog, and five arrows. Gobryas, the father-in-law of Darius, gave an ingenious explanation, which, however, seems somewhat incomplete to us. "Unless you become birds to fly through the air, mice to burrow under the ground, or frogs to take refuge in the swamps, you will not escape our arrows." That does not explain why the arrows were five in number. In the meantime the Scythians were negotiating with the Greeks that the latter might cut the Danube bridge; but the tyrants, after each proposal, refused, reflecting that their position at home depended on the support of the King of Persia. Darius recrossed the Danube without trouble and returned to Sardes, leaving some eighty thousand men in Europe under the command of Megabyzus, who reduced the Greek cities of Thrace and obtained the submission of Macedonia and its king Amyntas.

Hippias, tyrant of Athens, of the family of Peisistratos, had been driven out in 510 by the Spartans, and had retired to Sigeion in the Troad. He sought the help of Artaphernes, Satrap of Sardes, and intrigued against the city which had expelled him. Athens herself, fearing the Spartans, sent ambassadors to the same satrap, offering to recognize the overlordship of Persia, in exchange for effective help; but these agents were disavowed by their government on their return in 508. A second Athenian embassy arrived at Sardes in 506, with the request that the satrap Artaphernes should cease to protect Hippias; he replied that Athens should recall her former tyrant, and, since she refused, she might expect war. This was chiefly brought about by the revolt of Ionia (499-4).

Histiæos, tyrant of Miletos, who had been entrusted with the construction of the bridge over the Danube and had been rewarded by the gift of a town in Thrace, Myrcinos on the Strymon, aroused the suspicions of the Persian agent by fortifying it. He was summoned to Susa, and interned, though treated honourably, and his son-in-law Aristagoras took over the government of Miletos. To him Histiæos sent a slave who announced that his head must be shaved with the utmost secrecy ; when this was done, there appeared, tattooed on his scalp, a message calling for revolt against the Persians. The moment was well chosen. Aristagoras had advised the satrap to attack the island of Naxos, and this attempt had failed, as a result of treachery ; consequently the tyrant of Miletos expected to lose his crown and perhaps his life as well. When he abdicated, a popular rising seized the government ; the other tyrants, returning from Naxos with the fleet, were arrested by the rebels aboard the ships. Sparta, to which Aristagoras appealed, refused to help ; Athens sent twenty ships, and Eretria, in the island of Eubœa, five. Feeble as this support was, it encouraged the insurgents, who took the lower town of Sardes by surprise (498), but could do nothing against the strong citadel which dominated the city. Unable to hold the town, they retired, and were attacked by the Persians near Ephesos.[1] The Athenians then abandoned a cause which they considered lost.

This capture of Sardes was only an escalade, and led to nothing, but its repercussions were considerable. Darius in his wrath commanded that at every meal a slave should call the Athenians to his memory. The rebels were heartened, and had some success in Caria, at Pedasos, where a body of Persian troops was wiped out. But a Greek fleet of 353 ships was attacked off the island of Lade, near Miletos, by 600 Phœnician and Cypriote vessels ; the squadrons of Samos and Lesbos deserted the common cause, and the battle was won by

---

[1] Maspero (**XVIII**, p. 704, n. 5) shows that the statements of Herodotos (v. 99-101) are contradicted by Charon of Lampsacos, who, being nearer the events, speaks only of the retreat (Frag. 2, in Müller, *Fragmenta Hist. Græc.*, vol. i, p. 32). The dimensions assumed by events immediately afterwards seem to prove that the second version is nearer the truth.

the Persians (494). This disaster was followed by the fall of Miletos, the principal city of Ionia and the centre of the revolt ; the city was taken, the male population slain, and the women and children were transported to Ampe, at the mouth of the Tigris. To hold the Greek colonies of Asia Minor, the Persians had been compelled to withdraw their troops from Thrace and Macedonia, and these two provinces had become independent once again. Athens built the fleet which was to save Greece.

Darius decided to reconquer Thrace first, and entrusted this duty to his nephew Mardonius. In one campaign (493) Mardonius recovered the province and compelled Alexander, the son of Amyntas, King of Macedon, to renew the treaty concluded by his father. This success was to have been followed by an attack on Greece, but half of the fleet which carried supplies was destroyed by a storm, and the project had to be abandoned for the time. Mardonius was recalled (492).

A second expedition was entrusted to the Mede Datis and the Persian Artaphernes, the second of whom was the son of the Satrap of Lydia. The destruction off Mount Athos of the Persian fleet which was to convoy the army as it advanced by land caused the Persians to adopt the sea route, for many islands, including Ægina, had made their submission. The plain of Alaya in Cilicia was chosen for the assembling of the expeditionary force, which embarked on a fleet of 600 vessels.

The marine host appeared before Naxos, whose inhabitants were reduced to slavery. Delos was spared on account of its sanctuary, and the fleet made for the island of Eubœa, with the object of punishing the city of Eretria for its share in the attack on Sardes ; it was taken by treachery and burned, the inhabitants fled to the hills, and those who were captured were transported to Susiana. Athens does not seem to have raised a finger to save her ally.

Hippias, who had joined the Persian fleet, indicated the bay of Marathon (490) as an excellent mooring ; the cavalry could deploy with ease on the plain, and the tyrant expected his supporters to rise in his favour ; but no movement of the kind occurred. Athens was only twenty-four miles away. The Athenians had been joined by a thousand Platæans, but the Spartans, whose assistance was awaited, had not yet arrived, on the pretext that they must wait for the full moon before taking the field.

The armies remained facing each other several days. The Greeks wondered whether they should attack a force so much more numerous than themselves ; the generals hesitated, but in a council of war Miltiades persuaded the Polemarch, or commander-in-chief, that safety lay in the offensive. At his suggestion, in order not to be outflanked, the centre of the army was spread out and a very strong wing was formed on each side. The Athenians attacked suddenly ; the two wings were victorious, and fell on the centre, where the Persians and Sacæ had the advantage. The Persian host fled, and the Greeks pursued them to their ships. Not all the troops had landed ; Datis had been surprised on the way to Phaleron. Next day he doubled Cape Sunion, but, on approaching Phaleron, he perceived the victorious Greek army ready to meet him with stout hearts ; he took alarm, and sailed for Asia Minor. The Athenians had fought with the energy of despair, and they had defeated the troops of the Great King. The moral effect of the victory was enormous, and to this day the echo of it has not died away. The Asiatic forces had suffered a serious set-back, and Greece was saved.

Egypt was still governed by Aryandes, whom Cambyses had appointed, and this satrap tried to extend the frontiers of the province towards the west. Taking advantage of the fact that the Dorians of Cyrene had twice driven out their king Arcesilas III and had finally murdered him at Barca, Aryandes, moved by the lamentations of Pheretime, the deceased tyrant's mother, who ascribed the death of her son to his loyalty to the King of Persia, sent troops to besiege Barca, which was taken by treason after holding out nine months. The advanced guard of the army made its way as far as Euhesperidæ, which was later called Berenice and is now Benghazi. The occupation of Cyrene was contemplated, when orders came recalling the expeditionary force to Egypt. Although harassed by nomads, the Persian troops succeeded in bringing back with them part of the population of Barca, who were sent to Bactriana and there founded a city called after their own. Following on this unsuccessful expedition, Aryandes was put to death, either because he had issued a coinage of greater value than the royal darics, a certain prelude to a revolt, or because he had so angered the Egyptians by his extortion and corruption that the province was ready to rise. Darius visited Egypt in person, and, adopting an attitude exactly opposite to the senseless policy of Cambyses, he did everything to win the support of the priesthood. He brought back from Susa the high priest of Sais, Uzahorresenet, and entrusted him with the reparation of the havoc wrought by his predecessor. The traditions echoed by the Greek authors improve on his action still further, and make out that he was initiated in the mysteries, associated himself with the mourning with which the death of the Apis bull in 517 was celebrated, and promised a large reward to the man who should discover a bull worthy to take the place of that which was no more. Egypt was prosperous in the reign of Darius. It formed the sixth satrapy, with Cyrene, Barca, and Lower Nubia. The satrap, who was quartered in the old palace of the Pharaohs, had under him an army stationed in three fortified camps, at Daphnæ and Memphis on the Delta and Elephantine in the south. Apart from this military occupation, the country was unchanged, being divided between the properties of the temples and the domains of the nobles. Darius completed or reopened the canal connecting the Nile with the Red Sea, by which the fleets of those days could go from the Mediterranean to the Indian Ocean. In the Oasis of Thebes he built a temple of Ammon, the ruins of which still exist. The peasants, however, were discontented because of the heavy taxes which they had to pay, and revolted in 486. In the autumn of the same year Darius died, after a reign of thirty-six years.

XERXES

A little before his death, Darius had designated as his successor Khshayarsha, whom we know better by his Græcized name of Xerxes. His mother, Atossa, the daughter of Cyrus, had obtained his designation by the personal influence which she exercised over the old king and by the rank which she held at the court. It had long been expected that Artabazanes, one of the three sons whom Darius had had by his marriage with the daughter of his fellow-conspirator Gobryas, would be chosen, but when the king announced his wishes there was no opposition. Xerxes was then thirty-four years old, tall, and of noble bearing, but he was violent, sensual, weak and indolent.

Xerxes was at first disinclined to renew the expedition against Greece, regarding the defeat of the Persian army as quite unimportant; but Mardonius returned to the attack and persuaded him, pointing out the blow to the prestige of the great empire. First a revolt had to be put down in Egypt, where one Khabbisha had been in power for two years. The Egyptians were defeated (484) and punished, and the Delta was ravaged. Achæmenes, the king's brother, was appointed Satrap; the hereditary princes and the priests were left in possession of their property, and contributed to the restoration of peace in the country.

In the following year a certain Shamash-irba, of unknown origin, had himself proclaimed King of Babylon. A siege of a few months was sufficient to reduce the city, which was sacked. The temples were pillaged, the treasure of Bel-Marduk was seized, his golden statue was removed, and the population was led into captivity. Babylon never recovered from this disaster.

By the autumn of 481 preparations for the expedition against Greece were complete, and all the various troops called up assembled in Cappadocia and wintered in Lydia. Every people in the Empire furnished its contingent. At the head came the Persians and Medes, armed with the lance, bow, and sword, as were the Cissians and Hyrcanians; the Assyrians, wearing bronze helmets, followed, and after then came the Bactrians, Arians, and Parthians with their javelins and pikes and the Sacæ with their pointed caps and their axes, the cotton-clad Indians, the Ethiopians of Africa, with painted bodies, armed with long bows and flint-headed arrows, the Ethiopians of Asia (perhaps the negroid population of Makran), who wore extraordinary helmets made of horses' heads, and yet others, down to the inhabitants of the islands in the Persian Gulf. These were the infantry. Beside them there were men fighting from chariots, as there had been in the Egyptian and Assyrian armies. They were chiefly Persians and Medes, but there were also Sagartians from the country about Arbela, armed with lassos, Indians on vehicles drawn by wild asses, Bactrians, Caspians, Libyans, and Arabs on their dromedaries or one-humped camels. Each division was commanded by a Persian, and Mardonius was commander-in-chief.

The fleet was of the greatest importance, for the army depended on it entirely for supplies, and would have died of hunger if it had to live on the country. The 1,207 warships composing it were manned by Phœnicians, Egyptians and Greek subjects of Persia, and there were a few Persian, Median, or Sacian marines on board each. In addition to this fighting fleet there were 3,000 transports.

It must have been a fine sight when this immense host, whose true numbers are unknown (Herodotos's figures are obviously exaggerated), set forth from the neighbourhood of Sardes for the Dardanelles, the ancient Hellspont, where it was to cross the sea.[1] Preparations had been made in advance—two strong pontoon bridges over the strait between Abydos and Sestos, a bridge over the Strymon, and a canal north of Athos, to avoid the storm which had destroyed the fleet on the first expedition. In this canal three hundred darics were found in 1839.

Xerxes wished to be present at the crossing of the pontoons, which lasted seven days, and a marble throne was erected for him on a hill near Abydos. At sunrise the king poured a libation from a golden cup, which he then threw into the sea, with a golden bowl and a sword. This was a sacrifice to the sea-god[2]; the Persian royal house, as we saw in the case of Cyrus, paid great heed to the foreign gods whom it encountered in the course of its adventures. The 'Immortals', with wreaths of flowers about their heads, crossed the bridges the first; the planks were covered with branches of myrtle. The army was reviewed on the plain of Doriscos.

Thessaly had called the Greeks to her defence, but the ten thousand men sent to the Vale of Tempe, finding that the position could be turned, retired, and the Thessalians came to terms with the Persians. The Spartans wanted to evacuate the whole of northern Greece and to confine the defence to the Isthmus of Corinth; however, their plan was rejected, and they sent seven thousand men, commanded by Leonidas, to hold the narrow pass of Thermopylæ, between the hills and the sea, which was much narrower then than to-day. After

---

[1] M. Théodore Reinach has shown that the two lines in the *Persae* of Aeschylos, which were supposed to refer to the Bosphorus, really mean the Dardanelles, "Bosphorus" being simply used as a common noun signifying a narrow strait. Cf. *C. R. Acad. Inscr.*, 1923, p. 385.

[2] Compare the ceremonies performed in Rome when the first bridge was made over the Tiber, and the creation, in this connexion, of the office of Pontifex, "Bridge-maker."

waiting four days, perhaps for his fleet to join him, Xerxes gave orders to attack. The Medes and the Cissians, and then the Immortals, charged, but without success ; the defensive armour of the Greeks gave them a great advantage over the enemy. It was the same on the following day. Xerxes was wondering how he should take the position, when a way over the mountains was revealed by a traitor. The Phocian contingent which guarded it did not resist, but retired. When the news reached Thermopylæ all contingents retired from the struggle except the three hundred Spartans, the Thespians, and the Thebans, who would have liked to retire, but were forced to stay. Not waiting to be surrounded, Leonidas and his brave comrades advanced on the enemy and were killed to a man.

They did not prevent the Persians from marching on Athens, whose citadel, with its temple of the owl-eyed Athene, was fired to avenge the burning of Sardes. Meanwhile the Persian fleet had arrived, diminished in numbers by a storm off the coast of Asia Minor and a three days' battle near the northern point of Eubœa. It met the enemy at Salamis, and Xerxes, looking on at the battle from afar, where he sat on his throne, witnessed the utter failure of his undertaking.[1] The Great King decided to return to Asia, leaving his cousin Mardonius at the head of the army, which was stationed in Thessaly. The last force remaining on Greek soil was defeated at Platæa in the spring of 479 ; the death of Mardonius, killed while charging the enemy, decided the outcome of the battle. From this moment the Persians retreated, and Athens, by her successes, seized the hegemony of the sea.

In the reign of Xerxes an attempt was made to sail round Africa, a century after the Carthaginian admiral Hanno. The Persian Sataspes, who was sentenced to undertake this voyage in lieu of the death penalty to which he had been condemned, passed through the Strait of Gibraltar and sailed southwards for several months. He failed to circumnavigate the continent, and on his return to the court of Xerxes he was crucified by order of the king. Before he died he related that, on the furthest coast which he had visited, he had seen " little men,

---

[1] The Persian fleet was unable to deploy, and the ships collided, rending each other with their bronze rams. See the account of the battle in Aesch. (*Pers.*, 290-471), who was a contemporary. Cf. **XVIII**, p. 720.

clad in garments of palm, who left their towns and fled into the hills when they saw him approach ".[1]

Xerxes perished by a palace crime. In the summer of 465 he was murdered, with his eldest son Darius, by the eunuch Aspamithres (also called Mithradates), Prefect of the Palace, and Artabanus, Commander of the Body-guard. Seven months later Artabanus tried to deal with the youngest son, Artaxerxes, in the same fashion, but the latter resisted, and by his courage saved his life and won the crown. Artabanus, betrayed by Megabyzus, was slain with his accomplices.[2]

ARTAXERXES I

Artaxerxes I (Artakhshathra) was surnamed Longimanus or Long-hand. His reign of forty-one years was disturbed by no troubles except at the beginning. A son of the late king, Hystaspes, supported by the Bactrians, claimed the crown; after two defeats he disappeared (462). A new revolt in Egypt hardly constituted a threat to the State. Inarus, the son of the Libyan Psammetichus, blockaded the Persian garrison in the White Fort at Memphis. Athenian vessels from Cyprus were partly responsible for this achievement. To avenge the death of the Satrap Achæmenes, killed by Inarus, Megabyzus, Satrap of Syria, with a considerable army and the help of the Phœnician fleet, put down the revolt, except on the coast of the Delta (455). After some successful enterprises on the part of Cimon, Athens and Persia concluded an agreement known as the Peace of Cimon, under which the roadstead of Phaselis in Lycia was designated as the boundary between the spheres of action of the two navies (449). The Peloponnesian War relieved Iran of all fear from abroad, but the ambition of the satraps created new trouble at home, such as the revolt of Megabyzus, the viceroy of Syria, who, after twice defeating the troops of the Great King, concluded an advantageous peace with him.

Artaxerxes died in March, 424, on the same day as his wife Damaspio, and was succeeded by their son, Xerxes II. His brief reign of forty-five days ended with his assassination, but

---

[1] Hdt., iv. 43.
[2] According to Deinon (Plut., *Them.*, 27), Artabanus acted as regent during these seven months, probably in the name of Hystaspes, the king's brother.

his murderer, Sogdianus, the son of the concubine Alogune, barely profited by his crime ; another brother, Ochus (Vahuka), Satrap of Hyrcania, seized the throne without difficulty (7th December), and reigned under the name of Darius II. The Greeks surnamed him Nothos (bastard), because he was the son of a concubine. His wife was the abominable Parysatis, his aunt or stepsister,[1] who had a finger in every plot in the palace. At the beginning of his reign there were revolts ; they were quickly repressed, with the aid of bribes, and the leaders were executed.[2] Greece, taken up with her internal strife, could not defend her colonies, and the cities of Asia Minor had to pay tribute. Sparta made an alliance with the Great King, who, however, did not desire the complete annihilation of Athens ; a policy of balance of power was better suited to the interests of the Empire, in view of a possible coalition of all the Hellenes.

The Greeks were soon to show what useful help they could give to the man who asked for it. The death of Darius II at the beginning of 404 opened the field to claimants. Cyrus the Younger, his younger brother, who had obtained through the influence of Parysatis the chief command of the troops in Asia Minor, with the title of Karanos, had gone to his sick father in Babylon, and had left to take his place the Spartan Lysander, who had defeated the Athenian fleet at Ægospotami the year before. Cyrus had counted on the support of Parysatis to set aside his elder brother Arsaces, but when he arrived his father was dead and his brother was already enthroned as king at Pasargadæ. Cyrus, who had come at the head of an army, intended to assassinate his brother. He was suspected and arrested, and would have been put to death, if his mother had not intervened and folded him in her arms.

ARTAXERXES II

On ascending the throne Arsaces took the name of Artaxerxes II. He was known to the Greeks by his nickname of Mnemon, on account of his wonderful memory.[3] Cyrus the

---

[1] Aunt, according to Ctesias ; stepsister, according to Deinon, in Plutarch.
[2] His brother Arsites, supported by Artyphius, son of Megabyzus, and his cousin Pissuthnes, son of Hystaspes and Satrap of Lydia, who surrendered and was killed in 414.
[3] A translation of the Old Persian *abiataka, Persian yadah (written abietaka in a gloss of Hesychius), according to J. Oppert, Les Mèdes, p. 229.

Younger had hardly returned to his district in Asia Minor, when he took advantage of the fact that the end of the Peloponnesian War placed seasoned troops at his disposal, and formed a large army, with which he set out to conquer Asia (401). Going through Anatolia by Qoniya (Iconium) and the Taurus passes, he descended into Cilicia and, reaching the Euphrates, followed the river downwards. Near Babylon, at Cunaxa, the site of which is marked by the Khan Iskandariyah, on the Bagdad road, a great battle was fought (3rd September). The Greek troops were victorious, but Cyrus was killed in a cavalry charge which was repulsed by horsemen of Tissaphernes, eight of his defenders being hewn down about him. The king, who had been wounded in the fighting, caused the head and hand to be cut off his brother's corpse.

With the death of Cyrus the campaign ceased to have an object. The Asiatic troops broke up ; the Greeks, harassed by the Persian horse, transported their camp to the Tigris. All at once they found themselves leaderless, for their officers had been enticed into the tent of Tissaphernes, where they were arrested, conveyed to Babylon, and put to death. Then a volunteer who had followed the army for the love of the thing, Xenophon, took charge, and undertook to conduct them home, going up the Tigris and the Bitlis River, crossing the mountains near the springs of the Euphrates, and descending to Trebizond on the coast of the Euxine. This fine achievement is universally known as the Retreat of the Ten Thousand, and has been wonderfully described by the general himself in his *Anabasis*.

Persia had felt her military weakness ; henceforth when she intervened in Greek affairs her weapon was corruption. Athens combined her fleet with that of the Great King, Conon seized the island of Cythera, and the Long Walls connecting Athens with the port of the Peiræeus were rebuilt with the help of Persian subsidies. Egypt, after making several unsuccessful attempts to shake off the foreign yoke, succeeded about 405, under the grandson of an Amyrtæus, who had been independent for a time ; but it was not until six years later that the country regained its complete independence, under Nephorites. In Asia Minor, too, the native peoples were in revolt, and had to be reduced. In the autumn of 387 Artaxerxes dictated to his opponents the Peace of Antalcidas. The Greek colonies

of Asia and Cyprus fell once more under the Persian yoke.
It was a blow to Hellenic pride ; but the Persian rule was not
very burdensome, for it left great liberty of internal administration to these provinces, which were remote from the centre
of the Empire. Small local dynasties and free towns grew up,
from which no more was asked than that they should acknow-
ledge themselves vassals of the Great King and pay their
tribute regularly. The ancient Persians did not try to make
converts to their religion ; on the coins of the satraps we find
not only the image of Ahura-Mazda, but those of Baal of
Tarsus and of Pallas Athene.

Euagoras, a descendant of the Teucrians, took possession of
Cyprus, and the petty kings whom he dispossessed appealed
to the Great King for help. The work of Euagoras had been
facilitated by the fact that the Persians were busy with Egypt,
which was once more independent, and the King of Egypt,
Hacoris, sent him reinforcements, while Tyre furnished ships.
The Persians, led by Autophradates, Karanos of Asia Minor,
and the Carian Hecatomnos, at first met with no success ;
Tiribazus and Orontes had to take energetic steps to shut him
up in his capital, Salamis, of which he was eventually recognized
king, in return for a declaration of vassalage and the payment
of annual tribute (380).

The revolt of the satraps threw Asia Minor into confusion.
Ariobarzanes, Satrap of Phrygia and Mysia, who set the
example, was at first opposed by the Karanos Autophradates,
but the latter presently declared himself a rebel ; thence-
forward he could count on the support of the Greek cities and
the Pharaoh of Egypt. Treason relieved the king of some of
his enemies ; others, such as Orontes, made peace with him.
Datames, who had hitherto been loyal, carved out a great
kingdom for himself between the Euxine and the Mediterranean
but was slain by his own troops. These movements, forty
years before Alexander's conquest, showed the extreme
weakness of the central power.[1]

Domestic dramas were happening at the court. Parysatis
had poisoned Stateira, the wife of Artaxerxes, and had been
banished to Babylon in consequence. Stateira had three sons.

---

[1] A communication of M. Salomon Reinach to the Académie des Inscriptions et belles-lettres (*Comptes rendus*, 1923, p. 393). Cornelius Nepos wrote
a life of Datames, probably based on Deinon of Colophon.

Darius, the heir apparent, was made to believe that he was to be supplanted by his younger brother Ochus ; he made an attempt on the life of the king and was punished with death. Ariaspes believed that the king meant to make away with him, and committed suicide. Arsames, the son of a concubine, was assassinated ; he was the favourite child of his father, who died of grief at the age of eighty-six (358).[1]

It was in the reign of Artaxerxes that Ezra led a colony of Babylonian Jews back to Jerusalem, completed the construction of the Temple, which had been begun under Darius I in 520, and tried to organize a community on the basis of the Pentateuch as revised during the Captivity. In this he was aided by Nehemiah, also a Jew, who had been the king's cup-bearer and governor of Judea before the return of Ezra.

In the inscriptions left by this king we see for the first time the names of Mithra and Anahita, to whom he seems to have been especially devoted, particularly the latter, to whom he built temples in various parts of his empire.[2]

ARTAXERXES III

Ochus, the sole survivor of the three sons of Stateira, assumed the name of Artaxerxes III, and his first act was to put to death the princes of the royal family, in order to prevent any rivalry in the future. This drastic method has often been imitated since in the East. Asia Minor was not yet restored to tranquillity. The Karanos Artabazus, fearing to be charged with taking part in the revolt of the satraps, finally threw in his lot with them, and, with the aid of the Athenians, defeated the troops sent against him (356) ; but when he no longer had the support of Athens, he thought it wise to take refuge with Philip of Macedon. Egypt had a hand in all these adventures, and it was on Egypt that the king vented his wrath. A first attempt, in 353, was unsuccessful. Five years later, after two satraps had been defeated by Tabnit, King of Sidon, with the aid of Greek troops in the pay of Egypt, the king took command of his forces in person. As these advanced,

---

[1] According to the pseudo-Lucianic *Macrobius*, 15 ; ninety-four, according to Deinon, in Plut., *Artax.*, 30.

[2] In particular, at Babylon, Susa, and Ecbatana, according to Berosus in Clement of Alex., *Protr.*, v. 65. 3 (**LIX**, p. 67). This cult must have been peculiar to him, for his successor Ochus mentions only Mithra in his inscription at Persepolis.

Tabnit took alarm and surrendered the city ; this did not save him from being put to death with the citizens who had accompanied him. The rest shut themselves up in their houses and set them on fire. Mentor of Rhodes, who, with his Greeks, had been out of employment since the fall of Sidon, joined the Persian army which, thanks to his assistance, took Pelusium and Bubastis and so occupied Egypt, which was once more reduced to a Persisan province (345). The same mercenary helped Artaxerxes III to recover Asia Minor. The siege of Perinthos by Philip in 340 suggested to the Persians that the King of Macedon might have designs on Asia, and it is not impossible that they had a share in his assassination in 336. In the preceding year Artaxerxes III had died, poisoned by the eunuch Bagoas, who felt himself menaced by palace intrigues. The king was succeeded by Oarses, his youngest son ; he, too, fell victim to Bagoas, who set on the throne a great-grandson of Darius II,[1] Darius III Codomannus, in 335. He was the friend of the eunuch, but the latter was deceived in his expectations ; Darius refused to submit to his authority, and compelled him to drink the poison which he had prepared for the king. So Darius saved his life, but, whatever his personal courage may have been, he deprived himself of a man who might perhaps have averted the storm which threatened the empire of the Achæmenids.

DARIUS III CODOMANNUS

It was not for a mere matter of coinage, the struggle of the silver standard of the Greeks against the gold standard of the Persians,[2] that Alexander, Philip's son, plunged right into the heart of unknown Asia, where only a body of Greek mercenaries, that which Xenophon had brought back safe from Cunaxa, had yet penetrated. Taking up the projects of his father, which had been cut short by death, he saw in the huge Persian Empire the oppressor of Greece, and it was the liberation of Hellas at which he aimed, by carrying the war into the very heart of the enemy's country. He crossed the Hellespont in

---

[1] **XVIII**, p. 808, n. 3 ; Diod., xvii. 5. 5, makes him a grand-nephew of Artaxerxes II. According to Strabo, xv. 3. 24, and Plut., *Alex.*, 18, he did not belong to the royal line, and in his youth had been a courier.

[2] On this question see the authorities quoted by F. Justi, **IX**, vol. ii, p. 471, n. 2.

the spring of 334 at the head of 40,000 men, without receiving
any hindrance to his expedition. A victory on the banks of
the Granicus opened Asia Minor to him. The Greek colonies
were declared free. Halicarnassos resisted under a Persian
leader, Orontobates, and the admiral Memnon, who was still
in the service of Persia, but died at Mytilene at the beginning
of the next year.

Crossing Cappadocia, the conqueror came down into the
plains of Cilicia, and, following the coast, found the Persian
army formed up at Issus, ready to contest the way to
the Syrian Gates. Enclosed between the mountains and the
sea, the battle-field was too narrow for the Persian cavalry
to charge with success ; they were utterly routed, and Parmenio
seized the camp and the royal family at Damascus, with a vast
amount of booty. The victor did not accept the proposals
of alliance which Darius made to him, but advanced along the
coast, probably with the object of leaving no enemies in his
rear. In this way he subjugated Syria, where the city of Tyre
held him for seven months and Gaza for two. Egypt welcomed
him as a deliverer and bestowed divine honours on him. By a
stroke of genius he founded Alexandria on the site of Rhacotis,
and his city became one of the commercial capitals of the
world.

In the spring of 331 he left Memphis, and the battle of
Gaugamela delivered Babylon, Susa, and Persepolis into his
hands. Darius was obliged to fly east. Persepolis was burned
down, either because Alexander wished to avenge the burning
of Athens by Xerxes, or because he wished by this action to
mark that the empire of the Achæmenids was ended. It may
be that the conqueror was led, in the excitement of a carouse,
to an act which he secretly regretted afterwards, for he assumed
the inheritance of the Kings of Persia and made use of the
administration of the Empire as soon as he entered Persepolis,
and the destruction of the city could not serve a purpose of
that kind. His old comrades found that it was dangerous to
refuse to submit to his Oriental ways, and several paid for their
soldierly Macedonian frankness with their lives.

The plateau of Iran and the eastern districts still remained
to be conquered. Darius intended to collect a new army in
Media, but the project was cut short by the conspiracy of two
satraps, Bessus and Barsaentes, who killed him while he was

flying before Alexander's army (July, 330). The former of
the two murderers, who was of Achæmenid stock, attempted
to succeed his victim under the name of Artaxerxes IV, but
the advance of Ptolemy put an end to his enterprise. A revolt
on the part of the Mede Baryaxes was promptly put down by
the Satrap of Armenia. In the north, Alexander advanced
as far as the Jaxartes, took Cyropolis (Ura-Tubeh), and founded
an Alexandria which is to-day Khujandah. In 327, after
celebrating his marriage with Roxana, daughter of Oxyartes,
at Bactra, he descended into the valley of the Indus, and

Fig. 5. BATTLE OF GAUGAMELA, NEAR ARBELA

advanced as far as the Hyphasis (Sutlej). The Indian princes
Porus and Taxiles submitted. Sisicottus, another Indian
prince, was established in the fort of Aornos (Ranigarh), between
Kabul and the valley of the Sindarudh. Alexander descended
the Indus. Having been wounded at the attack on the fort
of the Malli, he destroyed the capital of Musicanus and crucified
the Brahmins who had raised the people against him. From
Patala the army returned to Persia, either through Arachosia
and Khurasan, or through Gedrosia, not without severe losses.
Nearchos conducted the fleet back along the coast, in the
autumn of 325.[1]

[1] A. W. Hughes, *The Country of Balochistan*, London, 1877, p. 177;
Tomaschek, "Topographische Erläuterungen der Küstenfahrt Nearchs,"
in *Sitzungsber.* of the Academy of Sciences of Vienna, 1890.

Alexander had hardly returned to Babylon when, worn out by hardship and excesses, he caught fever in the swamps of the lower Euphrates, and the sickness, aggravated by an orgy, carried him off in a few days. He died in Nebuchadnezzar's palace, now called al-Qasr,[1] at the age of thirty-two, on the 13th June, 323. His body was embalmed and conveyed to Alexandria, where it still is, but in a place which has long been unknown, perhaps beneath the tombs of the family of the Khedive of Egypt surrounding the Mosque of Daniel.

[1] E. Sachau, *Am Euphrat und Tigris*, Leipzig, 1900, Foreword, p. 1.

CHAPTER V

The Organization of the Achæmenian Empire

THE great empire founded by Cyrus and Darius I was no more ; nothing took its place, for the dying Alexander left the throne to the worthiest, and the result was general disintegration, and the reappearance of nationalities which had for two centuries been gathered together under the dominion of the Achæmenids.

The whole edifice rested on a single sentiment—loyalty of the subjects to the reigning house, whose representative was revered like a god and surrounded with imposing pomp of ceremony. The brilliant successes of the two founders had invested their memory with imperishable glory, and the Persians imagined this glory in material form when they believed that their kings were surrounded by the aureole which painters rightly call a ' glory ', the *hvareno* of the Avesta (*farr* in modern Persian). The king was an absolute autocrat, ruling from afar. The subject peoples retained their own organization, their religion, even their chiefs. The Phœnicians were still governed by kings ; the Egyptians had their chiefs of nomes ; the Jews went on with the establishment of their theocratic state in peace. So long as these vassal provinces recognized the king's authority and paid their taxes their people lived undisturbed. But all subjects without exception, even ministers and generals, were considered as slaves (*bandaka*, a slave) of the king. We have seen this notion survive, till times very close to our own, in the Ottoman Empire, which was organized, before the reforms of the XIXth century, on the same model as the old Asiatic monarchy.

This immense state, the first of its size to be seen on earth, which comprised the most diverse nationalities and languages, the admiration, the marvel, and the terror of the particularist Greeks in their tiny cities, was maintained by an administration inherited from Assyria and Babylonia, where the ancestors of Cyrus had gone for models for their small principality of Susa.

It was the scribes of these administrative offices who invented
a syllabary suited to the Indo-European language which the
Persians brought with them, simplifying the cuneiform
characters which had so long served the needs of the states
in the basin of the Euphrates and Tigris. In this script the
Iranian part of the great Behistun inscription is written, by
the side of the Babylonian and Susian translations of the text
in which Darius left to his remotest posterity the story of his
deeds.[1]

The Empire was divided into Satrapies or viceroyalties,[2]
each under a satrap (khshathrapa). This high official had with
him a secretary or chancellor, whose duty was to watch the
acts of the satrap and to report to the court. He was a
police-agent. The command of the troops was in the hands
of a general whose title—karanos—has been transmitted to us
by the Greeks. The citadels of the towns had a special
governor (arga-pat, fort commandant). These three high
officials, satrap, secretary, and general, were independent of
one another, and took their orders direct from the court.
These orders were borne by post-couriers, for ever going to and
fro over the paths which served as roads across those immense
tracts.[3] In addition to the secretary who supplied the court
with information (like the masters of the mounted post long
after, in the days of Islam and the Abbasid Caliphs), the
provinces were covered by an elaborate police organization.
Like the Missi Dominici of Charlemagne and the Délégués
Spéciaux of whom Napoleon dreamed on St. Helena, the
officials known as the King's Eyes and Ears went every year
to the most distant regions, to investigate the situation,

---

[1] See above, Introduction, chap. ii, "The Scripts of Persia."

[2] Herodotos gives twenty satrapies, the Persepolis inscription twenty-
four, and that of Naqsh-i-Rustam twenty-eight. At first there were twenty-
three : (i) Fars (Persis), (ii) Elam (Susiana), (iii) Chaldea, (iv) Assyria, (v)
Mesopotamia, Syria, Phœnicia, and Palestine (together Arabaya), (vi)
Egypt, (vii) the Peoples of the Sea (Cilicians and Cypriotes), (viii) Ionia
(Greek colonies in Asia Minor), (ix) Lydia and Mysia, (x) Media, (xi) Armenia,
(xii) Katpatuka (central Asia Minor, Cappadocia), (xiii) Parthiene and
Hyrcania, (xiv) Zarangia, (xv) Aria, (xvi) Chorasmia, (xvii) Bactriana,
(xviii) Sogdiana, (xix) Gandaritis, (xx) the Sakas (Sacæ), then in the Great
Plain of Tartary, (xxi) the Thatagus (Sattagydians) in the Helmund basin,
(xxii) Arachosia, (xxiii) the Makas, on the Straits of Hurmuz. At the end
of Darius's reign there were thirty-one. It will be noted that this list gives
the provinces in a circle round Persis, clockwise.

[3] The only road worth mentioning was that which connected Susa with
Sardes, over Asia Minor.

SACAE

AMYRGIAN SACAE

CHORASMIA

SOGDIANA

Oxus (OLD COURSE)

Oxus

Oxus

HYRCANIA

MARGIANA

BACTRIANA

GANDARITIS

DIA

PARTHIENE

ARIA

ZARANGIA

SATTAGYDIA

cbatana

SAGARTII

ARACHOSIA

INDIA

M

FARS

Indus

MAKA

followed by a company of soldiers to protect them and to give them effective help if required. On the bare report of these officials, the court took irrevocable resolutions. Governors were recalled, and sometimes put to death, without form of trial or right to present their defence. Often their own guards were ordered to execute the sentence on receipt of a royal command. There was no restriction on the omnipotence of the autocrat ; but this was not peculiar to Persia. In Asia it has always been so. In emergencies the satrap took over the direction of military affairs as well ; this practice, which had been exceptional at the beginning, had become normal by the time of Alexander.[1]

One of the chief duties of the satrap was to collect taxes, which were paid partly in kind and partly in money. Our only information on this subject comes from Herodotos. A fixed sum was laid down as the amount of tribute to be paid for ever. Small peoples were collected in great taxation-districts, to which the Greek historian gives the same name as the Egyptian districts—nomes. So Asia Minor was divided into four districts. The first, comprising the Ionians, Carians, and Lycians, paid 400 talents of silver ; the second, comprising the Mysians, Lydians, and other peoples, paid 500 talents ; the Phrygians, the Paphlagonians, and the Hellespont formed the third group, assessed at 360 talents ; and Cilicia paid 500 talents and 360 white horses. Phœnicia, Palestine, and Cyprus paid 350 talents.[2]

Egypt, in addition to the seven hundred talents which it had to pay with the dependent Cyrenaica and Barca, was obliged to supply the army of occupation with 120,000 measures of corn, worth 610 talents, and the fisheries of Lake Mœris in the Fayyum furnished 240 talents for the queen's private purse. In kind, Babylonia supplied 500 eunuchs ; Media, 100,000 sheep, 4,000 mules, and 3,000 Nisæan horses ; Armenia, 30,000 colts ; and India, in addition to the hunting-dogs which it sent to the king's palace, paid gold dust to the value of 40,680 talents of silver. Every three years the Ethiopians made a payment of gold, elephant-tusks, ebony, and five children ; the people of Cholcis furnished 100 boys and 100 girls every five years ; the Arabs supplied 100 cwt. of

---

[1] A. Buchholz, *Quaestiones de Persarum satrapis*, Leipzig, 1896.
[2] The silver talent was worth about £240.

frankincense a year.   The total amount thus coming into the Treasury in specie may be reckoned at £4,000,000, without counting the payments in kind, or the gifts offered to the king when he visited Persis, the present Fars, the inhabitants of which paid no taxes and were only obliged to make this gift. Plutarch relates that Darius made inquiries in the provinces to ascertain whether the taxes which were contemplated could be borne ; on receiving a reply in the affirmative, he halved the taxes, foreseeing that the satrap would have to take his share for his maintenance.   For the satrap was subjected to no control when levying taxes ; so long as he sent up the sum at which his province was rated, he was asked no questions about the rest.   So these minor potentates, to fill their own

Fig. 6.   DARIC OF DARIUS

pockets, did not hesitate to exploit the peoples delivered into their hands.   These methods have survived in the East to our own time.

By the time of Darius I coinage had been invented in Asia Minor.   Crœsus had already struck gold and silver money, and even the kings of Babylon may have caused ingots to be made representing shekels and fractions of skekels.   Darius made use of gold goins general, and struck money bearing, on one side only, the figure of an archer bending his bow, one knee to the ground.[1]

It is only fair to say that the viceroys, possessing this unrestricted power, put down brigandage and local warfare, kept the roads safe, and protected agriculture.   Darius congratulated the Satrap Gadatas, who had planted trees in

[1] E. Babelon, *Revue de numismatique*, 1901, p. 161 ; Pognon, *Journal asiatique*, xith series, vol. xvii (1921), p. 31.

PLATE I

ROYAL HUNT IN IRAN.

[face p. 76.

Asia Minor and formed a park reserved for hunting, the favourite amusement of the kings.[1]   The Achæmenids were fond of shooting game in the immense parks called 'Paradises', surrounded with walls and containing pavilions where the king and his suite could rest.   The ruins of one such pavilion have been found at Sidon, with a front of great kneeling bulls, like the protomæ of bulls, back to back, on pillar-capitals at Persepolis and Susa.[2]   These are probably the traces of the revolt of the King of Sidon, Tennes (Tabnit), against Artaxerxes III Ochus in 351, in which the insurgents destroyed the royal park.[3]

To protect the king's person a guard had been formed of Persians and Medes, and probably also of Susians, to judge from the friezes of the palace of Susa, now in the Louvre, in which the dark faces indicate inhabitants of hot countries. This guard, divided into three corps, contained 2,000 horsemen and 2,000 foot-soldiers, all of noble birth.   They were armed with lances with gold or silver apples at the lower end, on the strength of which the Greeks called them *melophoroi*.   The Archer Frieze shows that in addition to the spear, about seven feet long, they carried a bow and a quiver of arrows.   Next to them came a corps of 10,000 men, called the Immortals, forming ten battalions, the first of which bore lances adorned with golden pomegranates.[4]   They got their name, so popular tradition told, because as soon as one of them died he was replaced, so that the number of ten thousand never varied ; but it seems rather to be a case of popular etymology, explaining the name of the Amardi, a people of Persia, by its signification in Persian (*a* privative+*mereta*, to die).

This guard, with the garrisons of the more important strongholds, was the only permanent part of the army ; the rest came from levies made in time of war.   If the conflict was localized, it was carried on by the satrap of the district by means of contingents supplied by the peoples subject to him. If it was general, and the sovereign had to take command of

---

[1] *Bull. Corr. Hell.*, 1889, pp. 529 ff.

[2] Clermont-Ganneau, "Le Paradeisos royal achéménide de Sidon," communicated to the Acad. des Inscr. et belles-lettres, 17th Dec., 1920, and summarized in *Revue biblique*, 30th year (1921), pp. 106-9.

[3] Diod., xvi. 41-5.

[4] Heracleides of Cumæ, Frag. 1, in Müller, *Frag. hist. Graec.*, vol. ii, pp. 95-6.

his troops, his guard, which accompanied him, was surrounded by the reserves of all the provinces, a medley of peoples of different origin and speech, a confused mob, without cohesion between its various parts. When these confused, unorganized masses found themselves in front of organized armies and leaders who understood tactics, they could not stand, in spite of their numerical superiority. This was often seen during the Persian Wars, and was still more obvious when they had against them the Macedonian phalanx.

The administration of justice was indispensable to an empire of this extent. The king was the supreme judge, especially in penal matters. He gave sentence in the first and last resort in the case of crimes against the safety of the State or his own person. In civil cases he had delegated his powers to judges appointed by himself. We find this as early as the reign of Cambyses.[1] Sisamnes, one of the royal judges, was condemned to death by Cambyses and executed, because he had accepted money to give an unjust judgment. After his death he was flayed, and his skin was cut into straps, with which the seat from which he used to deliver justice was covered. Cambyses gave the appointment to the son of Sisamnes, and compelled him to sit on the seat thus barbarously adorned.[2] Artaxerxes I even improved on this ferocious treatment, for he caused judges who gave unjust sentences to be flayed alive ; their skins were likewise stretched over their seats.[3] Nevertheless, the law allowed no one, not even the king, to sentence a man to death for a single crime. Nor could any Persian inflict too severe a punishment on one of his slaves for a single fault ; but if, after careful consideration, he decided that the slave's faults were more numerous and more serious than his services, he might then give rein to his anger.[4]

High treason was punished by beheading and amputation of the arm. The great inscription tells us of the penalties meted out to the rebels. They were led to the royal court ; their noses and ears were cut off, and they were shown to the people ; then they were taken to the capital of the province where they had revolted, and were put to death. When Cyrus the Younger

[1] Hdt., iii. 31.
[2] Hdt., v. 25. See above, p. 46.
[3] Larcher's note in his translation of Herodotos, vol. i, p. 439.
[4] Hdt., i. 137.

was killed, his head and right hand were cut off. The whole
family usually suffered the same fate as its head.[1]

Private persons were often entrusted with the execution of
capital sentences. Orontes, condemned to death by Cyrus the
Younger for an act of treachery, was handed over to Artapates,
a sceptre-bearer, and no more was heard of him.[2] So, in the
middle of the XIXth century of our era, the Persian officers
of State were given the Babis to torture and put to death, at
the time of the persecution of the new sect.

[1] **CV**, iii, 649 ff.   [2] Xen., *Anab.*, i.6.

CHAPTER VI

The Religions of Persia under the Achæmenids

IN the immense empire which Cyrus had founded and Darius I had re-established in its unity, every subject people kept its own religion. The Great Kings were eclectics, who did not proselytize ; on the contrary, we find them being initiated into the worship of foreign deities and taking them for their protectors. What, then, were the inmost beliefs of these autocrats, which were sufficiently elastic to allow of such dealings with the patron gods of the conquered peoples ? Unfortunately the evidence at our disposal is too scanty to enable us to obtain more than an outline of an interesting subject, which affects the policy of these rulers, and would, if fully known, considerably affect our reading of history.

It seems to be certain that the Medo-Persian group had three religions—that of the king, to which the inscriptions testify, that of the people, our small knowledge of which comes from Herodotos, and that of the Magi, of which hardly any evidence survives but the *Gathas*, or hymns, preserved in the text of the Avesta.

The first of these religions places at the head of the universe Ahura-Mazda, the greatest of all the gods,[1] who created heaven and earth. The king reigns by the grace of Ahura-Mazda ; Ahura-Mazda gave him his power, and it is his support that has enabled him to conquer the rebels, as Darius proclaims in the Behistun inscription.[2]

If he is the greatest of all the gods, it means that there are others. But these are not designated by name ; clearly they did not enjoy the royal confidence. The difficult expression *vithaibish bagaibish* was for long explained as ' the gods of the clans and districts (*vith*), local gods, Penates ' ; but it should be noted that the two texts, Elamite and Babylonian, which

---

[1] *Mathista baganam* in an inscription from Persepolis, *baga wazarka* on the Tomb of Darius at Naqsh-i-Rustam.
[2] Col. 1, ll. 12, 24-6.

accompany the Old Persian text translate these words by
" all the gods ".   Since we cannot suppose that the translators
made a mistake, which would soon have been pointed out by
the other scribes, we must assume that *vith* is, as has been
conjectured, a dialect form corresponding to the Zend *vispa*,
' all '.[1]   We have no document which allows us to guess what
was the religion of Cyrus and Cambyses ; our information only
begins with Darius.[2]

The godhead not being visible, it was worshipped in the form
of a symbol.   Of this we have an irrefutable proof in the scene
sculptured on the Tomb of Darius.   The king is adoring a fire
on a stone altar ; the sun shines on the scene, which takes place

Fig. 7.   Ahura-Mazda on the Reliefs at Persepolis

in the open, since the ancient Persians had no temples ; and
an image of Ahura-Mazda, copied from an Assyrian type,
hovers over all.   It was only much later that the sacred fire
was protected from the rays of the sun.

In the inscriptions of Artaxerxes Mnemon and Ochus we
see for the first time the names of Mithra and Anahita.   The

---

[1] On this question, see the appendix added by L. H. Gray, of Princeton
University, to William Jackson's article, "The Religion of the Achæmenian
Kings," in the *Journal of the American Oriental Society*, vol. xxi, part. ii
(1901), p. 181.   The Aramaic version from Elephantine unfortunately does
not contain this passage.

[2] Cyrus appears in the Babylonian documents and the Bible simply
as worshipper of Marduk and King of Babylon.   As for Cambyses, the
inscription on the statue holding a temple in the Vatican refers to the re-
establishment of the Egyptian cult in the great temple of Sais.   There is no
reference to the personal beliefs of these two kings.

former, who was originally the ' God of Compact ', according
to M. Meillet, was at a certain date assimilated to the sun, and
later became the god of a secret religion which had devotees
all over the Roman Empire. Anahita, who may have been
taken from Assyria, was the planet Venus. The King's
religion had changed in character ; the notion of Ahura-Mazda,
alone in the sky, had grown old ; new deities sprang up by his
side, younger and therefore more active.

Mithra was worshipped by the Iranians in very early times,
although he was not introduced into the special religion of the
kings until the end of the Vth century. In the XIVth century
B.C. he is mentioned with Varuna, Indra, and the Nasatyas
as a god of Mitanni, in northern Mesopotamia.[1] In the pre-
Avestic religion he acts as mediator[2] between the upper world
of light and the lower world of darkness. From Artaxerxes II
onwards, the kings honour him as the bestower of the royal
glory, call him to witness in their oaths, and invoke him in
battle.

The introduction of Anahita into the Iranian pantheon
shows that the royal religion was becoming impregnated with
Chaldean astrology. It was in this form that it survived in
certain kingdoms of Asia Minor after the fall of the Persian
Empire.[3]

The people worshipped the four elements—light (divided
into the light of the day, or the sun, and that of the night,
or the moon), water, earth, and wind. The popular religion
included the sacrifice of animals, which was done in the presence
of a Magus, for, as Herodotos tells us, the presence of an
ecclesiastic of this order was necessary for the act to be valid.
The sacrificer led the victim to an unpolluted place, and, with
a tiara crowned with myrtle on his head, called upon the god
and prayed for the welfare of the king and all the Persians.
Next he cut up the victim, boiled the flesh, and laid the pieces
on a bed of soft grass, clover for choice. Then the Magus
chanted a ' theogony ', after which the sacrificer took away
the meat and did what he liked with it. It has been suggested
that by ' theogony ' Herodotos may mean the *Gathas*. Although

---

[1] Cuneiform inscription from Cappadocia ; cf. **XIX**, i, 2, pp. 589, 829.

[2] Μεσίτης. (Plut., *De Iside*, 46).

[3] **CXXXV**, p. 8, ll. 10-11 ; p. 121, ll. 13-17 ; F. Cumont, *Religions
orientales*, p. 258. Cf. J. Toutain, " Légende de Mithra," in the *Revue de
l'Histoire des religions*, xlv (1902), pp. 141-57.

there is no proof that the fragments of verse preserved under this name are the very hymns to which he refers, they have a very pronounced archaic character, and it may be admitted that, if they are not the same as the ' theogony ', they must have been very like it.

A fragment of a relief found at the village of Ergili, near the lake of Maniyas, in the neighbourhood of Dascyleion in Asia

Fig. 8. THE KING FIGHTING AN EVIL GENIUS. (Persepolis).

Minor, represents a scene of sacrifice. Two figures, one of whom is bearded and seems to be a Magus, stand on the right of a kind of architectural niche, the visible upright of which is surmounted by the *protome* of a bull. The two Persians are making a ritual gesture, with the right hand open and extended ; in the left hand they hold a long object, a bundle of rods or a short club. In front of them the heads of a ram and a bull are laid on a pile of brushwood. We find here a detail noted by Strabo :[1] the two persons, the Magus and his companion, have pulled the flaps of their tiaras up over their mouths. This monument dates from the end of the Vth century B.C., and was probably made by Greek artists working for the Persians. It should be observed that one of the two Satraps of Asia Minor had his residence at Dascyleion.[2]

The Magi were a tribe, belonging to the confederation of the Medes, just as the Levites of the worship of Jahveh were originally members of the Tribe of Levi. This tribe seems to have specialized in the knowledge and practice of a certain ritual. We have but little information about the ritual, but it must have represented a whole mass of very ancient traditions and beliefs, most of them dating from the prehistoric period when the Indians and Iranians were still one people. In the Sassanian period we find them co-ordinated in a single *corpus*, the Avesta, which was certainly not invented all at once, but must preserve very ancient memories. Since the surviving edition dates from the Sassanian period at the earliest, it is in connexion with that dynasty that I shall speak at greater length of the beliefs, dogmas, and rites preserved by the Magi for centuries and made an official religion only in the IIIrd century of the Christian era.

With reference to funeral practices, Herodotos declares that the Persians coated the body with wax and then buried it in the ground.[3] The Magi, on the other hand, only buried bodies after they had been torn by a bird or a dog.[4] Here we have

---

[1] xv.732-3.

[2] Collignon, *Bulletin de l'Acad. des Inscr.*, 6th Jan., 1914, p. 20.

[3] Cf. Cic., *Tusc.*, i. 45. 108 : *Persae etiam cera circumlitos condunt, ut quam maxime permaneant diuturna corpora.*

[4] *Ibid. : Magorum mos est non humare corpora suorum, nisi a feris sint ante laniata.* Herodotos says, " before the body has been *dragged* (ἐλκυσθῆναι) by a bird or a dog ". According to Strabo, the exposure of bodies that wild beasts might eat them was a custom of the hillmen of the Pamir, which was introduced into Bactriana in his day.

an appreciable difference between the two customs. The former is Persian ; so the kings caused tombs to be cut for themselves in the mountain sides, with architectural decoration on the exterior. The second is peculiar to the corporation of the Magi ; it is that enjoined by the Avesta, in respect of the bird but not of the dog (though the latter appears in funeral ceremonies, possibly as a survival of the early rite) ; it is the usage preserved by the Parsees, who build *Dakhmas*, or Towers of Silence, large circular charnel-houses open to the sky, in desert places near the mountains. The building of the *Dakhmas* is fairly recent ; the classical authors make no mention of anything of the kind, and no traces of them have been found.

The religion of the kings was that which the ancestors of Cyrus had had in their capital at Susa, when they ruled over an Anshanite people more civilized than themselves, from whom they probably took it. Now, this Anshanite civilization, in its later form, had been influenced by that of Babylon, which had subdued Elam. There was, therefore, without doubt, a pronounced influence of a Semitic religion on the beliefs of a race which was certainly Aryan.

With the Magi it is quite different. In Media, in the high mountains of Adharbayjan and Iraq Ajami, they were out of reach of any moral influence of the inhabitants of the plains. It can, therefore, easily be understood that they preserved through the centuries, down to the formation of the Avesta, a mass of beliefs and traditions which are obviously closely akin to those of India. In the time of the Achæmenids nothing was heard of them in the outer world, except the few scraps of information which the Greek authors have handed down to us ; the Persians employed the Magi only when offering sacrifice ; for the rest, the official religion recognized only one supreme God, and other unnamed gods beneath him.

The fact that the royal religion acknowledged only one God, whereas India knew of thousands and the Avesta, combining the two opposite principles, will still show us a populous pantheon, makes us conclude that the civilizing influence of Elam had been very potent ; had it not been for the traditions of the Magi, there was nothing left, except the language, to attach the official religion to its Aryan origins.

CHAPTER VII

The Arts under the Achæmenids

PERSIAN art in the time of the Achæmenids is neither primitive nor simple. It has undergone several influences, and it has been possible to determine the contribution of each of the foreign styles which have gone to form it. Chaldea and Assyria have given most; from them come the artificial platforms and the monumental stairways up their sides. In the valley of the Tigris and Euphrates Persia, like Chaldea, used brick. At Persepolis stone was used for basements, door-frames, and columns, but the walls were of clay, and therefore no trace of them is now left. As in Assyria, the reliefs run along the floor level, in the embrasure of doors and up the ramps. As in Assyria, colossi guard the entries; the god hovers in the air, surrounded by a ring " recalling the sun's disk "; the king sits on his throne, with his servants about him.[1]

But this architecture is distinguished from that of Assyria by one very marked feature, the preponderant importance of the column, which in Assyria was only an accessory. It is to Egypt, to the hypostyle halls of Thebes, that we must give the honour of having provided the model. Therefore it can only have been after the conquest of Egypt by Cambyses that the Persians thought of raising the majestic fluted columns of which some are still standing. The decoration of the Egyptian temples became that of the royal palaces, for the Persians had no temples to which to apply it. There is, however, one difficulty, presented by the curious capitals, which are of a form not found elsewhere; the origin of these should perhaps be sought in Assyria. We know from Diodorus Siculus that Egyptian artists worked on the buildings of Persepolis and Susa. An absolutely characteristic feature is the Egyptian *cavetto*, the hollow cornice peculiar to the land of the Pharaohs, which we find over all the bays, niches, windows, and doors.

[1] **XXII,** vol. v, pp. 884 ff. (English ed., *Persia*, pp. 487 ff.)

PLATE II

RESTORATION OF THE APADANA AT SUSA.
(After Dieulafoy.)

[face p. 86.

A further proof is supplied by the tombs of the kings. That of Cyrus, of which I shall speak later, is a built tomb; those of Darius and his successors are cut in the face of the mountain; the sculptured decoration outside recalls that of the fronts of the subterranean tombs of Egypt. But these façades are arranged in a special way, in that they present a copy of the façade of the palace, above which the fire-altar rises, with the figure of the supreme god, Ahura-Mazda, over all; it might be called an ingenious adaptation rather than an original creation.[1]

The contribution of Greek art is more difficult to specify. It probably asserted itself in sculpture. We must not forget that at this time sculpture in Greece " was still only breaking free from the trammels and groping of archaism ".[2] That there were Greek artists in the service of the kings of Persia, Pliny's testimony does not permit us to doubt; he speaks of Telephanes of Phocæa, who worked for Darius and Xerxes; either he did not accompany his fellow-townsmen when they emigrated after the Ionian Revolt, or he undertook of his own free will to work for the conquerors of Nearer Asia.[3]

The reliefs of Persepolis are astonishingly like those of Nineveh, but if one examines them more closely one will see, in spite of their superficial resemblance, appreciable differences in the movement of the draperies. In Assyria the garment seems to cling flat to the body, whereas in Persia the artist's conception has been largely governed by the study of the folds, and, indeed, at times these draperies are remarkably like those on the fragments of the earlier temple at Ephesos, which was built in the reign of Crœsus.[4]

Persian art has an original character, which consists in the proportion in which elements borrowed from foreign arts are combined, in the extraordinary size of the buildings, and in the richness of the decoration—I should say in the love of the colossal, if this word had not been brought into disrepute through the abuse of it by a modern European people. The artist did not have to consider private interests or those of the city, as in Greece, and later in the Roman Empire; he depended on a single master, the Great King. As has been

---

[1] **XXII,** vol. v, p. 887 (*Persia*, p. 491).
[2] *Ibid.,* p. 888 (*Persia*, p. 492).
[3] See Heuzey's note in *Bull. de l'Acad des Inscr. et belles-lettres,* Nov., 1886.
[4] **XXII,** vol. v, p. 827 (*Persia*, p. 430).

Fig. 9. CAPITAL FROM SUSA. (Louvre).

well said, Persian art was " a composite art born of the royal fancy, which had gathered into an artificial, powerful unity, like the Empire itself, every artistic form which had struck it in the provinces of Assyria, Egypt, and Asiatic Greece ; it was the caprice of an omnipotent dilettante with a love of size ".[1]

Persepolis had the advantage of being near quarries which supplied the materials necessary for these constructions—a close-grained limestone, easy to cut into large blocks, certain varieties of which resemble marble. To shape the blocks hewn from the mountain, the impressed labourers were not sufficiently skilled ; it required craftsmen, decorative stone-carvers capable of executing the bases and capitals of the splendid columns.

The capital of the columns is original, and is found nowhere else. It represents two half-bulls, or rather foreparts of bulls, *protomæ*, as they are called, back to back. Instead of the bull we find, in the eastern portico of the great palace of Xerxes, the unicorn with lion's feet and muzzle. This idea may have been taken from a kind of standard which appears in a relief at Khorsabad, the shaft of which is separated from the disk at the top by two heads of monsters, joined back to back, with a lion's muzzle and a single horn in the middle of the forehead.[2]

The column is fluted, the number of flutings being large. In the great hypostyle halls used for audiences, there is no central nave ; all aisles are of the same width, and all columns are equal. The roof-timbers, which bore the tiles, were of cedar, according to Quintus Curtius.

The monumental stairs by which the platforms were reached are composed of ramps rising to meet each other and then diverging again, with broad landings between.[3] The roofs were crowned with crow-stepped battlements, as in Assyria ; an enamelled brick of this shape has been found at Susa, and the Sassanian monument of Taq-i-Bustan also terminates in an ornament of this kind.

The facings of enamelled brick must have been a magnificent sight, veritable pictures, glowing with colour, as one can see

[1] J. Darmesteter, *Coup d'oeil sur l'histoire de la Perse*, p. 18.
[2] **XXII,** vol. v, p. 507 (*Persia*, pp. 107-8).
[3] *Ibid.* p. 531 (*Persia*, p. 131).

if one goes to the Louvre and looks at the Frieze of the Archers
and that of the Lions, from Marcel Dieulafoy's excavations at
Susa. The Babylonians had long known how to apply enamel
to clay and to fix its bright, strong colours by great heat.[1]
The Persians also used plates of metal ornamented with
hammered designs ; bronze was generally used, but gold and
silver were also employed. The Greeks knew of a golden
plane-tree which adorned one of the royal residences, but, so
far from admiring the beauty of the work, they laughed at it,
saying that it did not give enough shade to protect a grass-
hopper from the sun.[2] The existence of bronze facings is
certain ; at Susa a fragment of decoration of this kind has been
found, which was destined to cover a door.[3]

Near Mashhad-i-Murghab there is a building which the
natives call the Tomb of the Mother of Solomon, because its
gable roof recalls the tombs of women in Moslem cemeteries.[4]
It is generally agreed that it is the tomb of Cyrus ; Dieulafoy
alone took it for the tomb of Cassandane, the wife of the great
conqueror.[5] It consists of a small chamber borne by a
basement of six courses which diminish upwards, so as to form
steps. In ancient times it was surrounded by a portico, some
bases of which can still be seen. The difficulty about identifying
it is due to the description of Strabo,[6] who tells us that when
Alexander went through Pasargadæ he there visited the tomb
of Cyrus ; this, he says, was a tower of moderate size, in the
middle of a park, solid and massive below, and crowned by a
roof and a chamber with a very small entrance. The word
' tower ' might make it seem that this description does not
apply to the Murghab monument, which is not what we mean
by a tower ; but the inscriptions on the neighbouring monuments, in which Cyrus mentions himself by name, suggest that
the Greek word had a wider sense than our ' tower '.[7] The
contents of this tomb which Alexander visited were inspected
by Aristobulus, who entered the chamber at the command of
the King of Macedon. It was looted during the disorders

[1] **XXII**, vol. v, p. 549 (*Persia*, 149-50.)
[2] Xen., *Hell.*, vii. 1. 38.
[3] **XXII**, vol. v, p. 557 (*Persia*, p. 158).
[4] J. Oppert, "Pasargades et Mourghab," in *Journal Asiatique*,
xix (1872), pp. 548-55.
[5] LIa, i, 50.
[6] xv. 3. 7.
[7] On this question, see **XXII**, vol. v, pp. 603, 612 (*Persia*, pp. 204, 215).

which followed the conqueror's departure for Bactriana and
India, in spite of a permanent guard of Magi, who received a
sheep daily and a horse every month.[1] Arrian also has described
this monument in his *Anabasis* ;[2] he says nothing about a
tower, and his account agrees with those of modern travellers.[3]

Not far off is a ruined edifice, this time just like a tower on
a square plan. It is all the easier to restore because there is
an admirably preserved replica of it at Naqsh-i-Rustam.
Comparison with a funeral tower of the same type at Xanthos
in Asia Minor removes all doubt as to its purpose.[4]

Fig. 10. Tomb of Cyrus at Pasargadae

On the site of Pasargadæ, again, there is a relief carved on
a limestone block, representing a person seen in profile, who
wears a long robe falling to his ankles ; the border of the
material is adorned with a fringe and a band of rosettes. The
right arm, the only one visible, is bent, and seems to hold some

---

[1] The sheep was of course for the Magi to eat, whereas the horse was to be
sacrificed to the memory of Cyrus. The robbers were not able to remove
the coffin, and Alexander ordered Aristobulos to save the remains of the great
king. Cf. Harlez, *Religion persane sous les Achéménides*, p. 7.
[2] *Anab.*, vi. 29.
[3] **XXII,** vol. v, pp. 597, 600 (*Persia*, pp. 198 ff.).
[4] *Ibid.*, p. 381, fig. 268 (*Phrygia, etc.*, p. 374).

indistinct object. The hair, arranged in four locks, is cut
short at the level of the chin. Above the head two great
wild-goat's horns divide so as to hold a very complicated
head-gear, in which one can distinguish three solar disks,
surmounted by bunches of reeds and ostrich-feathers and two
snakes. The figure has four large wings, two turned upwards
and two down. On this monument it was once possible to
read, in cuneiform characters which have now disappeared,
the inscription "I am Cyrus, King, Achæmenid".[1] The
Assyrian style of the monument shows whence came the
craftsmen who were entrusted with its execution.

The funerary hypogæa where Darius and his successors lay
still exist ; cut in the virgin rock in the mountain side, they
are as Diodorus Siculus describes them.[2] They are in two
groups, three being behind the palaces of Persepolis, and four
others, three miles away, in the place which is popularly called
Naqsh-i-Rustam, 'Carving of Rustam', because one figure is
supposed to represent the national hero of whom Firdusi sings.
They are all arranged in the same way ; the visible part,
forming a picture, is divided into three portions, one above
the other, giving the appearance of a Greek cross, 80 feet high.
The lowest part is a perfectly bare parallelogram, without
ornament or moulding of any kind. The other two parts
together represent the front of a palace. Beneath a portico
of four columns with bull's-head capitals is a door with the
Egyptian cornice. The top of the monument presents a picture
in low relief ; the king stands on a pedestal of three steps ;
in his left hand he holds a bow, which rests on the ground ;
he extends his right hand, in sign of adoration, towards an altar
on which burns the fire, the symbol of Ahura-Mazda, whose
image hovers above the whole scene ; as we know, this is a
repetition of a familiar Assyrian motive. The solar disk appears
behind this image. Twenty-eight figures of men, arranged in
two bands, one above the other, support the flooring of the
platform ; these represent the various provinces of the Persian
Empire, as is shown by the inscription on the Tomb of Darius
at Naqsh-i-Rustam. Incidentally, this is the only inscription
found on these remains ; the others have no writing whatever.
The text runs "Look at the image of those who bear my

---

[1] **XXII**, vol. v, p. 668 (*Persia*, p. 270). See above, fig. 2.
[2] xvii. 71.

PLATE III

THE TOMB OF DARIUS.

[face p. 92.

Fig. 11.   THRONE OF DARIUS AT PERSEPOLIS.

throne, and you will know how great is the number of the countries which Darius the King has possessed ''.   MM. Babin and Houssay, of M. Dieulafoy's mission, managed to erect a scaffolding in 1885, and to observe, for the first time, that beneath the feet of seven of the figures the names of several satrapies were engraved.[1]   The interior of every tomb consists of a vestibule and a lower chamber, in the floor of which funerary receptacles are hollowed out, varying in number from one to nine.   The walls are absolutely bare, without trace of sculptures or ornament of any kind.

It is very likely that, as has been supposed, the idea of cutting a tomb in the mountain was suggested to Darius by his stay in Egypt, when he was with the army of Cambyses. The hypogæa of Beni-Hassan certainly impressed him.

The Persians had no temples, Herodotos tells us.   The historian of Halicarnassos, who came from a country where the ground was covered with temples, statues, and altars, was greatly struck by the fact that none of these familiar objects was to be seen among the hereditary enemies of Greece.   It is clear that there was no religious architecture.   But when he said that altars were unknown, the Father of History was thinking of those which, among his own people, served for blood-sacrifices.   As for the fire altar, on which the symbol of the supreme god burned, we know exactly what it was like, for we see it represented on the rock tombs.   In Cappadocia there were even temples, which Strabo saw, but these were oratories of the Magi, and one cannot infer anything from them with reference to the religion of the Persians in the time of the Achæmenids.   One may quote here the passage in the Greek geographer which bears on our inquiry.[2]   " In this country (Cappadocia) one finds what are called (in Greek) *Pyraetheia*, some of which are truly imposing sanctuaries, with an altar in the centre, on which the eternal fire, kept up by the Magi, burns among heaps of ashes."

In various parts of the present Iran one finds small monuments popularly known as *Atish-gah*, ' Place of Fire ' ;   the problem is, to what period they belong.   They are in the form of four-sided kilns, and there can be no doubt as to their purpose ; they are certainly fire-altars.   At Naqsh-i-Rustam, to the left

[1] **XXII**, vol. v, p. 622 (*Persia*, p. 222).
[2] xv. 3. 15.

of the necropolis, there are two altars of this kind, cut in the rock. They are unequal in size, and wider at the base than at the top ; on every face there is a semi-circular blind arch resting on pilasters engaged in the corners ; at the top is a square table, surrounded by triangular crenelations, and containing a depression in which the fire was laid. Now, these altars are of a different shape from those represented on the fronts of the hypogæa, and rather recall a small Chaldean edifice depicted on the monument known as ' Lord Aberdeen's Black Stone '.[1] It is possible that these two altars are earlier

Fig. 12. Two Fire-Altars at Naqsh-i-Rustam

than the building of Persepolis, and go back to the ancient Persian township before its elevation to the rank of capital.[2]

At Pasargadæ, not far from the Tomb of Cyrus, there are two pedestals which may have served as bases for fire-altars. They are called *Takht-i-Taus*, ' Peacock's Platform '. They are monoliths, cubical in shape, and hollowed out inside ; a stair of seven steps, likewise a monolith, leads to one block ; the other has disappeared. Why do these altars go in pairs ? No acceptable solution of the problem has been found. Single

[1] **XXII,** vol. ii, fig. 79 (*Chaldaea, etc.*, vol. i, p. 211).
[2] *Ibid.*, vol. v, p. 64 (*Persia*, p. 244).

altars have been found, such as that which existed at Firuzabad, the ancient Gur, but is now destroyed ; it was the only one of its kind.   These altars, therefore, were not necessarily in pairs.

The ruins of the royal palaces, at Persepolis and at Susa,[1] offer valuable material for study, and attempts have even been made to reconstruct their design.   The dwelling of the king was the true political centre of the Empire.   It was at the door of the palace, as at the Sublime Porte of the late Ottoman Empire, that affairs were settled.   Behind that door, in an inviolable sanctuary, surrounded by his harem and his servants, dwelled the autocrat who ruled over a great part of Asia. Official language retains traces of this ancient organization in the XXth century.   In British India, where Persian, under the Grand Moguls and even under the East India Company, was the official language of the Government, a State audience of the Viceroy is still called a Durbar ; this expression is simply the English transcription of *dar-bar*, a solemn audience (*bar*) at the king's door (*dar*).   It was on the royal edifices that the architects exercised their imagination.   Whereas the funerary monuments present only one uniform type, the palace-builder strove to vary his plans.   For every king wanted a dwelling of his own, and had no desire to use those bequeathed to him by his predecessors.   So to-day, in Persia, a son who inherits a house from his father prefers building a new one to using the old, which is not repaired and soon falls into ruins.   The ancients noticed this.   "At Susa," says Polycleitos, a contemporary of Alexander,[2] "on the top of the platform, each king builds himself a separate edifice, with treasuries and store-houses, which is intended to hold the tribute levied in his reign and to remain as a monument of his administration." What Polycleitos says of the royal treasuries is equally true of the dwelling of the sovereign.

Cyrus built at Pasargadæ, in memory of his victory over Astyages and the Medes, palaces which still existed when Alexander came ; it is believed that there are traces of them in the ruins north-east of the tomb of the founder of the monarchy, about half a mile away.   It is possible to reconstruct with fair probability a porch with four columns flanked by two lateral chambers, and a great hypostyle hall with two rows of columns.

---

[1] For the palace of Darius I at Susa see **XCI**.
[2] Strabo, xv. 3. 21.

Five human feet carved on one of the blocks show that there was a relief decoration similar to that at Persepolis.[1] The columns are not very large or numerous. Three piers are the best-preserved part of the building ; on one of them there used to be a short inscription in the three official languages, Persian, Susian, and Babylonian : " I am Kurash, King, Achæmenid ".

The ruins of the palaces of Persepolis stand on a high foundation, a platform (takht). There was a carriage road which went round its southern side to the mountain, and joined the platform on the east ; but the monumental entrance, which was used by persons who went to the Court on duty or at the king's command, was the wide stairway which is still intact. It consists of two double flights of steps, diverging and then converging, parallel to the retaining-wall. It is fourteen feet wide, and has 106 steps, 58 in the lower flights and 48 in the upper, according to Coste. This stairway ends on the second terrace, on which stand the propylæa and the hall of the hundred columns. Another terrace, ten feet higher, bears the remains of the hypostate hall of Xerxes, and behind, yet another ten feet higher, are the ruins of the palaces of Darius and Xerxes.

The propylæa consist of two huge piers on which the foreparts of man-headed bulls are sculptured in the round. This type is well known from the winged bulls in the Louvre, which come from Khorsabad near Nineveh ; they are, therefore, imitated from the Assyrian style, but freely imitated, for these have only four legs, whereas the Assyrian bulls have five.[2] This monument, about thirty-six feet high, was erected by Xerxes, as is shown by the trilingual inscriptions which it bears, describing it as " the porch which shows all countries "—that is, no doubt, the porch from which a vast stretch of country can be seen.

The hypostyle hall of Xerxes was the throne-room, where, on certain days, the king sat in great state, holding audiences and receiving foreign ambassadors. It was the grandest and most sumptuous of the monuments on the platform of Persepolis. Thirteen columns still stand, out of the thirty-six which formed the principal group ; in front of them and at the sides there were three more series of twelve columns each,

---

[1] **XXII,** vol. v, p. 666 (Persia, p. 269).
[2] Ibid., p. 782 (Persia, p. 386).

the bases of which can be counted—in all, seventy-two columns, 63 ft. 8 in. high. The walls of the stairs are sculptured with figures of soldiers, one to each step, facing towards the rise, as if they were going up the stairs to the palace. On the central terrace we see, on the left, servants leading horses and chariots, courtiers, and guards, and, on the right, figures representing the various peoples, bringing gifts of fruit or animals of their own country. There is no variety in the attitudes ; all are the same.[1] In these processions of tribute-bearers, guards, and great lords of the Medes and Persians going to the king's audience, all bodies are in the same pose, and the only variety is in certain details of costume. Among the lords, however, some turn round and extend their hand to their neighbour, or place it on his chest or shoulder ; but the position of the feet is not natural, and one sees the difficulties of the artist, who wanted to vary his attitudes but could only do so awkwardly. The king is almost always in one of three attitudes—worshipping at the fire-altar, felling a monster, a lion or griffin, or seated on his throne. In the last case he wears the *cidaris*, a smooth tiara, wider above than below, which was the sign of his high dignity, and the purple *candys*, the Median robe, falling to his feet. In one hand he holds the sceptre and in the other a flower. A servant stands behind him, holding a fly-flapper over his head.

The Frieze of the Archers, discovered at Susa by Dieulafoy, shows us the details of the uniform of the Persian troops. The soldier carries his bow on his left shoulder. To his back a quiver is attached, the deep lid being kept shut by cords ending in tassels of braid. With his two hands he holds a long pike off the ground, as if he was presenting arms. This pike has a head with a long socket at one end and a knob or apple of the same colour as the head at the other. These men wear a long tunic falling to the ankles, with wide hanging sleeves which cover the arms to the wrists. The tunic is adorned with a rich border and rosettes or lozenges which stand out against the colour of the ground. They wear laced boots of soft yellow leather, gold bangles on their wrists, rings in their ears, and a cap surrounded by a twisted fillet, as against the tiara worn by most of the guards at Persepolis.[2]

[1] **XXII**, vol. v, p. 829 (*Persia*, p. 431).
[2] *Ibid.*, p. 822 (*Persia*, p. 425).

PLATE IV

PERSIAN ARCHERS. CERAMIC FRIEZE FROM THE APADANA AT SUSA.

Other monuments complete the information which these figures give us regarding the Oriental garments which so intrigued the Greeks.   The Louvre possesses a series of intaglios in which we see Persians clad in the sleeved robe called the *candys*, and wearing on their heads the *cidaris*, a kind of turban which must correspond to the twisted headdress which we have just seen.   Others wear the seven-horned *cidaris* and a shawl. Among them we find archers, and even a mounted archer, turning round on his horse ; this last intaglio is Græco-Persian work.[1]

In the centre of this terrace is the hall of a hundred columns, none of which is standing.   Traces of paving in stones of different colours can be seen.[2]   To find another monument in which the walls enclosed such a vast area, and the roof was borne by so many columns, and the gorgeousness of the decoration was more in proportion to the huge dimensions, one would have to go to Karnak in Egypt.[3]   This hall of audience is probably older than the palace of Xerxes, and may have been built by Darius I.   It is also probable that this was the very hall which Alexander set on fire at the instigation of the courtesan Thais ; the ashes found in it are of cedar-wood.

The palace in which Darius resided is built on the terrace ten feet above that on which the colonnade of Xerxes stands. All the apartments open into the great roofed hall in the centre of the building.   Here the king had his harem.   In the Book of Esther the royal house is distinguished from the house of the women.

At the time of the Macedonian conquest the principal cities were no longer walled.   A long period of peace had caused the upkeep of the walls to be neglected, and, being built of sun-baked bricks, they had the more rapidly fallen into ruin. Ecbatana and Susa were open towns.[4]   Every city, however, had preserved its citadel, where the king could take refuge with his treasures behind a circuit of strong walls.[5]

---

[1] L. Delaporte, *Catalogue des cylindres orientaux*, vol. ii, p. 174 ; pl. 92, figs. 41, 42, 44 ; pl. 91, fig. 24 ; pl. 107, fig. 39.
[2] Cf. Esther, i. 6.
[3] **XXII**, vol. v, p. 727 (*Persia*, p. 329).
[4] Strabo, xvi. 3 ; Polyb., v. 48.
[5] **XXII**, vol. v, p. 765 (*Persia*, p. 369).

In sum, the study of the monuments shows that the art
of the Achæmenids was not born spontaneously of the genius
of the people.   One feels that it was done to order by artists
who were pupils of Assyria and Egypt, and, even at this early
date, of Greece to some extent.   Persia was a successful
upstart ;   a complete art had to be created to give brilliance
and dignity to the new monarchy.   The supreme will of the
Oriental despot, who must be obeyed at once, enlisted men on
all sides, whose business was to satisfy his caprices as quickly
as possible.[1]

Money had just been invented in Asia Minor,[2] but it was not
yet circulating in the central and eastern parts of the Empire.
None has been found in either Persepolis or Susa, whereas
quantities have been discovered belonging to the Parthian
and Sassanian periods.   The king's treasuries contained
precious metals in bullion ;   at Susa Alexander laid hands on
40,000 talents in ignots, and only 9,000 in gold coins.[3]   Darius
was the first to strike a gold coin, which was called the ' daric '
after him.   " Darius struck a coinage with gold which had been
made as pure as possible by refining."[4]   Indeed, the metal of
our specimens is almost pure.   The king is represented as an
archer, bending his bow, with one knee on the ground.
Agesilaos, when the Spartan Government recalled him from his
campaign in Lydia and Phrygia, exclaimed, as Plutarch tells us,
" Ten thousand Persian archers have driven me from Asia ! "
So, in our own time, we speak of St. George's Cavalry, who have
so mightily aided the undertakings of Great Britain.

In addition to the gold daric, silver Medic shekels were
coined, worth one-twentieth of the gold piece.   For subsidiary
money there were the silver and bronze coins struck by cities
and local princes in the mints of Asia Minor and Phœnicia.
Persian coins bore an image only on the obverse ;   on the
reverse there was a hollow square.   We may date the striking
of the first darics about 516 ;   but, since they bear no legend,
it is impossible to say for certain when or under what king any
coin was issued.   Nevertheless, by the study of the portrait

---

[1] **XXII**, vol. v, p. 845 (*Persia*, p. 448).
[2] The honour is shared by Lydia and Ionia.   Gyges, the founder of the
Mermnad dynasty, is accredited with the earliest issues, thick irregular
lumps with one or more punch-marks on one face.   **LXXXVI**, pp. 32-3.
[3] Diod., xvii. 66.
[4] Hdt., iv. 166.   Cf. **LXXXVI**, p. 33.

of the sovereign and the artistic character of the coin it has been possible to place certain issues.[1]

The Persians did not themselves practise the glyptic art, that of engraving seals of hard stone. We have a few intaglios engraved with inscriptions in Old Persian, but these are the work of the studios of Babylonia, where the art had been handed down from father to son from time immemorial. A curious relic of this distant time is Darius's own seal, in the British Museum. It is a cylinder of the Assyrian type, a green chalcedony, on which is engraved the figure of the king hunting lion, with the inscription in three languages, " I, Darius, the King ".

The inscriptions which the Achæmenids have left us are in three languages, Old Persian, Anshanite or Susian, and Babylonian, but there are some on which only one language is employed, the language of the court and the royal family, Old Persian. All these languages are written in cuneiform characters, but in the case of Old Persian the script is greatly simplified. The elements of Persian writing are evidently taken from Babylonian writing, but instead of the hundreds of signs and numerous ideograms characteristic of the latter script we find in Persian only thirty-six distinct characters, each having one single value, at least in principle, and a few ideograms, not much used on the whole. The writing of Anshanite or Susian on the Achæmenid inscriptions is also of a simplified type, but less so, and we find over a hundred characters. To transcribe Persian, then, cuneiform writing was enormously simplified. This was a considerable revolution, probably due to scribes who knew the Aramaic script, for the Persian script gives the impression of an Aramaic writing done with cuneiform signs ; only there are rather more characters, since cuneiform furnished unlimited resources for the transcription of sounds foreign to the Semitic languages. We do not know how or by whom the cuneiform system was thus adapted to writing Old Persian.[2] We may imagine that a royal command was transmitted to the offices of the administration taken over from the old kingdoms of Babylon, and that ingenious scribes exercised their wits to satisfy the wish expressed in high quarters to see the language of the conquerors

[1] **XXXI; LXXXVI,** p. 36.
[2] **LXXIX**a, p. 40.

take its place beside that of Susa, where the ancestors of Cyrus had reigned, and that of Babylon, which he had conquered.[1]

The language transcribed in the inscriptions must represent almost exactly the usual speech of the Persians attendant on Darius and Xerxes; it still had an archaic aspect on the whole, but it was the end of the early period.[2] As for the inscription of Artaxerxes III, there is reason to suppose that it was written by a foreigner who did not know the language; it is even asserted that this is the only possible hypothesis,[3] Probably no one read the Persian inscriptions; that of Behistun was a historical monument, but it was not meant to be read by passers-by, and one may ask whether there were ever many men who could read this type of writing. Accordingly Darius had copies and translations of it made, and these were sent to the different provinces, to judge from the Aramaic version found among the archives of the Jewish colony at Elephantine in Egypt. From this document it is inferred that the Behistun inscription cannot be later than 510. One of these copies, engraved on stone in Babylonian cuneiform, was recently found on the site of Babylon.[4] It is probable that the Babylonian text was the official version, for the papyrus corresponds to it. In any case, the papyrus is not the original, but a second copy made from the first by the Jews at Elephantine about 420.[5]

There is no proof that the Persian script was in current use or was employed, like the Babylonian, for practical purposes. If the Achæmenids had imitated their Ninevite and Babylonian predecessors, and had used plastic clay to write, in their own language, the history of their empire, we should have had a most precious document, usefully complementing the information which we owe to the Greeks. It is true that we hear of kings causing the annals of their forbears to be read to them,[6] but it is probable that the scribe read from a Babylonian, Susian or perhaps Aramaic text, translating it into Persian as he went on.

---

[1] **LXXIXa**, p. 19.
[2] *Ibid.*, p. 13.
[3] *Ibid.*, p. 20.
[4] *Veröffentlichungen d. deutsch. Orient-Gesellschaft*, iv, p. **24***.
[5] A. Cowley, *Jewish Documents of the time of Ezra*, London, 1919; *Aramaic Papyri of the Fifth Century B.C.*, Oxford, 1923, pp. 249-250.
[6] Esther, vi. 1.

PART TWO

THE PARTHIAN ARSACIDS.

CHAPTER I

PERSIA UNDER HELLENIC INFLUENCE

THE conquests of Alexander were divided among his lieutenants. While his half-brother Arrhidæos succeeded him in Europe, Perdiccas was chosen regent of the Asiatic empire pending the birth of an heir, the son of Roxana. The satrapies fell to various generals, Egypt to Ptolemy, Syria to Laomedon of Mytilene, Media to Peithon, Cappadocia to Eumenes, Cilicia to Antigonos. India continued to be governed by the native kings, Taxiles and Porus, while Adharbayjan remained under the Satrap Atropates, who gave it its name of Atropatene. There was no longer a central power to hold these diverse provinces together ; nationalities were re-awakened, and soon war broke out. Perdiccas, who wished to maintain the unity of the conquered state, was defeated by Ptolemy in Egypt and assassinated by his own men. The death of Antipater in 319 gave rise to a second war, and Eumenes was defeated by Antigonos in Susiana, not far from Shushtar.[1] The victor wished to make himself the successor of Alexander, but Seleucos gained the upper hand, and the last war of the Diadochi, or successors of the great leader, broke out in 310 and ended with the battle of Ipsus in Phrygia, where Antigonos, in spite of the support of his son Demetrios Polyorcetes, saw the end of his dream and lost his life. Asia remained in great part the possession of Seleucos and his successors.

The Seleucids dated the beginning of their rule in the year 312, the beginning of the era which bears their name. Their capital was first at Babylon, then at Seleuceia on the Tigris,

---

[1] At the confluence of the two arms of the Karun. Jane Dieulafoy, *À Suse*, Paris, 1888, p. 59.

a little to the south of the mediæval Bagdad, and lastly at Antioch in Syria. Seleucos maintained friendly relations with Sandrocottus (Chandragupta), who had his capital in Palimbothra (Pataliputra) and had founded the Maurya dynasty in India, and with Sophytes (Saubhuta), another Indian prince, at Lahore, in the kingdom of Taxiles. His ambassador Megasthenes brought home from his mission a treatise on India which is lost. Under Seleucos's grandson, Antiochos II Theos, who reigned from 261 to 246, Bactriana and Parthiene made themselves independent.

The Græco-Bactrian kingdom, which played such an important part in the penetration of Asia by Hellenistic civilization (probably influencing the Græco-Buddhist sculpture of Gandhara, and so all Indian sculpture), is only known to us through Justin's abridgement of Trogus Pompeius, himself an echo of Poseidonios of Rhodes, and through coins. Its founder, Diodotos II, who was called after his father, at first struck his tetradrachms with the profile of Antiochos II, and then, having declared his independence, substituted his own. His territories extended from Sogdiana to Margiana, that is, from Samarqand to Marv.

At the same epoch the kingdom of the Parthians was founded. Parthiene is mentioned as a province in the Behistun inscription. The people who inhabited it came from Scythia, where the nomadic Iranians had mingled with heterogeneous tribes. Arsaces, the founder of the Arsacid dynasty, made himself independent of the Seleucids in 250, with the aid of the nomad tribe of the Aparni, a branch of the Dahæ, to which he belonged himself. He fell in battle, perhaps against the Bactrians. The strife between the Seleucids and the Lagids gave his brother Tiridates (248-214) the opportunity to take possession of the kingdom of Hyrcania (Gurgan) and its capital Zadracarta (Astarabad). His alliance with Diodotos II enabled him to defeat the army of the Seleucids, to establish his independence, and to assume the title of Great King. With him the Parthian era begins (14th April, 247).[1] The ancestor-worship practised by the Parthians turned his brother Arsaces into a god, and the portrait of the latter, sitting on a throne, appears on the coins

[1] This date is established by a Babylonian tablet which gives both dates, Seleucid and Parthian. Cf. **IX**, ii, p. 483 ; G. Smith, *Assyrian Discoveries,* p. 389. Eusebius and Justin give different dates.

of the type copied from the Seleucid coinage. At the same time, the dynasty was linked up with the Achæmenids by the story that the two brothers were sons of one Phriapites, son of Artaxerxes II. So the Persian Empire was re-established ; but the conquest had left too deep a mark on Iran for this renovation to be a real re-birth. Only long afterwards could the Sassanids claim to take up the old Persian tradition.

Tiridates was able to proceed tranquilly with the consolidation of his power. He had a palace, named Dara, built near the mountain of Zapaortenum, probably near the modern town of Abivard ; but his capital was still Hecatompylos, in Comisene, the ruins of which are situated to the south-west of Damghan. He was succeeded by his son Artabanus, whom Justin calls Arsaces (214-196). This king took Ecbatana, but was driven back by Antiochos II, who forced him to give up his capital and overran the country as far as Hyrcania. The peace which followed enabled the Seleucid to attack Euthydemos of Magnesia in his Græco-Bactrian kingdom. The reign of Phriapites, who succeeded Artabanus, was quiet, for the Bactrians had designs on India and directed their forces to that side. His son, Phraates I, subdued the Mardi of Tapuristan (Tabaristan, Mazandaran), and gave them the Caspian Gates, leading from Khurasan to Media, to guard for him. He chose as successor his brother Mithradates (174-136), who, in his long reign of thirty-seven years, made the Parthian state into a great empire. The Seleucids were weakened by their wars with Rome and the rebellions of the Jews, the result of the maniacal persecution of Antiochos IV Epiphanes. Mithradates took Marv from the Bactrians, whose king Eucratides had his hands full with India, and Media from princes who were more or less independent. The latter province he gave to his victorious general, Bacasis. His activities extended to Elam (Susiana), to Persia, and to Babylonia.

Mithradates, who could boast that he had re-established the empire, and had taken the title of Great King, and his son Phraates II consolidated their power by the victories of their troops over the armies of the Seleucids. They defeated Demetrios II and Antiochos of Side in succession, and the latter was killed in battle. Phraates had to deal with a revolt of the Scythians, whom he had called to his assistance ; he attacked them, but a body of Greek prisoners went over to the enemy, and he was defeated and killed. His uncle Artabanus II died in 124 from a wound taken while fighting the Yue-Chi who, driven forward by the Huns (Hiung-nu), had recently driven the Græco-Bactrian kingdom back into India. It is at this time that we find the Sacæ (Sakas) establishing themselves in the north of Drangiana, and giving the country the name of Sakastana (now Sijistan).

Mithradates II, the son of Artabanus, did not succeed his father in peace. First he had to fight for his crown against two competitors, whose names are given us by their coins, Arsaces Nicephoros and Arsaces Dicæos Philhellen ; however he managed to dispose of them in the year of his father's death. Successful battles secured the eastern frontiers and extended his domains to the Euphrates and Armenia. It was at this time that the most famous namesake of the Parthian king, Mithradates, King of Pontus, had attempted to raise a barrier against Roman conquest by creating a powerful kingdom in Asia Minor. Not since Hannibal had the Romans had such a redoubtable opponent, but, after three long wars, they finally vanquished him.

The reign of Mithradates II was followed by an interregnum, until 76, when Sanatroices, an old man, the brother of Phraates II, or the son of Arsaces Dicæos,[1] assumed the title of King of Kings ; this did not prevent Tigranes, King of Armenia, from taking the capital of Atropatene and laying waste the country of the Tigris and Euphrates. His successor, Phraates III (69), intervened in the conflict between Tigranes and Pompey, from whom he obtained, for his colleague of Armenia, the restitution of Gordyene. Later, taking advantage of Tigranes' difficulties with Pompey, he recovered Mesopotamia, which his father had lost. He was poisoned by his sons, Mithradates III and Orodes, in 60. The former, after a reign of four years, was deposed and driven out by the nobles on account of his cruelty, and, after the fall of Babylon, where he had taken refuge, he was executed by order of his brother. It was during the reign of Orodes that the Triumvir Crassus, Proconsul of Syria, was defeated by the Parthians at the famous battle of

[1] Our authority for the interregnum is a passage of Trogus Pompeius in Justin ; for the difficulty involved, see Justin, IX, ii, p. 498. P. Gardner regards Sanatroices as the brother of Phraates II, while A. von Gutschmid takes him for a son of Arsaces Dicæos.

Carrhæ (Harran) in 53. On the advice of Abgarus II Ariamnes, Prince of Osrhoene, with his capital at Edessa, and a vassal of the Parthians, the Roman general engaged battle in the plains of Mesopotamia, where the Parthian cavalry could extend with ease, instead of following the foot of the hills. Harassed by the clouds of arrows which the Iranian troopers poured on them without interruption, the legions were broken by charges of the heavy mail-clad cavalry. During the negotiations which were opened in the course of the retreat Crassus was killed in a sudden mêlée, which was perhaps an arranged matter (9th June). Over 20,000 Romans remained on the field, and 10,000 prisoners were taken to Marv. Crassus's head was cut off and taken to Artaxata, where it appeared in a barbaric spectacle ; in a performance of the *Bacchæ* of Euripides it was thrown down before the king and his son Pacorus, who were among the spectators.

Orodes seems to have chosen Ctesiphon, on the Tigris opposite Seleuceia, for his capital ; this city was to remain the capital under the Sassanids. The defeat of the Romans encouraged him to attempt more distant ventures. He set out to attack Syria ; an expedition against Antioch in 51 cost his general Osaces his life, but this failure was avenged nine years later by the prince Pacorus. In the meantime the Roman Republican party had, in spite of the aid of the Parthians, lost the battle of Philippi (42), and Labienus, who had come to Ctesiphon, had persuaded the king to undertake the Syrian expedition. Pacorus reached Jerusalem without difficulty, and settled the difference between the two parties which divided Judea, giving the title of king to Antigonos, son of Aristobulos. Antony's general, Ventidius Bassus, formerly a muleteer in Picenum in central Italy, acted with great energy, driving the Parthian troops into the Taurus and finally defeating them at Gindarus, in northern Syria (9th June, 38).[1] Pacorus was slain. Orodes, weary of power, handed it over in 37 to his second son, Phraates IV, the child of a concubine.

Phraates IV employed drastic means to rid himself of possible rivals. He had all his brothers on the father's side put

---

[1] Jindaris in Arabic ; cf. Mehren, *Cosmographie*, p. 158 ; it is a very ancient town, called Kinalua in the Assyrian inscriptions ; cf. Sayce, in *Trans. Soc. Bibl. Archæology*, vii (1882), p. 292.

to death, and caused his father, who disapproved of his conduct, to be smothered in his pillows. Antony set out to avenge the defeat of Crassus ; he marched on the Euphrates with a large army and, finding himself resisted, turned towards the capital of Atropatene, which was at that time Phraata (Takht-i-Sulayman) ; there he was utterly defeated. His retreat into Armenia was effected under the most difficult conditions, but he eventually managed to save the greater part of his army.

For more than a century the Parthians were unmolested by Roman attacks. The Civil Wars, which ended with the battle of Actium and the triumph of Augustus, contributed greatly to this effect. Augustus presented Phraates with an Italian slave-woman named Musa, who did much to spread Roman influence in Nearer Asia, and the king sent his four sons to Rome, where they lived in princely style. The Italian lady, it is true, wished thereby to secure the throne for her own son, Phraates V, and with this end in view did not hesitate to poison the old king. She reigned conjointly with her son, and struck coins on which her image appears together with his, but their reign lasted only two years. A usurper followed, Orodes II, who was killed while hunting after a reign of four years.[1] The Parthians had to ask Augustus to send Phraates' eldest son, Vonones, but he had grown out of Oriental ways ; he was soon removed, and was replaced by Artabanus III, who reigned thirty years. This king was an Arsacid through his mother, and occupied the vassal throne of Media, which was once more separated from Armenia. A nephew of the princes in Rome, Tiridates, made war on him, and even succeeded in entering Ctesiphon, but only for a short time, for Artabanus soon reasserted himself (39). Artabanus wished to retake Armenia, but the Romans opposed this, and Tiberius even sent his nephew and adopted son, Germanicus, to the country.

On the death of Artabanus, his son Vardanes being absent, Gotarzes seized the capital, but was soon defeated by the lawful heir. However, he did the king a great service by revealing a conspiracy to him, and was rewarded by a reconciliation and the assurance that he should succeed to the throne on the death of Vardanes. Vardanes was assassinated about 45 A.D. Gotarzes was a cruel tyrant ; he vanquished Meherdates, a grandson of Phraates IV, whom the discontented party had

---

[1] Josephus, *Ant. Jud.*, xviii. 2. 4.

brought from Rome, and cut off his ears to prevent him from being made king. When Gotarzes died shortly afterwards (51), the crown was given to Vonones II, King of Atropatene. His origin is unknown, but some make him the brother of his predecessor. After reigning a few months he was succeeded by his son Vologeses I (51-75). Under this king war broke out against Rome. Corbulo took and destroyed Artaxata, and occupied Tigranocerta without a battle. Armenia thus became Roman once more, but not for long, for Vologeses, after a victory at Arsamosata, re-established Tiridates on the throne as a vassal of Parthia. This victory restored the hegemony of Persia over Nearer Asia and as far as the valley of the Indus. Accordingly we find the coins of Kings Turushka Kanerki, Ooerki,[1] and Bazodes bearing representations of Zoroastrian deities by the side of Greek and Indian deities, among whom Buddha appears.

Then came a series of kings whose origin is unknown, Vologeses II, his brother Pacorus III, and Artabanus IV.[2] They may have reigned over different provinces, for the dates of their coins overlap. Internal wars laid the country open to Roman intervention, which earned Trajan the surname of Parthicus. The successes of that Emperor on the Tigris and the capture of Seleuceia inspired him with dreams of conquering India, but he had not time to put his vast projects into practice. Osroes (Khosrau), who had been king since 107, had no resource but to flee, laying waste the country over which the Imperial army had already passed. Trajan caused Parthamaspates, the son of Osroes, to be solemnly crowned, and then retired ; falling ill at Selinus in Cilicia, he died there on 7th August, 117. Hadrian concluded peace with Osroes in 123.

After Osroes, who died seven years later, we have Vologeses II, his elder brother, who reigned eighteen years, and then Vologeses III (148-191).[3] The latter was not prevented by his agreement with Antoninus Pius from placing his brother Pacorus on the throne of Armenia in the stead of the protégé

---

[1] Sir Charles Eliot transliterates OOHPKI, KANHPKI as Huwishki, Kanishki (*Encyc. Brit.*, art. " Yue-Chi ").

[2] **CV**, vol. iii, p. 169.

[3] In the reign of this king we must place an Arsacid prince named Anshikan, who caused the Buddhist confession called *Triskandhaka* to be translated in 140-170 ; this is the most ancient translation. F. W. K. Müller, *Uigurica*, ii, p. 89.

of Rome, but this did not last long ; his troops, defeated at Europos,[1] could not prevent the Roman army from destroying the palace of Ctesiphon and burning Seleuceia. The plague which then broke out spread in Europe through Italy, whither it was taken by the soldiers who had not died of it. It is probably this Vologeses III who is mentioned in the *Dinkart* as the ' Huvafrita ' who restored the Avesta.[2]

War broke out again under his son, Vologeses IV. Septimius Severus made Nisibis into the great arsenal of the Romans in these parts, and for long the two peoples fought for its possession. The Roman army, coming along the Nahr-Malka canal by ship, appeared unexpectedly before Ctesiphon, which was looted and destroyed (199). However, the town of Hatra held out, under its king Barsemius, who made use of the Arab horsemen in his service and succeeded in destroying by fire the military machines set up against the place.

A conflict between two brothers, Vologeses V and Artabanus V, did not prevent the latter from defeating the Romans twice beneath the walls of Nisibis, and the Romans had to buy peace at a considerable price. This success marked the end of the Parthian Empire ; already, in Fars, a line of princes had grown up which would restore the ancient empire of the Achæmenids and for four hundred years would prevent the Romans from advancing eastwards—the house of Sasan.

---

[1] Dura, now Salahiyah, on the Euphrates.
[2] Avesta, *Yasht of Anahita*, 130 ; cited by F. Justi, in *Preuss. Jahrbücher*, lxxxviii (1897), p. 63.

CHAPTER II

THE RELIGION OF PERSIA UNDER THE ARSACIDS

THE absolute silence of the historians does not allow us to guess what was the religion practised by the Persians while the Arsacids, whose court was deeply influenced by Hellenistic ideas, were fighting against so many adversaries for the independence of the country. But we have a little light on what was happening in one, at least, of the confederate states which went to form the Empire of the Parthians.

In Persis, the modern Fars, thanks to the decline of the power of the Seleucids, an almost independent kingdom had been created, known to us only through its coins.[1] It was ruled by priest-kings. who preserved the traditions of the Magi of the time of the Achæmenids. On the reverse of the coins, the king stands, bow in hand, before the fire-altar, as in the reliefs of Naqsh-i-Rustam ; beside the altar the national standard is set up, the banner of the smith Kava, the Dirafsh-i-Kaviyani, which was afterwards, at the end of the reign of the Sassanids, taken and destroyed by the Arabs at the battle of Qadisiyah. Ahura-Mazda hovers above. The legends are in Aramaic script, replaced later by the Pahlavi of the Arsacids. On these coins, the princes take the title of Malka, that is, Shah (King) ; but the Arabian authors preserve a memory of their being called Hirbad (Æthrapaiti, Masters of Fire), which indicates their priestly character. The princes who took the title of Malka were two Dariuses, Piruz, and Vatafradat ; others are called Fratakara, Fire-maker, such as Bagakert, Bagadat, and Artaxerxes. Bagakert reigned about

---

[1] A. D. Mordtmann gave the name of Persepolitan to three series of coins struck by these local dynasties, whereas Blau held that they should be attributed to the Pyræthi or priest-Magi of Elymais (Susiana). Cf. E. Drouin, "Observations sur les monnaies à légendes en pehlevi," etc., in *Revue Archéologique*, 1886 ; C. Huart, art. "Persepolis," in *Grande Encyclopédie*, vol. xxvi, p. 886. On one of these coins the king's head is wrapped in a hood like that worn by Darius Codomannus in the famous mosaic from Pompeii ; the lower part is pulled over so as to hide the beard, like a Balaclava cap.

220 B.C. ; Artaxerxes IV, the last of these kings, about 220 A.D.[1]

In these or similar circumstances the very ancient traditions which had been preserved in Achæmenian times by the colleges of Magi continued to be maintained, and it was possible to put together, when Mazdaism revived under the Sassanids, the collection which we have in part under the name of the Avesta.

Certain writers have held that one of the Arsacids, Vologeses I, a contemporary of Nero, caused search to be made for the fragments of the sacred book of the Magi which survived either in writing or in the memory of the faithful ; we have seen above that this initiative should rather be attributed to Vologeses III. In any case, the attempt seems to have led to nothing, and we must wait for the arrival of the Sassanids, who based their State religion on the book, reconstituted by a ruling priesthood.[2]

THE RELIGION OF MITHRA

We have seen above that Mithra is mentioned, in the XIVth century B.C., in the cuneiform inscriptions of Cappadocia, and that Artaxerxes caused him to appear, by the side of Anaitis or Anahita, on the monuments of his reign. In the Ist century B.C. his religion expanded into Europe in consequence of Pompey's Eastern campaigns. Among the troops and the people he enjoyed immense popularity, and until the time of Constantine he was a serious rival to Christianity. Julian the Apostate (361-363) made a belated effort to substitute his worship for the religion which was now official, but without success. Monuments of the cult of Mithra are found, in countless examples, all over the Roman Empire. What, then, was this religion, which was so universally popular ?

Having developed in Asia Minor and Mesopotamia, it was not a purely Iranian religion. In Roman times Chaldea was the holy land of the Mithraists ; Mithra had a temple in Babylon, and Antiochos of Commagene (69-34 B.C.) raised a statue to him at Nimrud-Dagh. Nevertheless, in virtue of its

---

[1] Allotte de la Fuye, " Étude sur la numismatique de la Perside," in *Corolla Numismatica*, Oxford, 1906, pp. 63-96, pl. iii. A complete list of these princes will be found in J. de Morgan, " Note sur la succession des princes mazdéens de la Perside," in *C. R. Acad. Inscr. et belles-lettres*, 1920, pp. 132-40.

[2] **XVIII**, p. 576 ; **CXXXVII**, vol. iii, pp. xxii-xxiv.

origin, a word may be said of this religion in our account of the Arsacids. Colonies of Magi, emigrants from Babylon, lived obscurely in Asia Minor, chiefly in Cappadocia and Pontus, where the landed aristocracy was of Iranian origin, as is shown by the frequent occurrence of the name Mithradates in the ruling houses of those countries. Antiochos of Commagene,

Fig. 13.   RELIEF AT NIMRUD-DAGH

mentioned above, traced his descent to Darius I, son of Hystapes ; he instituted a cult and festivals in honour of Zeus-Oromazdes, Apollo-Mithras, and Hercules-Artagnes (Verethraghna) ; on the relief at Nimrud-Dagh he had himself represented facing Mithra, who stretches out his hand in sign of alliance, a motive which appears more than once on

Sassanian monuments. These Magi had no sacred book, but handed down their religious traditions by word of mouth, whereas in Lydia, from the IInd century onwards, liturgical books were used in the temples of Anahita. By the end of the Achæmenian empire the Magi were established in Babylon in great numbers, and already took precedence over the native priesthood in official ceremonies.

Fig. 14.　Mithra Sacrificing the Bull

This long residence of the priests of fire in the old capital of Chaldea explains the combination of Iranian elements with Chaldean (i.e., star-worship) which Mithraism presents. It was a syncretism, to which Greek sculpture came later to add new features. The Mithra of the Avesta presents only some of the elements which went to make the god, Sol Invictus, who had such a following in the Roman Empire.

The followers of the god often installed his worship in cuttings in the rock, choosing as sanctuaries, for preference, places containing a spring, or at least with running water near by.   In the apse of the temple a relief was set up representing Mithras Tauroctonos, the Bull-slayer, a composition which probably sprang from the brain of a sculptor of the Pergamene school, in imitation of the sacrificing Victory which adorned the balustrade of the Temple of Nike on the Acropolis of Athens.   The Bull was killed as follows ; Mithra subdued the savage beast and dragged it into his cave by the hind legs, and then stabbed it in the heart with a broad dagger ; he did this at the bidding of the Sun, which was conveyed to him by the Raven.   From the body of the victim all the races of plants sprang forth.

St. Jerome knew that there were seven degrees of initiation. To pass from one degree to the next, a man had to undergo certain ordeals ; with his eyes bandaged, and his hands tied with the inwards of a fowl, he leapt over a ditch full of water after which a ' Deliverer ' cut his curious bonds.   Tertullian tells us that the initiate who rose to the rank of Miles was presented with a wreath, *interposito gladio ;* he thrust it away with his hand, and henceforth renounced wearing it for ever, for it belonged to Mithra, the invincible god.   Some of these rites occur in the initiation of Freemasons.   The grades were Raven, Cryphius, Miles, Lion, Persian, Heliodromus, and Pater.   In the ceremonies masks were worn representing these different types, as is shown on the relief discovered at Konjica in Bosnia.

The hope of a glorious immortality reserved for the initiate certainly exercised a great attraction on them, and contributed to the diffusion of the Mysteries.   The excellence of their morality, which encouraged action, and afforded effective support in the struggles of life, assuredly made for their popularity.

Mithraism was always mainly a military cult, brought in by the Eastern auxiliaries of the Roman army and encouraged by the Emperors.   At the end of the second century Commodus was received into the number of the initiate, and took part in their secret rites ; in 307 Diocletian, Galerius, and Licinius, meeting at Carnuntum, restored a temple of Mithra.   I have already mentioned the unsuccessful efforts of Julian, who celebrated the mysteries of this cult in his palace in Constantinople.[1]

Such was the religion of Mithras in the West ; of its practice in Persia we know nothing. We find traces, however, of a festival called Mithrakana, which has become the autumn equinox, *mihrijan*, for the modern Persians. This feast did not follow the cult in its wanderings over Europe and northern Africa, but remained confined to the Eastern provinces.

---

[1] **CXXXV,** vol. i, pp. 4, 7 ff.   F. Cumont, art. " Mithra," in Daremberg, Saglio, and Pottier, *Dictionnaire des antiquités*, vol. iii.

CHAPTER III

The Arts under the Arsacids

THE Arsacids have left nothing but their coins and a few monuments of architecture. The ruins which may be attributed to their time number five—the temple at Kanguvar, the building at Hatra, the small edifice at Farrashband, the funerary chamber at Warkah, and the palace at Babylon, to which one may add the remains of a palace at Susa, built over the hall of audience of Artaxerxes Mnemon.

At Kanguvar, the ancient Concobar, remains have been found of a temple showing profound analogies of style and arrangement with those of Greece. It is composed of a central hall and a vast peribolus of bastard Greek style. According to Isidore of Charax it was a temple of Artemis. At Ecbatana, the present Hamadan, there was a temple of Anahita where the population still sacrificed to the goddess in Roman times. The columns are bastard Doric, and the building shows a medley of different styles.

Hatra is the present al-Hadr, forty miles from the Tigris, south-west of Mosul. The ruins are surrounded by a circular fortification, with a diameter of about a mile. The central edifice, which was built for the Arabian sovereigns who reigned in this district at the time, consists of three great vaults and four smaller vaults in a row, with a square hall behind. We find almost the same arrangement in the buildings at Sarvistan and Firuzabad. The decoration is of quite a special kind ; for the first time we find human heads, in the form of masks, adorning the round arches and pilasters. It is a Persian monument ; Roman influence is only seen in the construction of the vaults, the arrangement of the archivolts, and the design of the elevation.

Farrashband is three stages west (not east, as has been said) of Firuzabad, in the province of Fars, on the road from Shiraz to the sea. The small ruined building there was first reported by Marcel Dieulafoy,[1] who observes that it is " built of unshaped rubble " and that the dome rests on four piers connected by arches ; it represents, he says, " the last stage through which the old Persian dome was to pass before the transformation of the pendentive ".   Dieulafoy would make it an Achæmenian monument, but it is more probable that it is as late as the Arsacid period.

In the necropolis of Warkah certain sarcophagi may be attributed to the Parthian epoch.   At Behistun there is a

Fig. 15. Building at Farrashband, Arsacid Period

badly preserved relief of Gotarzes I, commemorating his victory over the combined forces of Meherdates and Cassius. This sculpture bears an inscription in the Greek language. The king is portrayed on horseback, brandishing a lance, while a winged Victory crowns him.

The most complete evidence on the state of sculpture is furnished by the coinage of these princes.   These coins were struck on the model of the Syrian drachma, from dies executed by native craftsmen.   The obverse bears the face of the king ; while the reverse varies.   Under the first Arsacids the reverse

[1] **LIa,** vol. iv, p. 77.

shows the founder of the dynasty, Arsaces, clad in military costume and holding a bow in his hand. Later the king is shown, deified ; Mithradates I appears in the attitude of Hercules, and Mithradates II and his successors receive a triumphal wreath from the hands of Victory. We also find elephants, horses' heads, and deer. The workmanship degenerates steadily as time goes on.

A horseman, clad, like his horse, entirely in mail, is represented

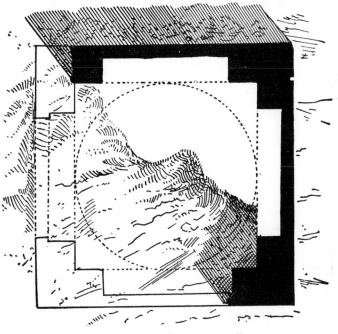

Fig. 16. PLAN OF THE BUILDING AT FARRASHBAND

on the column of Trajan in Rome. He is a *cataphractarius*, one of the heavy cavalry who charged at the decisive moment. Defensive armour of this kind did not exist in the time of the Achæmenids. The principal arm of the Parthians, which won them victory over Roman tactics in many a battle, was the bow, for which Catullus calls then *Parthi sagittiferi*.[1] So, too,

---

[1] Cat., ii. 6. Chapot, *La Frontière de l'Euphrate*, pp. 42 ff. F. Cumont, "Le Sacrifice du tribun romain," in *Monuments Piot*, xxvi, p. 44. Only the light cavalry, composed of Palmyrene natives, could hold its own against the Parthians and Sassanian Persians. F. Cumont, *ibid.*

the battle of Agincourt was lost by the French chivalry because of the bowmen on the English army.

It is outside the Iranian territory properly so-called that we must go to realize what the industrial arts were like at this epoch. There was a very thriving export trade with its centre at Palmyra, which dealt with the great ports of Syria and Phœnicia, and this prosperity, which was expressed in those magnificent buildings which still stand in the midst of the desert, was in great part due to the relations of the city with the Parthian kingdom. In India, at Taxila,[1] excavations have yielded objects dating somewhere between 700 B.C. and 100 A.D. Some of these objects are Greek and some Oriental, the latter being almost exactly like the Sarmatian objects found in South Russia.[2]

---

[1] Sir John Marshall, *Archæological Survey of India, Ann. Rep.*, 1912-13, pl. xxii, *a*, 7 ; 1917-18, part. i, pl. iv, *a* ; same author, *A Guide to Taxila*, Calcutta, 1919.

[2] Rostovtzeff, " Une Trouvailie de l'époque gréco-sarmate de Kertch," in *Mon. Piot*, xxvi, pp. 143 n. 2, 157 n.1.

PART THREE

THE SASSANIDS.

CHAPTER I

The Sassanian Dynasty

ARDASHIR I

SASAN, the old eponymous hero of the race, was a priest of the temple of Anahita at Persepolis. His wife Ram-behisht was the daughter of the king of the Bazrangi line, whose capital was the town of Nisayek, the white-walled citadel of which under Arabian rule bore the name of Bayda, made famous by the celebrated commentator of the Koran, al-Baydawi. Their son Papak (Babek in Persian) was a petty prince of Khir, a small town on Lake Bakhtigan, on the road from Sarvistan to Niriz. He obtained for his son Ardashir from King Gozihr the dignity of Argapat (fort commandant)

Fig. 17.
ARDASHIR I

of the town of Darabjird. This was the beginning of the fortunes of his house.

Ardashir conceived the great project of re-establishing the autocracy of the Achæmenids, who had held all the provinces of Iran united under their absolute sway, and were remembered under the Seleucids and Arsacids as symbols of Persian nationality. His undertakings began in the time of his father, who killed Gozihr, declared himself king, and demanded from Artabanus V that his elder son Shapur should be acknowledged as his successor. Artabanus refused, but none the less Shapur reigned after his father and compelled his brother Ardashir to recognize him as his overlord. The opportune collapse of a vault in the palace of the queen Humai rid Ardashir of his elder brother, and the new

king at once commenced a career of conquest. He conquered a certain Vologeses, Prince of Kirman, and installed
as governor in his stead his own son Ardashir, from whom
the capital of the country, which to-day has the same
name as the province, was called Bih-Ardashir, ' the good
city of Ardashir ', Bardasir in Arabic.[1] The princes of Susiana,
Isfahan, Mesene, and even Oman were defeated and subjugated one after another.   At length Artabanus V,
Ardashir's overlord, set out at the head of a considerable army,
and was defeated and killed in the plain of Hurmizdagan in
Susiana, in 224. Two years later Ctesiphon fell into the
conqueror's hands. A relief carved on the rock of Naqsh-i-
Rustam bears witness to these achievements. The king, on
horseback, receives from Ahura-Mazda, likewise on horseback,
a great ring, the symbol of kingship, while Vologeses and
Artabanus lie under the horses' feet. Inscriptions in Pahlavi
and Greek, which Silvestre de Sacy has deciphered,[2] are written
on the shoulder of the charger.

The defeat and death of Artabanus delivered Persia into
Ardashir's hands. But Armenia and Georgia were still
unconquered.   The war of revenge against Rome was a national
idea.   The new king resumed the endeavour, but the presence
of Alexander Severus at the head of the legions and the
resistance of the town of Hatra and of the princes of Edessa
checked his ambition. He succeeded, however, in taking
Nisibis and Harran in 237. Two years before, the Roman
Emperor had been murdered in Gaul by his mutinous troops.

Ardashir found a potent instrument of government in the
religion of the Avesta, the old Mazdaism which had been given
new life by Zoroaster and elaborated by the colleges of the
Magi during the long silence of the reigns of the Seleucids and
Arsacids. He and his successors made it a State religion,
and the high priest was one of the chief dignitaries of the
Empire. Later we shall see how this religion was codified.
In addition to obtaining the moral support afforded by this
religion, Ardashir was a great builder of cities, and many towns
in the early Middle Ages, and even after the Moslem conquest,
bore his name with some qualifying term.

---

[1] Nœldeke, *Geschichte der Araber*, p. 10 n.   Istakhri, in *Bibliotheca
geogr, Arab.*, vol. i, p. 161.
  [2] **CLXV,**

SAPOR I

He was succeeded in 241 by Shapur I, whom the Romans
called Sapor. The war went on in the north, and the Persians
advanced as far as Antioch. Sapor was defeated in the second
year of his reign by the Emperor Gordian III, but nevertheless

Fig. 18. Sapor I and Valerian. Sassanian cameo in the Bibliothèque
Nationale

concluded a peace with Philip the Arabian by which he was
left in acknowledged possession of Armenia and Mesopotamia,
where he had taken Hatra. The great military feat of his
reign was the defeat and capture of the Emperor Valerian at
Edessa. The prisoners were interned in [the
city of Jundi Shapur, recently founded by the
king in Susiana, on the site of the ancient
Beth-Lapat, between Shushtar and Dizful.
There they were employed on the
construction of a huge granite dam,
intended to hold the water needed
for irrigation and to raise the level
of the Karun. It was called the Shadhurwan,
the 'Joyfully Flowing', a name which was
later used for fountains, and it exists to this
day. Sapor's victory is commemorated at Naqsh-
i-Rustam, near Persepolis, by a sculptured relief, on which
Roman craftsmen must surely have worked. The story of the
indignity with which the King of Persia treated the Emperor,

Fig. 19.
Sapor I

Fig. 20.
Valerian

which, according to Lactantius, went all round the world, is
quite improbable, and is just an old wives' tale.

Sapor was less successful in his attempt to subjugate the
Palmyrenes, who defied him and invaded Mesopotamia. It
was a mistake to quarrel with them, and so to risk throwing
them into the arms of the Romans ; but, luckily for Sapor,
Odenathus was assassinated and succeeded by Queen Zenobia,
who counted on Persian help in her plan of founding a great
Syrian kingdom.   However, she could not resist Aurelian, who
took Palmyra in 271 and banished the queen to Tibur.

Fig. 21.   Portrait of Sapor at Naqsh-i-Rustam

The *Georgian Chronicle* names a son of Sapor, Mihran, as the founder of the so-called Chosroan, i.e., Sassanid, dynasty in Georgia. It is said that he was converted to Christianity. A brother of the King of Persia, Peroz, is known as the protector of Mani or Manes, the founder of the Manichæan religion, which for a long time had a following in Central Asia, and attracted the attention of the outside world, when it was regarded as a mere Christian heresy. It was at the coronation of Sapor, on the 20th March, 242, that Mani preached for the first time in public. But the Mazdean religious authorities could not, any more than the Christian church, allow dogmas which were based at the outset on the absolute equality of light and darkness, of good and evil. They persecuted Mani, and were not satisfied until they had caused him to be executed at Jundi Shapur, in the reign of Bahram I, the son and second successor of Sapor. If the kings of Persia had continued to favour this religion instead of fighting it, it is certain that, in view of its extraordinary expansion over the old continent, it would have given the successor of Cyrus and Darius the political hegemony of Asia. As it was, the cause of Manichæism served that of Iran, and contributed to the spread of Iranian ideas and civilization even on the high table-lands near the Desert of Gobi.

After Sapor, who died in 272, we have, in rapid succession, his son Hormazd (Hormisdas) I, who offered Mani a refuge from persecution in his castle at Dastagird and reigned only a year, another son of Sapor named Bahram I, who reigned three years, and his son Bahram II, who reigned eighteen. In the reign of this last king the Emperor Carus led an expedition as far as the neighbourhood of Ctesiphon, where he died suddenly in 283. Bahram III, who reigned only four months, in 293, owed his surname of Saganshah, ' King of the Sacæ ', to the fact that his father Hormazd I had made him viceroy of Sijistan after the conquest of the country from the Sacæ or Sakas, a Scythian people who dwelt there.

Narses, the son of Sapor I, had succeeded in driving Tiridates, the protégé of Rome, out of Armenia, but he was defeated twice by Galerius the Cæsar, whom Diocletian had sent against him. He managed, it is true, to beat Galerius between Callinicon and Harran in 296, but in the following year he lost Armenia, his family was taken prisoner, and his treasures were pillaged.

He died of grief soon afterwards.   Tiridates recovered Armenia,
and the Romans penetrated as far as Georgia.   Narses was
succeeded by his son Hormazd II, who was defeated and killed
by the Arabs ; his eldest son and successor Adhernarses,
distinguished himself by his cruelty, which cost him his life
in 310 ; another son, Hormazd, after being kept in prison for
thirteen years, escaped to Byzantium and only returned to
Persia later, in the wake of the army of the Emperor Julian.

Fig. 22.   Sapor I presenting the freedman Cyriades to the Roman
Army.   Sculpture on the road from Shiraz to the Sea

There were no more sons of Hormazd II by his lawful wife,
but a concubine was expecting an heir.   This heir, crowned
before he was born, reigned in Persia for seventy years under
the name of Sapor II.

SAPOR II

The conversion of the Emperor Constantine to Christianity
affected the relations of the Roman Empire with Persia.   The
many Christians who lived on the territory of the Persian

Empire were tempted to look outside the frontiers for protection against the persecutions to which they were subjected by Mazdaism as the State religion ; many, on the other hand, who were regarded as heretics by the orthodox Church, came and sought freedom to maintain their faith under the Great King. Furthermore, Tiridates, King of Armenia, had recently been converted by the preaching of Gregory the Illuminator. Persecutions were political rather than religious. When the Nestorians came and settled on Persian soil, vexations ceased ; having been driven out of Roman territory, the heretics could no longer cause offence at the court of Ctesiphon. This settlement of the Nestorians was the starting-point for an evangelization of Asia which carried their influence far beyond the confines of the Empire of Iran, to the north of the continent and into China. With their teaching went the use of the Syriac script, which, after having been employed by the Uighurs, is still used to-day to transcribe the sounds of Mongolian or Manchu ; but it would seem to be rather with the Manichæan script, which is of the same origin, that one should connect these alphabets.

The struggle with the Roman Empire went on. The Persians still had their eyes on Armenia, where they would have been glad to establish themselves. Sapor II took possession of that country, but could not hold it. In 340 he invested Nisibis, but was unable to maintain the siege for more than two months. He had to conclude peace, but did not give up his pretensions to Armenia, on the throne of which he set Arshak, who paid tribute both to the Persians and to the Romans. After an armistice, a victory of the Romans at Singara in 345 cost the king's son, Narses, his liberty and his life ; but this success was followed by many defeats. Fourteen years later Amida (Diyarbakr) was taken and the population put to the sword.

Constans II had been succeeded by Julian the Apostate. The campaign on which he embarked, at the head of allies such as the Armenians and the Sassanid Hormazd, took him to Ctesiphon. Starting from Harran, his army went down the Euphrates, accompanied by a war-fleet. The Emperor perceived that he could not overcome the fortifications of the capital. He was about to start across Media, when, during a battle, while he was exhorting his tired men, on the 26th June, 363, he was killed by a javelin thrown by a Persian trooper.

Jovian was elected Emperor by the army, and hastily concluded peace in order that he might be able to take his troops back to the frontiers of the Empire. This is probably the event commemorated in the relief carved on a rock near the town of Shapur.[1] By the side of the titanic conflict which continually brought the Romans back, never with success, to the country of the lower Euphrates, the everlasting bickerings provoked by the question of the Armenian throne, which was always open, and the struggle against the Kushans established in Bactriana are of minor importance.

The long reign of Sapor II ended in 379. There was nobody to succeed him but an old man of seventy, his half-brother

Fig. 23.
TRADITIONAL
PORTRAIT
OF SAPOR II

Ardashir II, who had in the past persecuted the Christians in his province of Adiabene. He was deposed by the Persian nobles after reigning four years, and was succeeded by a son of Sapor II, named Sapor III. This king, who had made peace with Theodosius, fell in a mutiny of the troops. He was followed by his brother Bahram IV, sur-named Kirman-Shah, ' King of Kirman ', because he had been viceroy in that region. He reigned eleven years. With him Theo-dosius settled the Armenian question in an entirely novel manner, by dividing the country into two halves, one under the influence of Constanti-nople and the other under that of Ctesiphon.

YAZDIGIRD I

In 399 Yazdigird I (Isdigerd) ascended the throne. He was the son of Sapor II (or possibly of Sapor III), and was called *Beze-ger*, ' the Sinner ', because he had drawn on himself the hatred of the priests by his equity in religious matters. The historian Procopius has left us a portrait of him in which he speaks of his magnanimity and of the admirable sentiments which had made him popular even before his accession. Arcadius placed his heirs under Yazdigird's protection. His

---

[1] Texier, *Description de l'Arménie*, pp. 146-7 ; **CVII**, pl. 141. Cf. Mordt-mann, in *Sitzungsber. der Münch. Akad.*, 1874, p. 260, and *Zeitschr. d. deutsch. morgenl. Gesellschaft*, xxxiv, 67.

death, in 420, is a mystery; according to a legend, he was
killed by the kick of a horse which he was trying to saddle,
but this story may have been invented to conceal a murder.
His own son, Sapor, who was governor of Armenia, hastened
to claim his father's inheritance, but was put to death at once,
in the fear that he might follow in his father's footsteps. A
distant kinsman, Khosrau, was made king, but could not keep

his throne, for another son of Yazdigird,
Bahram V, succeeded in making himself master
of the kingdom with the aid of Nu'man, the
Arabian king of Hirah, at whose court he had
been brought up.

Bahram was surnamed Gur, the ' Wild Ass ',
because, it was said, he had, while hunting,
killed a lion and a wild ass which it was
attacking with a single thrust of his spear, or it

Fig. 24.
BAHRAM V

may have been because of his strength and speed. At the very
beginning of his reign he had to attend to the Turkish invasions
which were commencing to threaten the north-eastern frontiers
of his dominions. The Ephthalites or White Huns had invaded
Bactriana ; he defeated them near Marv and killed their king
with his own hand, and the crown of the vanquished king was
set up as a trophy to adorn the fire-temple of Adhar-Gushnasp,
at Shiz in Atropatene. His persecution of the Christians, in
which he followed the example set by his father, obliged many
of them to take refuge on Roman territory, and led to the
rupture of the peace. The Persian campaign, which was led
by Mihr-Narseh, a great personage of royal origin, descended
from the viceroy Hystaspes, Darius's father, was not successful ;
in spite of the defence of Nisibis, Persia was compelled by several
defeats to conclude peace in 421. Religious liberty was proclaimed, and Acacius, Bishop of Amida, sold the ornaments of
his church and the sacred vessels to ransom seven thousand
Persian prisoners and to send them home with clothes and some
money in their pockets.

In 438 Bahram was succeeded by his son Yazdigird II. He
would have liked to resume the struggle against the Romans,
but the Ephthalites were still threatening Bactriana, and he
had to combat them. He wanted to compel the Armenians
to embrace Zoroastrianism, in order to bind them more closely
to Persia by a common religion, but the Armenians had invented

an alphabet in which to write their language,[1] and this powerful means of propagating ideas was the best defence of their nationality against foreign assaults. The minister Mihr-Narseh wrote a proclamation in which he attacked the dogmas of the Christian religion and the organization of the community. Eighteen bishops refuted him in their turn. Measures were taken to cause Zoroastrianism to triumph ; a revolt was the result. Yazdigird had just been defeated by the Kushans; nevertheless, he hurriedly returned to Armenia and vanquished the rebels at the bloody battle of Avarair (2nd June, 451). Their general, Vardan Mamikoni, fell on the field of battle ; the Patriarch Joseph and ten ecclesiastics were imprisoned and executed three years later. Nevertheless, peace was quickly restored, showing that the mass of the people was not imbued with fanaticism, and, without any religious constraint, numerous fire-temples were erected.

On the death of Yazdigird II in 457, his son Hormazd III succeeded, but had to fight another pretender, his younger

Fig. 25.
PEROZ

brother Peroz, who did not hesitate to ask the Ephthalites for help, giving them two cities in Bactriana in return, Taliqan and Tirmid. While the two brothers were fighting, their mother Dinak ruled in Ctesiphon as regent. Peroz (Firuz) defeated and slew his brother in 459. His reign, which lasted twenty-five years, was unfortunate. To combat the famine which ensued from a long drought, he bought food-stuffs abroad, decreased taxes, and compelled the rich to share their supplies with the poor. The feast of Abrezagan, the Falling of Water, was instituted to commemorate the rains which put an end to the disastrous drought.

If the barbarian invasion, by occupying all the energies of the Roman Empire, made it impossible for the Romans to take up the century-old struggle with the Persians, the latter enjoyed no peace, being more and more threatened by the Ephthalites. Two expeditions were led against the chief of these tribes, Akhshunvaz, or Khush-nevaz, whom Priscus

---

[1] The Armenian script was invented in 397 by Mesrop, a man from Hassik in Tarun (died 19th Feb., 441), and was popularized by the Catholicus Sahak Parthev (Isaac the Parthian). Cf. Justi, **IX**, ii, p. 528.

calls Cunchas (Κούγχας), and neither was successful. In the
first, the army was lost in the desert by a spy, and perished
miserably ; in the second, Peroz lost his life, and for two years
his empire paid tribute to the White Huns. In the course of
his long reign, in spite of the anxieties with which he was beset,
the luckless king had been able to found or to rebuild cities
to which he gave his name, and had opened the territory of his
empire to the Nestorians, who were persecuted by the Monophysites at Edessa and in Armenia and driven out of the Roman
Empire by Zeno the Isaurian in 489.

Persia was without a king. The general Zarmihr, called
Sokhras in the Persian chronicles, who had returned from the
Armenian war, gave the crown to the brother of Peroz, whose
name was Balash, another form of Vologeses. Balash successfully disposed of the rival pretensions of his brother Zareh, but
the exhausted treasury did not permit him to meet the demands
of the financial representative of the Ephthalites. Zarmihr,
who was a true soldier, got together a small force by his own
efforts and compelled Akhshunvaz to conclude peace, the claim
for tribute being abandoned and prisoners returned. Among
these prisoners was Kavadh, a son of Peroz, who had been held
as a hostage. Zarmihr's success resulted in the complete
effacement of King Balash, who was deposed and replaced
by Kavadh in 488. Kavadh, or Kobad, was to reign forty-three
years.

KAVADH

One of those Utopians to be found in all countries and climates,
who imagine that they can establish social justice by a levelling
process in defiance of the most evident natural laws, a socialist
named Mazdak, developing the ideas of Mani, founded a
religious sect which believed in community of goods and
women, abolition of all privileges, and prohibition of the
slaughter of living things for food. The king saw in these
doctrines a weapon with which to break the power of the
nobles, and he encouraged their propagation. The nobles, in
self-defence, imprisoned Kavadh and replaced him by his
brother Jamasp (497), who was not suspected of favouring the
subversive ideas of the Mazdakites.

Kavadh, with the aid of his wife, escaped from the prison of
Gilgird and went over to the White Huns. He married his

own niece, the daughter of the King of the Ephthalites and the Princess Firuzdukht, who had been taken prisoner in the previous wars. After this marriage, Jamasp restored the throne to his brother. Kavadh showed himself ungrateful to the two men who had contributed more than anyone else to his escape from Gilgird, the general Zarmihr and Seoses, who had held a horse ready for his flight. In the fall of Zarmihr we must doubtless see the hand of the Mazdakites, whom he had persecuted ; he was replaced by his rival Shapur, a man of birth equal to his own, being of the Mihran family.

Money was needed to pay for the help of the Ephthalites. Kavadh tried to negotiate a loan in Constantinople, but the Emperor Anastasius refused to furnish the hereditary enemy with means to procure arms which might be turned against himself. The King of Persia declared war, entered Armenia and Mesopotamia simultaneously, and took Theodosiopolis (Erzerum) and Amida (Diyarbakr) after three months of siege (503). These successes were not lasting ; Kavadh was recalled by disturbances and an invasion of the Huns in the following year. He had made peace, of which the Romans took advantage to fortify Dara opposite Nisibis and several points defending the passage of the Euphrates—Birtha (Birah) and Europos (Dura, Salahiyah).

Many years later, in 527, the Persians, making the fortification of Dara their excuse, recommenced the war. It was the first year of the reign of Justinian. Belisarius, his general, first lost a battle, but had his revenge three years later, and finally was beaten at Callinicon, in 531. Sittas, his successor, finding the Persians occupied with the siege of Martyropolis (Mayyafariqin), spread the report of an inroad of Massagetæ, and so caused the investment to be raised. Kavadh died in the same year, at the age of eighty-two, having in his time rebuilt some cities.

CHOSROES I

His son Khosrau I, the Chosroes of the Greeks, had been declared heir presumptive since 513. His subjects gave him the surnames of Anoshak-ravan (Anushirvan), ' of the Immortal Soul ', and *Dadgar*, ' the Just '. He was beyond dispute the greatest king of his line, and his memory has survived in Arabic and Persian literature, which are both much later than his own date. Menaced by a conspiracy at the very beginning of his reign, Chosroes disposed of it. A party had tried to place on the throne, not his elder brother Zames, who was blind in one eye and therefore ineligible for kingship, but Kavadh, the son of Zames. Executions restored order.

The victories of Justinian's generals in the West, by which the kingdoms of the Vandals and the Ostrogoths were destroyed made it unlikely that the Romans would abide by the terms of the peace of 531, by which they had had to pay a war indemnity and to evacuate Mesopotamia. Justinian had intervened as arbiter in a quarrel between two Arabian kings of the Syrian desert, the Ghassanid al-Harith ibn Amr, the protégé of the Romans, and al-Mundhir ibn Nu'man, who reigned at Hirah as vassal of the Great King. Chosroes took Antioch in 540, and transported the inhabitants to a new city which they built near Ctesiphon and called Bih-az-Andio-Khusrau, ' Chosroes' Better Antioch '. The Arabs knew it as Rumiyah, ' Roman '. Chosroes also took Callinicon, but his efforts were checked by the resistance of Belisarius. Then peace was made. Some years later, on a false report of the king's death, his eldest son Anushazad revolted at Jundi Shapur (Beth-Lapat) ; he was punished by blinding with a hot iron. The campaigns of Chosroes in the country of the Lazi ended disastrously with the defeat of his troops at the mouth of the Phasis in 553. Nine years later a fifty years' peace was concluded with Rome.

In the east, Chosroes advanced the frontiers of the Empire to the Oxus by the defeat of the White Huns, with the aid of the Turks of the Shao-vu branch under their chief Sinjibu (the Silzibulos of the Greeks) ; but the Turks, having conquered Transoxiana, were soon to show themselves the enemies of the Iranians. Accordingly the king had new fortifications made in the Darband Pass above the Caspian Sea and in the Pass of Darial, or Alans' Gate, while other fortifications were erected to close the access to Gurgan or Hyrcania. Having been summoned by the Arabs to deliver them from the Ethiopians, who had conquered them in 529, the Persian troops occupied Yemen in 570, under the leadership of Wahriz. The general and his troops married women of the country, and their descendants, staying there, were later known by the Mussulmans as *Abna*, 'the Sons ' (of the conquerors). The last years of Chosroes, who died in 579, were saddened by the defeat of his army at Melitene (Malatiyah), from which the king barely escaped with his life, crossing the Euphrates on an elephant.

His reign was marked by the completion of the survey of the Empire, which had been commenced under his father Kavadh. Children, women, and old men were exempted from the land-tax, while people without land, Christians and Jews, paid a poll-tax.[1] In his time, also, the book of *Kalila and Dimna* was brought from India and translated from the Sanskrit, and the game of chess was introduced.

Hormazd IV, the son of Chosroes by the daughter of the Khan of the Turks, after whom he was called Turk-zad, resumed the war against the Romans without success, and had to combat the revolt of the satrap Bahram Chubin, a descendant of the Mihran family. That officer, having defeated the Turks in Svanetia, but having been less successful against the Romans in Armenia, did not forgive Hormazd for recalling him, and seized the capital. Hormazd fled to Bih-Qubadh, but the army which was fighting the Romans in Mesopotamia declared for the king's son, Khosrau II Parviz, who had taken refuge at the court of the Roman Emperor Maurice. With the support of Constantinople Khosrau was placed on the throne (590). Hard pressed in Adharbayjan, Bahram Chubin had to fly to the Turks, by whom he was subsequently put to death.

CHOSROES II

Taking the assassination of Maurice by Phocas in 602 as a pretext, Khosrau Parviz, or Chosroes II, invaded Mesopotamia and Armenia. Within a few years his general Shahr-Baraz, the 'Boar of the Empire', took Edessa, Antioch, Damascus, and, lastly, Jerusalem (June, 614), whence he carried off the Holy Cross in triumph to Ctesiphon ; then he took possession of Egypt. In Asia Minor, Shahin entered Cilicia, took Cæsareia, and laid siege to Chalcedon (Kadi-Keui) opposite Constantinople ; but he fell into disgrace and was put to death, and Shahr-Baraz completed the capture of the city. If the Persians had had a fleet, Constantinople was theirs. In the meantime Heraclius had become Emperor, and his reign was the signal for a successful campaign against the Persians, who restored Asia Minor and Armenia to him (624). Four

---

[1] **IX,** p. 538.

years later, he took Dastagird, where he found three hundred Roman eagles which had been carried off as trophies of former victories. He did not, however, attack Ctesiphon, fearing that his communications would be cut. Falling ill at Bih-Ardashir, Chosroes designated as his successor his son Merdan-Shah, whose mother was the Syrian Shirin, but he was not followed by the nobles, who preferred his other son, Siroes (Shiroe). Siroes made away with his brother and threw his father into the prison which Theophanes calls the House of Darkness ; there the old king was murdered to satisfy a private vengeance (628). Terrible disasters marked this period ; the Tigris and Euphrates rose and flooded the whole of Iraq, converting it into a vast swamp ; plague broke out, and carried off Siroes after a reign of six months.[1]

Before Siroes died he had obtained peace from the Romans, but hardly was his infant son Ardashir III on the throne, when the Khazars invaded Georgia and Armenia. The general Shahr-Baraz was defeated at Uti, near Lake Gegham, but, in co-operation with Heraclius, he succeeded in deposing the young king and usurping the crown. His triumph was short ; a month and a half later he was put to death. A grandson of Hormazd IV, Chosroes III, had risen against him in Khurasan ; but it was a sister of Chosroes, Puran, who was crowned at Ctesiphon. The peace concluded with Heraclius provided for the restoration of the True Cross, but it should be observed that it had already been returned, for the Feast of the Exaltation had been instituted on the 14th September, 629. Puran, disheartened by the defeats suffered by the Empire, abdicated after reigning a year and five months, and was succeeded, after a short interregnum under Gushnaspberdeh, a brother of Chosroes III, by one of her sisters, Azarmi-dukht. Hormazd V, a grandson of Chosroes Parviz, had himself crowned at Nisibis, and maintained himself there until 632, when he was massacred by his soldiers and succeeded by Yazdigird III. No less than twelve persons wore the royal tiara from the death of Chosroes III in 628 to the accession of Yazdigird III, son of Shahryar,

---

[1] According to the Arabian historian, Tabari, Chosroes Parviz gave orders in 607 that a statement of the Imperial revenues should be made. The amount was reckoned at 420,000,000 *mithqals*, a weight corresponding, roughly, to 600,000,000 drachmæ, according to the calculation of E. Blochet, " Les Manuscrits orientaux de la Collection Marteau," in *Notices et extraits* vol. xli, p. 102 n. ; cf. **IX**, p. 538.

on the 16th June, 632, the first day of the era which bears his name. There was anarchy in the upper classes and in the royal family, and a catastrophe was about to overthrow the ancient fabric of the Iranian monarchy—the Arabs were at the gates.

THE ARABIAN CONQUEST

Muhammad had just died ; but the triumvirate which then assumed the command of the Moslem nation, Abu Bakr, Omar, and Abu Ubayda ibn al-Jarrah, had decided, after putting down the Bedouin attempt at independence known as the Apostasy, to recommence the raids by which the religious and political legislator of Medina had founded a power, the extension of which was far beyond his dreams. After the success of the expeditions in Syria, those which were directed against the Iranian Empire offered the greedy warriors, most of whom were not even Moslems, the prospect of still richer booty. The battle of Dhu-Qar had shown that regular troops like the Persians could be beaten by the impetuous charges of the Arabs. After four battles by the advanced guards, in which the Persians were successful, a decisive battle was fought at Qadisiyah, not far from Hirah, a day's march south of Karbala, in 636. One of the Companions of the Prophet, Sa'd ibn Abi Waqqas, commanded the Arabs ; the general Rustam, son of Farrukh-Hormazd of Ray, was at the head of the Persian forces. After a battle lasting three days, in which Rustam was killed and the standard of the Empire, the banner of the smith Kava, the Dirafsh-i-Kaviyani, was taken, things seemed about to turn in favour of the Persians, when reinforcements arriving unexpectedly from Syria brought about the defeat and rout of the Iranian army. The way to the capital was open ; the king fled and Seleuceia was taken. In the next year Ctesiphon fell, with its citadel, the White Castle.

A bloody battle at Jalula opened the passes of the Zagros to the Arabs, and the battle of Nahavand, between Behistun and Burujird, destroyed the hopes which the king had placed in the great army collected by Firuzan (642). It was the last effort. The citadels all over the country fell one after another, in spite of the gallant defence of the commandants. Taking refuge in Marv, in the east of his former possessions, Yazdigird had called on the neighbouring kingdoms for help, and the

Turkish chief of Sogdiana had hastened up with an army ; but, displeased at the way in which the king received him, he intrigued with Mahoi, the Satrap of Marv, and annihilated the much reduced Royal Guard. Finding himself without friends, Yazdigird fled, and was murdered in his sleep by a miller with whom he had sought shelter, in the autumn of 651.

Persia ceased to exist as a state. At the same time she lost her national religion, which, under the assaults of continued and energetic proselytism, finally disappeared almost entirely. There remain only a few groups of its adherents about Tihran and at Yazd, in addition to the colony which went to India and settled in the Bombay district, where it has thriven down to our own day. It was here that Anquetil-Duperron found the original text of the Avesta and learned the language from the *dasturs* who preserved the tradition.

Yazdigird III had a son, Peroz III, about whom the Chinese historians give us some details. His father had vainly tried to obtain the help of China ; in 638 he had sent an embassy to the court of the Middle Empire, evidently without success. On the death of Yazdigird, Peroz succeeded him as King of Persia, and was recognized as such by the Emperor of China ; taking refuge in the mountains of Tukharistan, he continued to claim the throne of his fathers. He sought help from the Emperor Kao-tsung, who, however, decided not to intervene, the distance being too great for a military expedition, but the King of Tukharistan was more helpful, and took advantage of a moment of respite which the Arabs gave him to restore the prince theoretically in his possessions. In 661, when China organized the administration of the western countries of which she had become suzerain after her victories over the western Turks in 658, she set up a government of Persia, the direction of which was entrusted to Peroz, whom the texts name Pi-lu-sseh. The seat of this government was Tsi-ling. In reality, China did no more than consecrate facts already accomplished, confining herself to giving a kind of investiture to Peroz, who resided at Tsi-ling and called himself King of Persia. Where was this Tsi-ling ? It can hardly have been in Persia proper, for Peroz was never able to return to the country. If the King of Tukharistan succeeded in restoring Peroz, it can only have been by placing him in one of the easternmost provinces of Persia, probably the town of Zaranj, the capital of Sijistan, as has been suggested by Yule[1] and admitted by Chavannes.[2]

Peroz, attacked by the Arabs, could not hold out long in Tsi-ling ; driven from Tukharistan, he fled to China.   In 674 he appeared as a suppliant before the Emperor, and was well received.   In 677 he asked for and obtained authorization to build a Persian temple, consecrated to the Mazdean worship, at Ch'ang-n'gan.[3]   He died soon after, leaving his son Ni-nie-sheh (Narses ?) at the court of China.

Ni-nie-sheh went to Tukharistan, where he lived over twenty years, but in the end, deserted by all, he was compelled to abandon his vain hopes, and returned about 707 to the capital of China, where he presently died of an illness.   The Chinese also mention, in 722, a certain Pu-shan-hwo, whom they call King of Persia ; in 728-9 we hear of a Chosroes, a descendant of Yazdigird ; and lastly, in 732, an unnamed King of Persia sends the Nestorian monk, Ki-lie, as ambassador.[4]

Small dynasties continued for some time to maintain their independence on Iranian soil.   Those known as the Ispehbeds or Aspahbeds, ' Leaders of Armies ', reigned in the mountains of Tabaristan.   Even in the time of the Sassanids these distant provinces were beyond the power of the king   The lords of Gilan, by paying tribute, had protected themselves against invasion and reigned for a long time ; in the XVIth century, at the beginning of the Safavid conquests, Gilan was still almost independent.   The rest of the Empire became a field of exploitation for the conquerors ; each took his share, and soon forgot the arid deserts from which he had come.   Iranian society had no longer a political centre, but the Iranian spirit was not dead, and the language of the people, as states more and more independent of the power of Bagdad arose on the soil of Persia, was to flourish again in a magnificent poetical literature, one of the finest and most attractive in the world.

    [1] *Cathay and the Way Thither*, vol. i, p. lxxxvii, n. 1.
    [2] *Documents sur les Tou-kiue occidentaux*, Petrograd, 1903, p. 257.
    [3] *Journ. Asiatique*, Jan.-Feb., 1897, p. 68.   Cf. E. Blochet, *Messianisme*, p. 42, and " Textes pehlevis historiques et légendaires," in *Rev. Archéol.*, 3rd series, xxviii (1896), p. 179.
    [4] Chavannes, *Documents*, pp. 172, 257 ff.   Cf. Abel-Rémusat, *Mémoires de l'Institut*, viii, pp. 86-8 ;   F. Hirth, *Wiener Zeitschr. f. d. Kunde des Morgenlandes*, x, 233.

CHAPTER II

The Organization of Persia under the Sassanids

THE CLASSES OF SOCIETY

THE population was divided into four classes—priests, warriors, office employees, and farmers and craftsmen together. There were further a great many sub-divisions, covering the representatives of every function in society. Thus, the priests were divided into judges and various priestly officials ; the bureaucracy included not only the scribes, but the physicians, poets, and astrologers ; and the last class comprised also traders and business men. Each class was placed under the authority of a chief, who had under him a controller who dealt with the census, an inspector who investigated fiscal matters, and an instructor who supervised the work of the apprentices. This information we have from the Arabian historians and Pahlavi theological literature.

The priesthood were recruited among the Median tribe of the Magi, and were called accordingly Mobeds (*Moghbedh=Magupat*, ' Chief of the Magi '). The high priest was the Chief Mobed, who had the supreme direction of religious matters and a decisive voice in questions of dogma and church policy. He was nominated by the king, and himself nominated the members of the priesthood. This gave him extraordinary influence in the affairs of the Empire, since he was the director of the king's conscience.

It is less easy to define the functions of the Herbed, whose name means ' chief of fire '. When Chosroes II Parviz built a fire-temple, he attached twelve thousand Herbeds to it, to recite prayers and invocations. The Chief Herbed was certainly their head and representative at court, but his rôle does not seem to have been clearly defined, or at least our information about him is incomplete.

The bilingual inscription in Parthian and Pahlavi at Hajjiabad, in which Sapor I records a feat of bowmanship performed by himself in the presence of the nobles of his court, mentions the Shatradars (Princes of the Empire), the Vispuhrs (Sons of the Clans), the Wazurgs (Grandees), and the Azats (Freemen, or Nobles). The first, who held the rank of king (whence the expression ' King of kings '), were the vassal princes who governed distant provinces, and vassal kings like the Arab kings of Hirah, the Armenian kings down to 430, and the kings of the Chionites and Albanians beyond the northern frontier. In the same category were the wardens of the marches, the Marzbans, and, of course, those satraps who belonged to the royal family, who were given provinces in which to learn the art of government, regardless of the possibility of their revolting—a disastrous system which has survived in Persia until the present day. The Vispuhrs comprised, first, the seven privileged families, of whom the three foremost, the Karens, the Surens, and the Aspahbeds, were of Arsacid descent, and bore the surname of Pahlav, ' Parthian ', while the others, such as the Spendiyars and Mihrans, also claimed Arsacid blood, in order not to seem inferior. These families held hereditary offices ;[1] for example, the Argabeds had the privilege of placing the crown on the king's head, and it was only later, when the power of the priests was at its height, that they lost it in favour of the High Priest. In addition, there were three military offices and three civil. The military offices were those of Generalissimo (Eranspahbed), of General of the Cavalry (Aspabed), and of Director of Supplies (Eranambaragbed) ; the civil offices were those of Director of Civil Affairs, of Arbitrating Judge, and of Director of Taxes and Inspector of the Royal Treasures (the last two functions being combined). These were purely honorary offices, the holders of which lived on the revenues of their fiefs and had no part in the administration of the State ; it is in the following category that we shall find the officials who guided the destinies of the Empire.

The Grandees (Wazurgs) and the Nobles (Azats) assembled, at the coronation of the new king, to do homage and to hear the coronation speech ; sometimes they deposed him, and sometimes they also put him to death. They were " the great officials of the Empire, the highest representatives of the bureaucracy ".[2]

---

[1] Theophylactus, iii.8.
[2] **CXXXIII**, p. 30.

According to the Arabian historian Ya'qubi,[1] there were, next to the king, the Wazurg-framadhar or Grand Vizier, the Mobedan-mobed, or High Priest, the Herbed or Guardian of the Sacred Fire, the Dabirbed or Chief of the Secretariat, and the Spahbed or Chief of the Army. Mas'udi[2] gives rather a different order, placing the High Priest before the Grand Vizier ; this is because his sources of information were less ancient than his predecessor's, and referred to a time when the priests had acquired predominance in the State.

The Grand Vizier was at first called Hazara-pat, ' Leader of a Thousand ', because he originally commanded a battalion of the Guard composed of a thousand men. The Greeks were acquainted with this title of $\chi\iota\lambda\iota\alpha\rho\chi\circ\varsigma$, which was held by Hephæstion, Perdiccas, and Cassandros, and the Armenians continued to give the Vizier this title, even after it had been changed into that of Wazurg-framadhar, or ' Chief Commander'. Since the office of Prime Minister created by the Abbasid Caliphs was copied from the Sassanian model, we may infer from the former what were its duties under the Persian kings. This minister had complete control of all affairs, referring to the king when he thought it necessary. " The Vizier is he who manages our affairs," the kings of Persia used to say ;[3] " he is our tongue with which we speak, and our weapon which we hold ready to strike our enemy in distant countries." He was a catholic person ; he had to be crammed with knowledge and a fund of anecdote, so as to supply all the information demanded by the king ; he had to amuse him, to interest him, and, if required, to act as astrologer or physician.

Until the reign of Chosroes I Anushirvan, the army had only one Generalissimo, the Eranspahbed. Then the post was abolished, and its duties were divided among four generals-in-chief, each entrusted with a quarter of the kingdom, which was properly the domain of a viceroy, called the Padhghospan.

For the Empire was divided into four equal parts called *padhgos*, which were named after the four cardinal points— Awakhtar (North), Khwarasan (East), which still survives in the name Khurasan, Nimroz (South), and Khwarwaran (West).

---

[1] Houtsma's edition, i, p. 202.
[2] *Kitab at-Tanbih* ("Book of Indication "), in *Bibliotheca geogr. Arabic.*, viii, 103.
[3] *Viziers' Guide*, in Enger, *Zeitschr. d. deutsch. morgenl. Ges.*, xiii, p. 240.

The viceroys were at the head of the civil administration and probably commanded sufficient military forces to maintain order at home and to defend the frontiers against attack from outside. Under Chosroes I, and not before his time, the Padhghospan was subordinate to the Spahbed, or military chief.

There were no longer any satraps, except in Armenia, Adharbayjan, and the districts bordering on India.[1] The governors of provinces were called Marzbans, a title originally given to the military commanders of the marches, the 'Margraves', but extended later to the civil heads of districts which were smaller than the satrapies of the Achæmenids. But governors of royal race were still called Shah, or King.

The gift of a silver throne was a mark of especial honour. The hereditary governor of the Alano-Khazar march, who was a vassal king, was an exception; he had the right to sit on a golden throne, like the Great King himself. This ancient custom was revived by Mardawij, the leader of Daylamite bands who founded the Ziyarid dynasty, and aspired to restoring the vanished Sassanian Empire in the IXth century, when he had a golden throne made for himself and silver ones for his lieutenants.

We also find in certain districts governors called Ostandars, who seem originally to have been administrators of the royal estates, called from the Armenian *ostan*, which at first meant land or a town belonging to the king. In time of trouble these officials had been changed into military governors.

Towards the end of the Sassanian Empire, all civil and military powers were concentrated in the hands of the Generalissimo, the Spahbed, who had become the superior of the Padhghospan or combined the two functions. His title was to survive the disappearance of the monarchy; in Tabaristan, which for a long time escaped the Moslem conquest, native chiefs maintained their independence, with the title of Spahbed, which was Arabized as Isfahbad.

When, in prehistoric times, the Aryans settled in the territories which they occupy to-day, they appear to have distinguished themselves from the aborigines by the name of Azat, 'Freeman', which later became synonymous with 'Noble'. This must be the class to which the Knights

[1] J. Marquart, *Eranshahr*, i, 110, 112.

belonged. From the earliest times the Persians had been great horsemen.[1] It was natural that the Knights should come immediately after the higher nobility. In peace time these Knights lived on their estates and supervised the farming of their land by their peasants. Some, however, stayed at court,

Fig. 26.
ARTANES,
SON OF TAMET,
A PERSIAN
HORSEMAN.

for example, those who were entrusted with looking after the sons of Chosroes II.[2] Their instructor was one of the high officials. When Yemen was conquered under Chosroes I, Wahriz, who was appointed governor of the country, was a Knight. Some of the expedition remained there, married native women, and founded families.

The Dihqans, or Headmen of villages, formed a class lower than the nobility ; they lived on their estates and were not very different from the real peasants, except in education and perhaps in dress. Among them the Shahrigh, or administrator of the canton (*shahr*), was chosen. The chief business of the Dihqan was the levy of taxes ; he was like the modern *kadkhuda*. When the Moslems became masters of the country, they needed the assistance of these headmen and land-owners to get what they could out of the land-tax. It is among these provincial nobles that Firdusi, in the *Shah-Namah*, declares that he collected the traditions which make up the mythological history of ancient Persia.

Fig. 27.
INTAGLIO OF
A PERSIAN
NOBLE.

The nobility, thus graded, was divided from the people by an impassable barrier. It was distinguished by the magnificence of its horses, its clothes, and its armament ; the women wore robes of silk ; fencing, riding, and hunting were its privileges. The Knights held an honoured rank and enjoyed all sorts of favours.[3] It was an exception for anyone to pass

---

[1] The horse was domesticated in prehistoric times. See the representation of Equus Przewalski on an Elamite ivory plaque found at Susa, in Jéquier, **LXXXVII**, vol. vii, p. 26, fig. 15, which may be compared with the ornament incised on a silver vase from Maikop in Kuban, S. Russia (Rostovtzev, *Rev. Archéol.*, 5th series, xii, 1920, p. 27.) Innumerable proper names of the Achaemenian period contain the word *asp*, ' horse ' (Skt. *açva*).

[2] Nœldeke, *Geschichte der Perser und Araber*, p. 357 (Tabari's *Annals*).

[3] **CXXXIX**, pp. 226, 531.

from one caste to another. If a commoner distinguished himself in quite an entraordinary way, he was summoned by the king, who had him examined by the priests, and the latter took him into their body or placed him among the warriors or secretaries, according to his qualifications.[1]

The peasants were attached to the soil, were liable to impressed labour, and served in the army as footsoldiers, without the inducement of pay or other reward, as Ammianus Marcellinus tells us.[2] The townspeople were better off; they paid poll-tax, like the peasants, but were exempt from military levies.

THE KING AND COURT

The king's garments were at once impressive and gorgeous. Hormazd IV is described in detail by Theophylactus,[3] who shows him sitting on the royal throne. "His tiara was of gold, adorned with precious stones. The carbuncles set in it gave off a dazzling brilliance, and the rows of pearls all round it mingled their shimmering light with the loveliness of the emeralds, so that the eye was as it were petrified in wonder that could never have its fill. His trousers were covered with gold ornamentation, hand-woven and of great value, and altogether his dress displayed as much luxury as love of ostentation could desire."

The tiara varied in shape, as can be seen if one examines the reliefs of these kings, and their coins, of which we have a complete series. Ardashir I still wears the Arsacid tiara with pearls, but later his headgear has a balloon-shaped top, symbolizing the terrestrial or celestial globe. Sapor I has a dentate crown of a peculiar shape, with the ball above, adorned with pearls or precious stones. This type of headdress, with slight modifications, is maintained by his successors. Sapor II, however, wears a tiara without the ball, adorned with three rows of big pearls. Then bows of ribbon are added. In the time of Bahram V Gur and Yazdigird II, the ball, completely spherical, is raised above the crown by a stem (at this time it seems to have been regarded as the symbol of the sun); and a crescent has been added, its horns enclosing the lower half of the globe.

---

[1] **CXXXIX**, pp. 215, 520.   [2] xxiii.6.83.   [3] iv.3.

The crescent had begun to appear in front of the tiara in the time of Bahram IV, and Chosroes I added a star. After Kavadh, the globe dwindles until it is almost entirely enclosed by the horns of the crescent, and it disappears completely with Chosroes II, being replaced by a star.

There used to be manuscripts, now lost, which contained miniature portraits of the kings. The Arabian historian Mas'udi saw one of these manuscripts in 915 at Istakhr, the ancient Persepolis, in the possession of a nobleman of Fars. The portrait of the king used to be painted on the day of his death ; his clothes and his crown, the cut of his beard, and the expression of his features were depicted, and the portrait was then deposited in the royal treasury, in order that his appearance might not be unknown to posterity. The manuscript seen by Mas'udi was a copy of one which was found in the royal treasury in 781. Hamzah of Isfahan made use of it in his history when describing the features of the Sassanid kings.

By etiquette, the king remained hidden, inaccessible and invisible even to the highest dignitaries of his court. Between the sovereign and his household there hung a curtain, concealing him from view ; this curtain was ten cubits away from the king and ten cubits away from the position occupied by the highest class in the State. The keeping of this curtain was entrusted to a Knight's son, who had the title of Khurram-bash, ' Be Joyful '. When the king received his favourites privately, this Knight's son ordered a servant to go on to the roof of the palace, and to cry, at the top of his voice, so as to be heard by all present : " Watch over your speech, for to-day you are in the presence of the King ". The same ceremonial was observed at feasts and concerts ; the courtiers stood silently in order of rank, and the Khurram-bash commanded one to sing this piece or that, and another to play an instrument in such-and-such a mode.[1]

Musicians were in great demand at the court, and appeared in ceremonies ; they even accompanied the king out hunting ; they were summoned to celebrate the inauguration of a dam on the Tigris in the reign of Chosroes II ; we hear of a famous singer in the same reign, Barbed (contracted from his real name, Fahlabed, which has been preserved by the Arabian authors, and means etymologically ' Chief of the Parthians '), who

[1] **CLXIV,** vol. ii, p. 158.

enjoyed such favour with the king that the courtiers, having
been threatened with execution if they informed the king of
the death of his favourite black horse Shabdiz, made use of
Barbed to break the news of the calamity in veiled terms.
The names of celebrated tunes are mentioned, we hear of
' royal modes ', and we have lists of the instruments used—
lute, flute, mandoline, oboe and harp.

The chief amusement of the kings was hunting, as it had
been in the days of the Achæmenids, and as it has been since
Persia changed religion. It was done in great walled parks,
formerly called ' paradises ', in which lions, boars, and bears
were preserved. Theophanes[1] tells us that the soldiers of the
Roman Emperor Heraclius found, in the gardens abandoned
by Chosroes II, ostriches, gazelles, wild asses, peacocks,
pheasants, and even lions and tigers. Two reliefs of this epoch
show us a boar-hunt and a stag-hunt, over ground surrounded
by nets ; the king and his companions, clad in sumptuous
stuffs and pearl-embroidered coats, pursue the game with
arrows, while women play the harp for the entertainment of
the party.

We can imagine what a State audience of the king must have
been like, for the hall in which this ceremony took place still
stands, and, moreover, has been seen and drawn by many
travellers, so that we have the less cause to regret that a few
years ago an earthquake destroyed the great pointed arch
which was such a conspicuous object. This is the Taq-i-Kisra,
the ' Arch of Chosroes ', south-east of Bagdad on the right
bank of the Tigris, which during the last war was often called
the Salman-i-Pak, after one of the companions of Muhammad,
whose mausoleum is near by. It constitutes the remains of the
White Castle which Chosroes I built at Ctesiphon about 550.
The front, adorned with niches, has no windows ; there were a
hundred and fifty openings in the roof, five or six inches in
diameter, which allowed a mysterious light to filter in. The
throne stood at the end of the hall, and when the curtain was
drawn back the king, splendidly clad, seated on his throne,
wearing on his head the heavy bejewelled tiara, which was
attached to a golden chain hanging from the ceiling to
take the weight, presented such a marvellous spectacle that

---

[1] p. 495.

the man who saw it for the first time involuntarily fell on his knees.[1]

Foreign ambassadors were received with especial honours, and this is so in modern Persia. When a high official of this kind presented himself at the frontier, the governor of the province ascertained the object of his mission, and at once reported to the king, in order that there might be time to prepare a reply. Then the sovereign sent an escort to conduct him to the royal residence ; the same escort is to-day commanded by the Mihman-dar. The governors of the provinces traversed on the way saw that suitable accommodation was in readiness. The escort of honour had to take care that the envoy did not examine the condition of the country too closely, for Persian ambassadors had instructions to take note of the state of roads and passes, of rivers and wells, of land providing forage, and of the character of the sovereign and of his associates, and the court of Ctesiphon reasonably supposed that the representatives sent to it would receive similar instructions from their governments. In a solemn audience, the king, seated on his throne and surrounded by his high dignitaries, questioned the ambassador on his name and his journey, on his mission, on his august master, and on the arm which the last-named might have at his disposal. Then the king conducted him to his palace with great pomp, entertained him at his table, took him hunting, gave him a robe of honour, and dismissed him with the customary ceremonial.

The king showed himself in public on rare occasions, such as the feasts of the equinoxes. When grave affairs of State were discussed, or a high court was held to judge one of the lords, the assembly was public, so the Armenian writers say ; that is, not only were the king, the Magi, the courtiers, and the soldiers of the private guard present, but the people were allowed to enjoy the show from outside the enclosure. All this pomp and all these assemblages of high dignitaries were only intended to impress the onlookers, for nobody durst raise his voice in the presence of the king. When Chosroes I reformed the taxes and established new principles of collection, he assembled his council and asked twice whether anyone had any objection to the new arrangement. On the third time of asking, for

---

[1] **CXXXIII,** p. 102, following Nœldeke, *Geschichte der Araber und Perser*, and Zotenberg's translation of Tha'alibi, *Histoire des rois de Perse*.

everyone had remained silent, a man asked respectfully whether the king had meant to establish a tax for perpetuity, which, as time went on, would lead to injustice. " Accursed and rash man ! " cried the monarch, " To what class do you belong ? " The man replying that he was one of the secretaries, the king ordered him to be beaten to death with a writing-case ; this was done, and the beholders exclaimed " O King, we find all the taxes which you have laid on us just ! "

The usual rewards for merits were titles, gifts of money, and posts at court. The gift of a tiara brought with it the right to be admitted to the royal table and to the king's council, even if one was a foreigner, like the Roman citizen who, according to Ammianus Marcellinus, had betrayed his countrymen in the time of Sapor II. There were titles of honour, such as Mihisht, ' Greatest ' given by Yazdigird I to Mundhir, the King of the Arabs, Wahriz, borne by the general who conquered the Yemen in the reign of Chosroes I, Hazaraft, which we find attached to the names of Zarmihr and the Spahbed Bistam, and Hazarmard, ' (Strong as a) Thousand Men ', which Chosroes II gave to a Byzantine general sent to his help by the Emperor Maurice. Some of these titles even contained the king's own name, with an epithet or substantive attached, such as Tahm Shapur, ' Sapor is Strong ', or Javid-han-Khosrau, ' Chosroes is Eternal '. An ecclesiastic was honoured with the appellation of Hamak-den, ' Knowing All Religion '.

The gift of a robe of honour from the king's wardrobe was a very ancient custom, and survived in the East until our own time, when it was superseded, in the XIXth century, by orders of knighthood copied from Europe. Sapor II gave the Armenian general Manuel, according to Faustus of Byzantium,[1] a royal garment, an ermine fur, a gold and silver pendant to attach to the eagle on his helmet, a diadem, breast ornaments, a tent, carpets, and gold vessels. To reward the Grand Mobed who had brought him some good news, Ardashir I filled his mouth with rubies, gold coins, pearls and jewellery.

To meet such prodigalities as these, the king's treasury, which was at the same time the public treasury, had to be well stocked. One treasure of Chosroes II, who had several, was called Ganj-i-badh-award, ' the Treasure brought by the Wind '; the Roman Emperor had put it on board ship at the time

---

[1] V. Langlois, *Historiene arméniens*, i, p. 301.

when the Persians were threatening Constantinople, and the ships had been cast by the wind on the coast of Egypt, where the Persian general Shahr-Baraz had seized it. Another was the Ganj-i-gav, the 'Treasure of the Ox', found by a peasant as he ploughed with his oxen ; it contained a hundred vases full of gold, silver, and precious stones, which were believed to have been buried by Alexander. The king rewarded the peasant with the gift of one of the vases.

When the Arabs captured and looted Ctesiphon, the masses of booty which they took gave them a high impression of the luxury which reigned at the court of the Sassanids. Among the royal treasures they found the crown of Chosroes II, his wardrobe, every article in which was embroidered with gold and adorned with precious stones, including one coat woven of gold thread and strewn with rubies and pearls, the king's cuirass and helmet, both of pure gold, and a carpet, three hundred ells by sixty, of silk brocade bordered with emeralds and adorned with flowers done in precious stones.

Of all this luxury, only a few scattered remnants survive. There are two cups in the Cabinet des Médailles in Paris ; one is adorned with enamel rosettes, red and white alternately, in three bands, in a setting of gold which shows at the bottom Chosroes I sitting on a throne borne by winged horses ; the other, which is of silver, represents Chosroes II indulging in the pleasures of the chase.

THE ARMY

The army which fought the Romans and won the Sassanids some fine victories, and in any case defended the territory of the Empire so that enemies could not invade very far, deserves to be known. It is to Western authors, and Ammianus Marcellinus in particular, that we owe our knowledge of its organization and armament. As in Mediæval Europe, its strength lay in its cavalry, composed of noble knights, who held the first place in the order of battle. A relief has preserved for us the costume of the Persian knight. He wears a coat of mail which goes down to the knees, with sleeves and a high collar concealing the whole face ; his head is protected by a helmet adorned with floating ribbons ; in his right hand he holds a lance about six feet long, and in his left a target ; a quiver is attached to his belt ; the head, tail, and breast of the horse are likewise covered with coat of mail.

The Arabian authors and the memories preserved in the epic permit us to add to the arms represented in this relief a straight sword, a mace attached to the belt, an axe, and two ropes attached behind the helmet, which probably formed the *kamand* or lasso by which an enemy could be pulled off his horse.[1] Ammianus Marcellinus (xxiv. 6. 8) describes the cavalry charges which the Persians made against the Roman infantry ; the heavy-armed horsemen advanced in ordered masses, in such close formation that the scales of their armour, turning as their bodies moved, gave off a dazzling light. Procopius (*De Bello Persico*, i. 18) observes that the Persians were almost all bowmen, and masters in their art, but that their shots were lacking in force, because their strings were not stretched tight enough.

There was a body of cavalry called the Immortals, as in the time of the Achæmenids, which, we may suppose, was composed of ten thousand picked men, like its ancient prototype. The corps of the Jan-apaspar, the ' Seekers of Death ', mentioned by the Arabian historian Tabari, may perhaps have been composed of mercenaries ; the name of one of their leaders, Jalinus, is more likely to be Greek than anything else.

The infantry was of very little importance ; it consisted of a mass of unorganized peasants, armed with oblong wicker-work shields covered with raw hides, who acted as troops of the baggage train. Being of no military value, drawing no pay, and never receiving any reward, they were ready to throw down their arms. The Emperor Julian compared them to disgusting goats, covered in filth.

By the side of the Persian cavalry fought auxiliary troops, also mounted. These were the feudal cavalry, led by native princes, as in the time of the Achæmenids. Among them were Sacæ of Sijistan, Gelli of Gilan, Daylamites, who were more skilful with the sword, spear, and dagger than with the bow, peoples of the Caucasus, Hunnish or Chionite mercenaries, Chuls of Gurgan (Hyrcania), transported into Adharbayjan by

---

[1] In the time of the Achæmenids the Sagartians, a nomad people of Persian origin and speech, had this weapon. They were horsemen, who in war used ropes woven with straps, at the end of which were nets (instead of slip-knots) ; when they entangled a horse or a man, they pulled him to them and killed him. Cf. Hdt., vii. 86.

Chosroes I, and Armenians, who were the object of especial attention.

The reserve of the army was formed of elephants from India, which inspired the Romans with a certain amount of terror. They carried great wooden towers full of soldiers and adorned with flags. During the battle they stood in a line at the rear of the army, in order to give it confidence.

The reliefs of the period give representations of the flags. In particular, we see a long narrow standard of cloth, like a banderole, flying from a shaft. Elsewhere we find a standard-bearer holding a shaft at the top of which is a wooden cross-piece with three balls above it and two underneath. The national banner, the palladium of the Empire, was the famous Dirafsh-i-Kaviyani, the flag which was said to have been made of the apron of the smith Kava, who in mythical times raised the popular revolt against the Semitic oppressor Dahak and placed Feridun on the throne. This flag had attained enormous dimensions, twenty-two feet by fifteen, and was studded with precious stones by kings who made it a point of honour to embellish it. It was taken by the Moslems at the battle of Qadisiyah, cut up, and sold in pieces at Medina.

There were stores and arsenals (*ambar*) in which, in peace time, arms were kept ready for issue to the troops. The city of Anbar on the Euphrates, which was for a time the capital of the Abbasids before Bagdad was built, took its name from the magazines which held the arms needed to fight the Romans, whose frontiers were not far away.

Ammianus Marcellinus says[1] that the signal for battle was given by trumpets; by these we must probably understand the long trumpets with a straight tube which tradition has preserved until our own time in countries subject to Iranian civilization, called *kurra-nai*, 'colt-flutes'.[2] The *Dinkart* mentions the detail that before battle the nearest water-course was consecrated by a libation of holy water and a stick which had been blessed was fired as the first arrow. The general was expected to exhort his troops to fight bravely, reminding them of the sacred duty of fighting the infidel and the rewards for

---

[1] xix. 2. 5. Cf. Elisæus, in V. Langlois, *Historiens arméniens*, vol. i, p. 221.

[2] C. Huart, "Musique persane," in A. Lavignac's *Encyclopédie de la musique*.

which they might hope in this world and the next. It was also customary for him to summon the enemy to surrender and embrace the Mazdean religion, or else he challenged them to single combat with the cry "*Mard o mard*!"—"Man to man!" The modern game of Prisoners' Base seems to be copied from the cavalry battles which began with a duel of two champions of equal worth, the rival hosts keeping their ranks, and ended with a general charge on both sides, and a mêlée which decided the victory.

When the king commanded in person, a throne was set up in the centre of the army, and he was surrounded by his suite and a body of devoted soldiers, while a second circle of footsoldiers and archers formed an outer ring. It was unprecedented for the king to hurl himself into the fray, but Sapor II did. If the king was not present, the Commander-in-Chief occupied the throne and directed operations from it, as Rustam did at Qadisiyah.

The Persians were experts in siege-craft, which they seem to have learned from the Romans. When Muhammad was beset in Medina by the Meccan troops, he found among his people a slave of Persian origin, a Christian converted to the new religion, named Salman al-Farisi, who taught him the art of digging a moat round an open town. The Sassanians knew the use of the ram, the *ballista*, and movable towers for attacking strongholds, and when defending them they used to catch the ram in a slip-knot (the *kamand* or lasso), poured down molten lead, and threw flaming stuff on to the machines.

Procopius[1] tells us how they established their statistics of casualties. Before taking the field, the army was passed in review before the general who was to command it. Each soldier marched past separately, and threw an arrow into a large basket placed for the purpose, Then the baskets were sealed with the royal seal. After the campaign, the baskets were opened, and each soldier took out an arrow. So the number of arrows left at once showed how many soldiers had been killed or captured.

THE PRIESTHOOD AND EDUCATION

Mazdaism being a State religion, the priests had become of great importance in the Empire. Agathias[2] remarks on the

---

[1] *De Bello Persico*, i. 18.   [2] ii. 26.

veneration with which the Magi were treated ; public matters were settled in accordance with their advice and predictions. " Among the Persians," this author says, " nothing is considered lawful and just unless it has been approved by a Magus ".

The influence of the priests was the greater because they owned large landed estates, chiefly in Adharbayjan, the ancient Media Atropatene, and religious fines, tithes, and voluntary gifts supplied them with abundant resources. The Magi lived by their own laws, Ammianus Marcellinus tells us ; that is, they were accepted as a state within the State, having canonical institutions different from the laws of the kingdom. They were organized in a hierarchy about which we have not complete information. The lowest class consisted of the plain Magi (Moghs), above whom came the Herbeds (Chiefs of Fire) and Mobeds (Chiefs of the Magi), among whom we may place the priest who gabbled prayers (Zot) and him who kept up the fire (Raspi). An instructor of the Magi also held a higher post, and at the very top of the scale were two high dignitaries, the Herbedan-herbed, who may have been the Chief Justice, and the Mobedan-mobed or High Priest.

The chief business of the priests was the service of the temples. Whereas the Achæmenians had no temples, to the astonishment of the Greeks, the Sassanians built oratories or fire-temples, in which they worshipped fire, the symbol of Ahura-Mazda. There was a House Fire in every house, a Clan or Village Fire (*adheran*), and a fire for each canton, which was called Bahram's Fire. The first was kept up by the head of the family, but the service of the *adheran* required at least two priests, and the Bahram's Fire even more. Above these fires, and far more honoured by their worshippers, were the three fires which were quite especially venerated in the territories of the Empire—Adhar-Farnbagh, belonging especially to the priests, at Kariyan in Fars, Adhar-Gushnasp, the Warriors' or Royal Fire, at Ganjak in Adharbayjan, and Burzin Mihr, the Farmers' Fire, on Mount Ravand in Khurasan.

The kings showed themselves generous to these sanctuaries. Bahram V Gur presented the temple of Adhar-Gushnasp **with** the precious stones which adorned the crown taken from the Khan of the Turks, together with the wife of the conquered potentate ; Chosroes I was equally liberal ; and Chosroes II, having, in his struggle with the usurper Bahram Chubin, promised gold ornaments and gifts of money to the same temple, kept his word when he triumphed.

The priests attached to the temples had much the same duties as their Parsee successors to-day. They tended the fire and saw that it did not go out ; they prepared the *haoma*, a sacred herb which was passed through a strainer to make the communion drink of the priest ; they dealt with the offerings of bread and meat ; they gabbled prayers and litanies. In their dealings with laymen, they performed ritual purifications, heard confessions, gave absolution, passed sentences of fine, and conducted the ceremonies pertaining to birth, to the presenta-tion of the *kusti* or ritual belt, to marriage, to funerals, and to religious festivals. Since religion came into the smallest events of daily life, and the layman was in constant danger of sinning through heedlessness, one may imagine that the priests, in order to wash away moral stains, were intervening the whole time.

Teaching was done by the priests alone. Was it extended to the middle class and the people ? Our evidence does not permit us to say. The nobles learned to read, write, reckon, and play polo, and also chess when this game was introduced from India in the reign of Chosroes I, and their chief occupation was fencing.

Sport was not the business of the priests ; so it was the teaching of reading, writing, and arithmetic which was especially reserved to them. It is probable that the Mobeds taught the wealthier townsmen, the merchants. The reading of Pahlavi was difficult, for the Persian verbs, pronouns, and prepositions were represented in writing by their Semitic equivalents. Thus these words became mere ideograms, numbering about a thousand. People wrote in Aramaic and read in Persian. The Manichæan manuscripts found at Turfan have for the first time given us a Pahlavi language without these artificial ideograms.

The priesthood was intolerant and fanatical. This is only too clearly proved by their persecution of heretics and men of other religions, in particular the Christians, who were accused of betraying the Empire in the interest of Rome.

ADMINISTRATION

An administration inherited from earlier times and composed of offices called Divans formed the structure of the State. We have no direct information about the number and duties of the various departments, but, since the Abbasid Caliphs in the Moslem period adopted an organization copied from that of the Sassanids, we may attempt to reconstruct it. We know, moreover, that the king had different seals for the privy department, for the secretariat for the despatch of letters, for criminal justice, for the award of distinctions and offices, and for finance. It is probable that, in addition to these departments, there were others for military affairs, the post, the coinage, weights and measures, and the royal domains.

The Arabian historian al-Baladhuri, who got his information from a convert from Mazdaism to Islam named Ibn al-Muqaffa, the author of the Arabic version of *Kalila and Dimna*, gives some details about the administration of finance. Reports on the sums levied were read aloud to the king ; the chief of the craftsmen handed him yearly a statement of the return of the various taxes and of the balance of the Treasury ; the king placed his seal on the documents submitted to him. Chosroes II Parviz introduced, in the place of parchment, paper dyed with saffron and scented with attar of roses. Paper must have been brought into Persia by trade, for it was a monopoly of China and was only manufactured in the country where it had been invented ; it must have been rare and expensive. Orders given by the king were drafted in his presence by the royal secretary, and another official entered them in his day-book, which was made up every month, sealed with the royal seal, and deposited in the archives. The order itself was passed to the Keeper of the Seals, who sealed it and handed it to the executive agent. The latter re-drafted it in the special style of the bureaucracy, and this version was sent to the secretary, shown to the king, and compared with the day book. If the two versions agreed, the secretary placed the royal seal on the executive agent's document, in the presence of the king or his most intimate confidant, and the order was then in force.

The royal seal consisted of a ring bearing the engraved image of a boar. When a document involved obligations to another state, whether independent or dependent on the Empire, it was accompanied by a small bag of salt, bearing the royal seal, as a sign of the immutability of the oath. The Arabian historian Mas'udi describes in detail the four seals of Chosroes I Anushirvan and the nine seals of Chosroes II Parviz.[1]

---

[1] **CLXIV,** vol. ii, pp. 204, 228.

The postal service was used only for Government communications, not for those of private individuals. It must have been very like that of the Achæmenids, which we know from the Greeks, and that of the Abbasid Caliphs, about which the Arabian authors tell us. It was a horse post, which took persons as well as letters. The roads were well kept up, and there were sufficient horses and personnel at the relays to maintain the service. In mountainous country foot-runners were employed, and in the plains mounted couriers on horses or, in the deserts bordering on the Arab country, on camels.

The revenues of the State consisted chiefly of the land-tax which was probably called *kharag*, an Aramaic word which appears in the Talmud and is the origin of the Arabic *kharaj*, and the poll-tax, called the *gezit*, whence comes the Arabic *jizya*. The latter took the form of a fixed annual amount, which was distributed among the tax-payers. The land-tax was also distributed among the tax-payers ; it was assessed for each canton according to the harvest, each canton paying from a sixth to a third of the yield, according to the fertility of the soil (or, as some writers say, from a tenth to half), the distance from a town being taken into account. Children, women, and old men were exempted from the land-tax. The poll-tax was levied on tax-payers who did not own landed property, namely, Christians and Jews.[1] Chosroes I completed the survey begun by his father Kavadh. Under Chosroes II in 607, the yield of all taxes amounted to six hundred million drachmæ.[2]

The uncertainty of the basis on which each man should pay gave a pretext for the exactions which have been the rule in the East from the earliest times to the present. We have definite proof in a document preserved by the Christian authors —an order issued to the governors of the Aramæan countries by Sapor II, who needed extraordinary taxation in order to maintain the war against the Romans.[3] " On receiving the present order of our godhead, which is contained in the

---

[1] F. Justi, **IX**, vol. ii, p. 538.
[2] *Ibid.*, and see above, p. 135 n. 1.
[3] **CLVIII**, pp. 45-6.

enclosure sent by us, you will arrest Simon, the chief of the
Nazarenes. You will not release him until he has signed this
document and agreed to collect, for payment to us, a double
poll-tax and double tribute for the whole people of the Nazarenes
which is in the country of our godhead and dwells on our territory. For our godhead has only the troubles of war, and they
have only rest and pleasure ! They dwell on our territory and
share the sentiments of Cæsar our enemy ! " At first sight, the
moral implied in this document may appear curious, and raise
doubts of its authenticity, but, if one remembers that the
kings of Persia declared themselves of divine race, *minoi-
chitra*, and that the measure ordered has been frequent in the
East, one will regard it as a valuable example of the unbridled
autocracy of the potentates of the Orient. It is probable, too,
that the methods employed to raise money were not confined
to the Christians, and that the other subjects of the Empire
were subjected to similar exactions.

The farmers, for example, did not dare to touch the ripe fruit
until taxation had taken place. If the collector arrived late
to make his assessment, the fruit went bad and the peasant lost
heavily, if he was not ruined. This is exactly what went on
in the Ottoman Empire in the XIXth century ; the corn
remained on the threshing-floor until the assessing official
arrived, and a storm might destroy the whole harvest. To
remedy this state of things, Kavadh is said to have decided to
change the system of taxation, and Chosroes I Anushirvan
succeeded in establishing a new basis for collecting the land-tax.
By this system, the *garib*, an area equal to about half an acre,
was taxed at a *dirhem* a year for wheat and barley, eight
dirhems for vines, seven *dirhems* for lucern, which provided
fodder for horses, no doubt combined with the usual chopped
straw, and five *dirhems* for rice. Dates and olives were taxed
by the tree. All other produce, for example, isolated date-
palms not forming part of a continuous plantation, were exempt.
In spite of defects in its practical application, the new system
was a relief for the general public, and it was perhaps this
reform which earned Chosroes I the name of ' the Just ' in the
memory of the Persian people.

The poll-tax was also reformed. It was applied to all men
between twenty and fifty years of age, who were divided into
classes according to their means. The highest class paid

eighteen *dirhems*, others eight or six, and the mass of the people four. These taxes were paid to the Treasury every three months. The nobles, soldiers, priests, secretaries, and, in general, officials in the king's service, were exempt. The judges of the cantons had to see that the royal orders were properly carried out.

These regular taxes were not the only burdens which the people had to bear. There were also customary gifts, called *ayin*, and compulsory presents which were given at the two equinoctial festivals, Nauruz (spring) and Mihragan (autumn); these usages have survived to our own time.

In spite of the methods of pressure used to bring in the taxes, there were always considerable arrears. Sometimes the kings, to relieve the tax-payer, remitted them. Bahram V Gur, on his accession, proclaimed a remission of all arrears, and reduced the taxes by a third for the first year of his reign. Complete dispensation from land-tax, poll-tax, impressed labour, and other burdens was proclaimed by Peroz on the occasion of a famine.

JUSTICE

The judges were held in high respect. The great privileged families were entrusted with the office of mediator and arbiter, probably in cases arising between nobles, but the normal functions of a judge seem to have been reserved for the priests, who were the sole depositories of legal science. There were these judges in all cantons, as was natural, and it is probable that the Headman of the village, the Dihqan, exercised the functions of judge or arbiter, if there was no special office for this duty. There was also a judge attached to the army.

" The laws were much feared among the Persians," says Ammianus Marcellinus. " Those against deserters and ingrates were especially cruel, and some were quite abominable, such as those by which a whole family suffered for the crime of one of its members." This last was a survival of the primitive custom by which first the clan, and then the family, was collectively responsible for one man's misdeeds. Three kinds of crime were distinguished : against God, when a man turned away from religion ; against the king, such as rebellion, treason, or flight in battle ; and against one's neighbour, when one man injured another. At the beginning the laws had been very severe, the two first crimes being punished with death and the third with talion. In the time of Chosroes I the penalties were modified. Before heretics were put to death, they were kept in prison and catechized for a whole year. If they repented, they were set at liberty. This law applied chiefly to the Manichees and Mazdakites, who were guilty of making innovations affecting the State religion. Crimes against the king were punished by the death of only some of the rebels or deserters, who were executed as an example to the others. Crimes against one's neighbour were punished by fine and mutilation.

Theft was very frequent. According to the *Dinkart*, a thief taken in the act was led before the judge, with the stolen article hung to his neck ; he was put into jail and laden with chains proportionate to his crime ; on conviction, he was taken to the gallows and hanged. Detention pending trial might last months or even years, but imprisonment does not seem to have been used as a punishment. It was, of course, employed as a means of removing dangerous men. The Castle of Oblivion near Jundi Shapur in Susiana was so called because it was forbidden to mention in the king's hearing the persons imprisoned there.

Blinding was a very common penalty, applied especially to princes who revolted, and it was practised all through the Middle Ages. It took the form of an artificial cataract, induced by passing a red-hot flat needle before the cornea, or by pouring boiling oil on the eyes. According to the Armenian historian Moses of Chorene, Sapor II punished a cowardly general with death by making him drink bull's blood, a penalty which had already been applied in Achæmenian times. The most usual form of execution was beheading with a sword. Treason against the State or against religion was punished by crucifixion, as in the case of Mani, whose skin was afterwards stuffed and hung up at one of the gates of Jundi Shapur. In the *Acts of the Christian Martyrs* we see that stoning was sometimes practised.

It is, again, in the account of the persecution of the Christians, who were regarded as the hereditary enemies of the State on account of their alleged or real dealings with the Roman Empire, that we can read the frightful description of the tortures reserved for those held to be criminals. The same treatment was meted to the Manichees and Mazdakites, as traitors to the State religion. But when studying Mr. Arthur Christensen's gloomy picture,[1] one should add that the Persians were no innovators in this respect ; their Semitic forerunners and their Moslem successors did as much, the ' question ' practised by Roman law authorized cruelties nearly as bad, and these barbarous methods did not disappear until the French Revolution.

In case of religious persecution, the ordinary courts were not competent. Royal commissions, composed in great part of Mobeds, investigated the matter and pronounced the penalty. Sometimes, too, the provincial authorities took it upon themselves to order a prosecution. The case of the Bishop Abdhisho was first referred to Prince Ardashir, who reigned later as Ardashir II but was at the time governor of the province of Adiabene with the title of King ; then the Grand Mobed, assisted by two Magi, dealt with it ; and finally the Chief Eunuch, the master of all the elephants in the kingdom, took it over. One Grand Mobed was converted to Christianity ; to judge him, a commission was appointed under the Inspector of Stores. This official, not venturing to take the responsibility of passing a death-sentence, submitted the case to the king, who ordered accusations of lese-majesty to be made. The Grand Mobed was then condemned to die of hunger in a remote and desert spot.

The ordeal was frequently employed in cases of doubt to prove the guilt or innocence of an accused man. It was effected either by means of the sacred bundle of twigs used in religion (baresma) or by fire, as in the episode of Siyavush in the Shah-Namah, where the hero rides through a fire on his horse, and in the romance of Wis and Ramin (p. 136).

The King was the supreme judge. The Siyasat-Namah of Nizam al-Mulk relates that on certain occasions the kings appeared on horseback on a platform from which they overlooked the crowd, and rendered justice to those who complained of oppression. The first Sassanid kings held public audiences, to which all were admitted, twice a year, at the equinoxes. These were announced by public criers some days beforehand, and on the prescribed day a herald proclaimed that no one should be prevented from attending.

[1] CXXXIII, p. 71.

This custom was abolished by Yazdigird I, or, according to the *Acts of the Martyrs*, by Yazdigird II. It is none the less true that most of the Sassanid kings had, in different degrees, a deep sense of justice, and tried to remedy the abuses ensuing from the unbridled tyranny of the nobles and provincial governors.

THE FAMILY AND PROPERTY

Society was based on the family and property. Polygamy was usual, and in addition to their lawful wives the Persians had concubines, slaves bought or taken in war. The wife had to pay absolute obedience to her husband, but had a more honoured position than elsewhere in the East. Betrothals often took place in childhood, and men were advised to marry young (at fifteen, according to the *Dinkart*).

A question about which, though it has been much discussed, the unanimity of our sources allows no room for doubt, is that of the marriage between close relations, the *Khwetuk-das*. Unions of this kind, which were regarded as incestuous by all other religions except the Egyptian, is recommended by the Avesta and Pahlavi theological literature. " The *Khwetuk-das* neutralizes mortal sins," says the author of the *Shayast-la-shayast*. Many historical instances show how frequent was marriage between brother and sister, regarded by the *Dinkart* as being accompanied by the divine splendour and having the value of an exorcism. Such unions were naturally regarded with horror by the Christians subject to the Empire, as they were by the Moslems when they conquered Persia.

After the communistic upheaval and the ravages done in society by the application of the theories of Mazdak, thanks to the support of Kavadh, Chosroes I had to prescribe new arrangements to restore order in the Empire. As far as possible, confiscated property was returned to the former owners, and it was ordained that anyone who had damaged another in his property should make full repayment, without prejudice to the penalty which he had incurred. A child whose origin was uncertain (Mazdak having prescribed community of women) was to be regarded as belonging to the family with which it happened to be, and would inherit from the father to whom it was attributed, if, at least, the latter recognized it. Married women were to be handed back to their husbands. A woman who was single at the time of the promulgation of the communistic law might choose as husband the man who had then been assigned to her, or another ; but the former was obliged to give her the usual marriage-present. The king undertook the guardianship of noble children without parents. The boys were attached to the court and received a marriage gift enabling them to choose a wife, and the girls were dowered from the State funds ; so a new nobility, devoted to the king, was created.

The marriage regulations, handed down by tradition, are rather obscure. There seem to have been five forms of marriage. (i.) The woman married with the consent of her parents ; the children which she bore her husband belonged to him in this world and the next ; she was called the *padheshah-zan*, or ' privileged wife '. (ii.) A wife who was an only child was called the *ovagh-zan*, or ' only-child wife '. The first child which she bore was given to her parents to take the place of the daughter who had left the family ; after that she became, like the first, a ' privileged wife '. (iii.) If a man of marriageable age died single, and his family gave a dowry to a strange woman and married her to a stranger, this woman was called the *sadhar-zan*, or ' adopted wife '. Half of her children belonged to the dead man, whose wife she would be in the next world, and the other half to the living husband. (iv.) A widow who married again was called a *chaghar-zan*, or ' servant wife '. If she had no children by her first husband, she was considered as an adopted wife, and half of her children by her second husband belonged to the first, whose wife she would again be in the next life. (v.) The woman who married without her parents' consent was the least considered of all. She was called the *khud-sarai-zan*, the ' wife who has made her own house '. She could not inherit from her parents until her eldest son was of age and had given her as ' privileged wife ' to his own father.

There was a relic of marriage by purchase in the custom by which the future husband paid the girl's parents a certain sum of money, or goods to that value, which must be returned " if the girl is not in marriage worth the amount paid ", in the words of the *Dinkart*, that is, if she remained barren.

The birth of a child was attended by the celebration of certain rites and the presentation of pious gifts, especially if the child was a boy. When he was given a name care had to be taken to avoid those used by idolaters. The child owed

obedience to its father, and if it did not fulfil this duty part of
its inheritance might be given to the mother, if she was more
worthy. The education of young boys (up to the age of seven
among the Moslems, who may have taken this limit from the
Persians) was done by the mother. If she died, the duty fell
on the fathers' sister or his grown-up daughter. The daughter
remained beside her mother, but the father alone could give her
in marriage, and was obliged to do so as soon as she was of
marriageable age. If he died before, the privileged wife could
give her in marriage, and, failing her, the lawful guardian ;
girls could not choose their husbands.

To ensure the maintenance of the family, that it might have
a posterity and the dead man's name might be preserved, the
law ordained marriage by substitution. When a man died
without male issue, leaving a widow, she was married to his
nearest kinsman. If there was no widow, this kinsman
married the dead man's daughter or nearest female relative.
In both cases the child of the new marriage was regarded as the
offspring of the deceased. But if there were no available women
in the family, the money left by the deceased was employed to
obtain a woman, whom one of his relations married. The
concordance of the letter of Tansar with the evidence of
al-Biruni in his book on India makes it impossible to doubt the
existence of these legal arrangements.

Adoption was subject to very strict regulations. If a man
died without leaving a grown son to take his place, the minors
were put in ward, and, if he had possessed a certain fortune,
the administration of the inheritance was given over to an
adoptive son. Where there was a privileged wife, she assumed
the direction of affairs under the title of adoptive son. If there
was only a servant-wife, she, having no authority, had to be
put in ward like the minors, and in that case the guardian would
be either her father, if he was alive, or her brother, or some other
near kinsman. If there was no privileged wife or only daughter,
the charge of adoptive son fell, successively, on a brother, a
sister, a brother's daughter, a brother's son, and other near
relations.

What conditions were to be fulfilled by the adoptive son ?
He must be of age, of the Mazdean religion, and intelligent ;
he must have a numerous family, and must not have committed
any mortal sin. If a woman was called upon to do this office,

she must neither have a husband nor desire one, she must not live in concubinage or by prostitution, and she must not have been adopted by another family, for a woman could only be adopted once, whereas a man might be adopted by several families, without limit.

There were three kinds of adoption. The ' existing adoptive son ' was the privileged wife or sole and unmarried daughter, who was adopted ipso facto and without special formality. The ' predetermined adoptive son ' was he who was appointed for the purpose by the deceased. The ' constituted adoptive son ' was the man chosen among the near kin.

There were supervisors to see that the laws regarding inheritances were observed. These were probably priests, for the division of the goods of the deceased among the heirs was within the competence of the Mobeds, and they, should the deceased have left no property, had to look after the funeral and the future of his children.

Provision could be made for common ownership by contract. If a man had two wives, and enjoyed common ownership with them by contract, each wife held her goods in common with the man, but exclusively with reference to the other wife. This common ownership might be cancelled by the man, but not by a wife. Lawful heirs could not be deprived of the goods falling to them, except for the payment of a debt or the maintenance of a wife, children, a father, or any other old man dependent on the deceased, in which case the attribution of part of the property to these dependents was valid. In making a testament, a man was obliged to set aside a portion of his goods for each unmarried daughter and two portions for his privileged wife, if he had one.

INDUSTRY AND TRADE

Industry and commerce enabled those who practised them to live in a certain comfort. The manufacture of textiles was highly developed. Many stuffs woven with ornaments of conventional flowers and fantastic animals were imported into Europe either by trade in the early Middle Ages, or by the Crusaders, and were used to wrap relics of the Saints, thus being preserved until our own day. This industry by no means disappeared on the Moslem conquest, and the Arabian authors have preserved for us the names of the factories of Tavvaz,

Shata, Ray, and Marv. In winter feathered garments were worn, such as those made of cormorant, or garments of silk and wool padded with coarse silk stuffing.

Silk came from India by sea. The overland routes by Central Asia, where regular transit was maintained by the Sogdians, put Persia, and so the Roman Empire, in communication with China, whence silk was also obtained direct. The Chinese, for their part, prized the valuable Persian eyebrow-dye, and imported it for the use of the Empress.[1] Babylonian carpets were in great demand in the land of the Great Wall.[2] The precious stones of Syria, the corals and pearls of the Red Sea, and the textiles of Egypt were conveyed to China by caravan, along the southern edge of the Desert of Gobi.

The Persian Empire had adopted the Assyrian practice of transporting vanquished peoples far away from their homes. Imitating Darius I, who had settled foreign colonists in Susiana,[3] the Parthian Orodes had transported the Roman prisoners taken at Carrhae to Marv, and Sapor I established the companions of the Emperor Valerian at Jundi Shapur, where the engineers of the Roman army built the so-called Emperor's Dam to hold the water of the river. When Sapor II took Amida (Diyarbakr) he distributed the captives among the towns of Susiana, at Susa, Shushtar, and elsewhere, and these introduced the manufacture of new kinds of brocade and silk goods.

GENERAL CHARACTERISTICS OF THE SASSANIAN PERIOD

The special feature of the government of the Sassanids as compared with that of their immediate predecessors, the Arsacids, was the centralization of the powers of the State in the hands of an absolute autocrat, supported by an exclusive religion. The administration, inherited from the previous governments and preserving ancient bureaucratic traditions going back to the Assyrians and Babylonians, had remained the same ; but it was more stable, and the governors of provinces, being kept in dependence on the central power, less often felt inclined to revolt ; indeed, for centuries no satrap rose against his king. The old spy-system, organized by the

---

[1] Hirth, *Chinesische Studien*, Munich and Leipzig, 1890, etc., pp. **235** ff.
[2] Hirth, *China and the Roman Orient*, Leipzig and Munich, p. 253.
[3] Hdt., vi. 119.

Achæmenids, worked wonderfully, and was the basis of the internal policy of the monarchy.

The strength of the army lay in the heavy mail-clad cavalry which we have seen charging the Roman legions. The knights who composed it were small feudal lords whose domains, held direct from the Crown, were scattered about the surface of the Empire. The great vassals had only levies of peasants, badly armed and of small courage, to lead into battle. Moreover, the feudal nobility had reserved to themselves hereditary offices through which they retained considerable influence when the power of the bureaucracy became preponderant ; they had it should be added, valuable support in the priesthood.

For it is the priesthood, as Mr. Christensen observes,[1] which gives the dominant note of the Sassanid government, " in striking contrast with the syncretism of the time of the Achæmenids and the Hellenism fashionable under the Parthians ". Mazdaism, having become the State religion, gave its ministers the highest place in the hierarchy, but the king was the supreme head of the religion, for he was endowed with divine majesty and surrounded with the luminous glory (*hvareno*, Persian *farr*) which marked out his person for the respect of mortals.

The constitution of the Empire was despotism tempered by dethronement and assassination. As Tabari remarks, only Ardashir I, Sapor I, Sapor II, Kavadh, and Chosroes I chose their successors. Later the kingdom became an elective monarchy in the Sassanid family ; the designation of the king was referred to a board composed of the Grand Mobed, the Chief of the Secretaries, and the Commander-in-Chief ; and in case of disagreement the Mobed decided, after taking counsel secretly with his retinue of priests.

Ammianus Marcellinus[2] has left us an excellent description of the Persian aristocracy. The Persians were almost all slender, with dark or livid complexions, hard, ' goat-like ' eyes, arched eyebrows meeting in the middle, carefully tended beards, and long fuzzy hair. They were incredibly wary and suspicious ; in hostile countries they would not touch the fruit on the trees, for fear of poison or spells. They wore golden bangles and necklaces, precious stones, and above all pearls.

[1] **CXXXIII,** p. 78.
[2] xxiii. 6. 75-84.

They always wore swords, even at banquets and entertainments. They were talkative and boastful, stern and ferocious, threatening whether things went well or ill with them, wily, proud, and cruel. Their bearing was easy, their gait ambling. They were the best fighters in the world, cunning rather than dashing, and especially dangerous in long-distance combat, that is, with the bow. On the whole they were brave, and bore the hardship of campaigning easily. They arrogated to themselves the right of disposing of the lives of slaves and common people, and no servant durst open his mouth in their presence. They indulged in sexual debauches without restraint. In brief, the great men divided their time between the exercise of arms, in war or sport, and the joys of love. They were courteous, too, and chivalrous in character.

The Arabs always had a profound admiration for the Empire of the Sassanids, which seemed to them a model of the art of government. They admired the perfect management of the State, the methods of warfare, the sound intelligence, the cleanliness, the extreme correctness of conduct, the veneration in which the king was held ; they admitted the superiority of the Persians in the arts of dress and cooking and medicine. Since the Arabs had known nothing of the Roman Empire at its best, and had no point of comparison but the Greeks of Constantinople, it can be understood that they formed a fairly high opinion of the great empire which a happy fortune had enabled them to overthrow.

CHAPTER III

The Religion of Persia in the Time of the Sassanids

ZOROASTER

THE life of the law-giver of Iran is nothing but a tissue of legends in which vain efforts have been made to disentangle some historical basis. His very name is impossible to explain in at all a satisfactory manner. In the Avesta he is called Zarathushtra, sometimes preceded by Spitama, which seems to be a family name and connected with *spit*, meaning ' white '. *Ushtra* is a camel. But it is the first part of the name, *Zarath*, which causes all the difficulty, especially the mute spirant dental *th*. If it were not for this, one would think of *zara*, and the whole name might mean ' Owning golden camels ', but it is highly unlikely.[1]

The time at which he lived is hard to determine. The Greek and Latin writers, who obtained their information from people among whom the legend had already formed, place him six thousand years before the Christian era ; this is quite absurd. The Parsee tradition, as we find it in the Pahlavi text of the *Bundahish*, places his life between the VIIth and VIth centuries B.C., and this date is now almost universally accepted, for the *Gathas* mention the name of the Prophet, and, in view of the archaic character of the language in which they are composed, it is hard to place them after the time of the first Achæmenids, at the latest. The Orientalist West is even more precise, and specifies a period from 660 to 583 B.C.

Media, the centre of the Magi, and in particular Media Atropatene, the present Adharbayjan, saw the birth of Zoroaster, but it was in the east of Iran, at Bactra, that he seems to have found the powerful protector who defended his reformation and was the first to adopt it. It is very tempting to see in Vishtaspa the same person as Hystaspes, the father of Darius I. Hystaspes was not a king, it is true, but viceroy

---

[1] **CLIV**, pp. 1-22, reproduced in **CLIII**, pp. 150-78.

of Bactriana. This hypothesis, which is not favoured by the specialists, was propounded very long ago by Anquetil-Duperron himself.[1]

The Parsee traditions tell us that Zoroaster was the son of Pourushaspa and Dughda. His life is a succession of miracles. Magicians and necromancers tried to compass his end, but in vain. At the age of about twenty, he retired from the world, in order to prepare himself for the mission which he felt called to fulfil. When he was thirty his career was decided by a revelation, which took place on the bank of the river Daitya, which tradition places in Adharbayjan. The Amshaspand Vohu-Mano, ' Good Thought ', appeared to him and led him to the throne of God, with whom he conversed. The mention of an Amshaspand shows that the legend is late.

Six other apparitions followed the first, within ten years. During this time he preached reform, both outside Iranian territory, in Turan, and in Sacastene, the modern Sijistan, but all in vain ; the priests of that day, whom the Avesta calls *Kavi* and *Karapan*, opposed him with all their might. On the command of Ahura-Mazda, he went to the court of Vishtaspa and devoted two whole years to the conversion of the king, in spite of obstacles of every kind. The Prophet was then forty-two years old (in 618, according to West's reckoning).

The *Gathas* give us details about the protectors whom Zoroaster found at the court of the king. These were Jamaspa, a minister, and his brother Frashaoshtra, a councillor of the king. The former married the Prophet's daughter, Pouruchista, and Frashaoshtra's daughter, Hvovi, became Zoroaster's third wife. The later chapters of the Avesta and the Pahlavi texts add to these names those of the king's sons, including Spento-data, who became Isfandiyar in the epic, and his brother Zairi-vairi (Zarir).

Conversions then took place in masses, and extended all over Iran. The tradition, which is quite without value, even makes this preaching extend to Turan, and to certain parts of India and Greece or Asia Minor ; and, since we know that this was certainly not the case, we may ask whether these comparatively late traditions do not contain some recollection of the expansion of the worship of Mithra. The last years of the Prophet are said to have been occupied with holy wars ;

[1] **LXXVI,** p. 309.

in the last of all, against an invasion of the Hyaonas, Zoroaster lost his life. The enemy were commanded by Arajataspa (Arjasp), and the man who killed the Prophet was named Tur-i-Bratarvakhsh. Zoroaster was seventy-seven years old (563).[1]

It has not yet been determined how much fact is contained in these traditions, most of which are late. The strange thing about the Greek accounts of Persia, is that neither Herodotos, who is so well-informed, nor Xenophon, who went up the Tigris with the Ten Thousand from Cunaxa, mentions Zoroaster. We only find his name in authors of whom, though they are ancient, we have nothing but late versions—Xanthos of Sardes, who was earlier than Herodotos, and lived in the time of Artaxerxes I, but is only quoted in Diogenes Laertius, in the time of Alexander Severus ;[2] Hermippos, who wrote about 200 B.C., but is only quoted by Pliny,[3] like Eudoxos, a pupil of Plato, and Aristotle himself ; and Ctesias, whose information on the subject only appears in Diodorus Siculus.[4] All that they tell us is very uncertain ; but the mention of the Prophet's name in the *Gathas* takes us back at least to the time of the Achæmenids, as do the Greek authors cited, and that agrees well enough with the tradition which places the reform which decided the religious future of Persia in the VIth century before our era.[5]

The Avesta is the sacerdotal code of Zoroaster's reformation. In the text itself and in the Pahlavi commentaries we have an exposition of the cosmogonic notions of its adherents, giving the widest conceptions and the smallest details. The language in which it is written is not the Old Persian of the Achæmenian inscriptions, but a sister-tongue ; by the side of the idiom of ancient Persia we have that of Media, which is closely akin to Sanskrit. It is not written in the same language throughout, and represents three successive stages—the *Gathas* or hymns, the early parts, and the later parts. The hymns take us, in respect of language, to the time of the first Achæmenids, while the later parts recall the deformations of the language of which

---

[1] **CLIII**, chaps. ix, x ; West, *Sacred Books of the East*, xlvii, Introd., §55.
[2] **XLI**, p. 74.
[3] *N.H.* (Mayhoff's ed.), xxx. 1. 3 ff., in **CLIII**, p. 42.
[4] Vogel's ed., i. 94. 2, Ζαθραύστην. A list of the ancient authors, Greek and Latin, in chronological order, is given in **CLIII**.
[5] **XLII**, pp. 11 ff.

we already find traces in the inscriptions of the last descendants of Darius I.

In the *Gathas* Zoroaster says himself that his intention was to restore the ancient purity of religion,[1] and the *Dinkart* seems to show him fighting against superstitions, magic, the invocation of the evil spirit. His teaching is based on the existence of two principles, light and darkness, good and evil; these two are at war, and one and the other gains the upper hand alternately. The universe is divided into two by an immense gulf, from the two sides of which the forces of the two enemies fight. Ormuzd creates everything good, and Ahriman creates all the bad, in order to destroy his adversary. Aristotle, who does not mention the name of Zoroaster, knows of the war of the two spirits, Oromazdes, whom he calls Zeus, and Areimanios, whom he compares to Hades.[2] In the end Ormuzd will be the victor, good will overcome evil.

In the time of the Sassanids a monotheistic tendency becomes clearly apparent in dissident sects. The expression ' infinite time ', *zrvan akarana*, which is found in the later parts of the Avesta, was used as the basis for the idea of a single God, superior to the two principles. This doctrine was known to Theodorus of Mopsuestia in the IVth century of our era, and to the Armenian writers Eznik and Elisæus in the Vth century.

The spirit of good and the spirit of evil are not the only combatants. Each has an army, the army of Heaven and the army of Hell, and the two forces are opposed. The head of the heavenly army is still Ahura-Mazda, ' the wise Lord ', but he does not rule the lower gods by himself; he is surrounded by a council of six ministers, of which he is the president. These are the six Amshaspands (Amesha Spenta, ' Holy Immortal ') making seven with Ahura-Mazda, who is the first of them. They are abstractions without reality, the Archangels who stand before the throne of God, the eager ministers of the orders of the Great King. Vohu-Mano (Bahman) is Good Thought, Asha-Vahishta (Ardibihisht) is Best Virtue, Khshathra-Vairya (Shahrivar) is Desired Empire, Spenta-Armaiti (Sipendarmidh) is Generous Renunciation, Haurvatat (Khordadh) is Health, and Ameretat (Murdad) is Immortality. J. Darmesteter has

---

[1] *Yasna*, 44, 9.

[2] Diog. Laert., *Lives of the Philosophers*, Introd., 8. Cf. Plut., *De Is. et Osir.*, 46-7 ; Agathias, *Hist.*, 2. 24 ff.

suggested that the conception of the Amshaspands was borrowed from the Neo-Platonists of Alexandria, and that they were an adaptation of the ' forces ' of Philo ; if so, the *Gathas* cannot be earlier than the Ist century after Christ. But it seems that this idea of a hierarchy of seven moral energies, without being quite the same as the Vedic Adityas, is nevertheless more ancient than the speculations of the Hellenized Jews ; it bears a remarkable resemblance to the notion of the Archangels in the later portions of the Bible—Gabriel, Michael, and Raphael.[1]

The Amshaspands are the protectors of various creatures ; the useful animals are under Vohu-Mano, fire under Asha-Vahishta, the metals under Khshathra-Vairya, the earth under Spenta-Armaiti, and water and plants under Haurvatat and Ameretat. Certain months, certain days of the week, and certain flowers are especially consecrated to them.[2]

Lower down in the hierarchy are the innumerable Yazatas, ' Those who deserve to be worshipped ', inferior gods or geniuses. These are the twenty-four gods of whom Plutarch speaks in his treatise *On Isis and Osiris*, but in the Avesta they are beyond numbering, and may be reckoned in thousands,[3] Diogenes Laertius knows that, for the Persians, the air is peopled by spirits.[4] But there are some, more important than the rest, to whom a day of the month is dedicated in the *Siruzas*, the books of the Parsees. These geniuses are divided into two classes, one celestial and one earthly ; Ahura-Mazda is the greatest of the celestial Yazatas and Zoroaster is at the head of the terrestrial. They are the tutelary geniuses of the sun, the moon, the stars, the earth, the air, fire, and water, or personifications of abstract ideas, such as victory, truth, peace, power. Atar, Fire, is the son of Ahura-Mazda, the fire of the sky and that which is enclosed in the veins of wood. Apo, Water, is the object of especial devotion. Hvare-Khshaeta, the Shining Sun, is the eye of Ahura-Mazda, and is drawn by swift horses. Next to them come Mah, the Moon,

---

[1] J. Darmesteter (*Ormazd et Ahrimane*, pp. 38-86) had compared the Amshaspands to the Adityas, but later he gave up this theory and ascribed the origin of the idea to Philo. See the references on this question in Jackson, IX, ii, p. 634, §34, n. 4.

[2] This idea is found in the *Bundahish* (27, 24, in West, *Sacred Books of the East*, v, 103-4).

[3] *Yasht*, 6, 1.

[4] Introd., 6. 5.

and the star Tishtriya, whom Plutarch calls Sirius. Mithra, originally the god of compact, is the god of light and truth ; he is mentioned with Anahita in late Achæmenian inscriptions, and he was adopted by the mysterious sect which propagated his worship in the furthest provinces of the Roman Empire. Mithraic reliefs, representing a male figure in a Phrygian cap cutting the throat of a bull, have been found in many places, for example, in Paris, and quite lately at Capua.[1]

Sraosha, the Obedient, is, with Mithra and Rashnu, one of the angels who will give judgment in the next world ; he is also the guardian angel of the world. The Fravashis are also guardian angels ; they exist in heaven before a man is born, and they are united to the soul after death. They are a kind of *Manes*, who aid Ahura-Mazda in the war against evil. They are not mentioned in the metrical *Gathas*, but that means nothing, for these hymns only exist in a fragmentary condition. In the Median period we find the name Fravartish, Phraortes.[2] They gave their name to the first month of the year, Farvardin.

Verethraghna, the genius of victory, became the name of the planet Mars in the form Bahram, through the Pahlavi Varahran. Vata, the Wind, Asman, the Sky, and Zem, the Earth, were likewise personifications in the ranks of the Yazatas.

Haoma is a deified plant, yielding the nectar which may only be drunk by the priests, and is prepared in a manner for which there are many ritual prescriptions. It is the *soma* of the Indians ; this shows that its worship is very ancient, being earlier than the separation of the two branches of the Indo-Iranian linguistic group ; it is not, however, mentioned in the *Gathas*. Plutarch knows it under the name *omomi* ($\H{o}\mu\omega\mu\iota$).

Against the army of good stands the army of evil, the infernal hosts let loose for the conquest of the universe. Its leader is the bad spirit, the spirit of pain, Angra-Mainyu, or Ahriman.[3] He commands the Divs or demons, whose name, *daeva*, in Sanskrit and Latin designates the gods (*deva, divus*). Aristotle knows his name in the form Areimanios. He is evil

---

[1] See above, pp. 112 ff.

[2] On this question cf. N. Söderblom, *Les Fravashis*, Paris, 1899, pp. 1-79.

[3] *Mainyu* means ' thought ', but *angra* is not clear. Darmesteter associates it with a root *ang* which would give the word the sense of ' constriction ', ' necessity,' ' pain,' but Geldner, Jackson, and Bartholomæ are in favour of a hypothetical root *ans* with the sense of ' oppose ', ' hate '. Cf. the references in **IX**, ii, p. 649 nn. 5, 6.

thought, rebellion, the lie, already fully named in the Behistun inscription[1]—every form of evil in the universe. He interferes with the good creation, and, if he cannot annihilate it, he at least tries to neutralize its effect. He is the evil creator, and his inventions are 'impediments' (*paityara*) ;[2] when Ahura-Mazda created life, Angra-Mainyu created death. His dwelling is darkness without end. But this war without mercy will one day end with the triumph of good and the annihilation of evil, at the Last Judgment.

Hell is peopled by Divs, Drujes, Darvants, Peris (*pairika*), dragons, and monsters, all created by the bad spirit to fight the good creation of Ahura-Mazda. They dwell in the North ; the gate of Hell is Mount Arezura, in the Alburz range, and the province of Mazandaran, on the shores of the Caspian, is their ordinary abode. These Divs are the personifications of sins, faults, and sicknesses ; they are innumerable, as are the forces which assail man. The light of day puts them to flight, and they can be constrained by religious ceremonies, for Zoroaster is one of their great enemies. According to Clement of Alexandria, the Magi used to boast that they could compel evil geniuses to serve them. A whole book of the Avesta is consecrated to the war against the demons ; this is the *Vendidad*, properly the *vidaeva data*, or 'Law against Divs'.

The *Bundahish* mentions beside Ahriman a group of six demons, whom parallelism required as 'opposite numbers' and adversaries to the six Amshaspands. The artificiality of the arrangement is apparent.[3] Three of these demons bear the names of Indian deities, Indra, Sarva, and Nasatya, easily recognizable in the forms, Indra, Sauru, and Naosihaitya. Aka-Mano, or Bad Thought, is naturally the opponent of Vohu-Mano, or Good Thought. Special mention may be made of Aeshma, the demon of rage, of devastation, better known under the name of Asmodeus, who, from the book of Tobit, passed into Christian demonology.[4] The Yazata Sraosha, the incarnation of religious obedience, of devotion, has the

---

[1] *Drauga* ; but there is nothing here suggesting the opposition of two principles, or that the lie is opposed to the truth.

[2] In the Iranian epic, *patyara*, monster, diabolical creation.

[3] It is hardly earlier than the latest parts of the Avesta.

[4] **CV**, vol. ii, p. 132. Cf. Windischmann, *Zoroastrische Studien*, pp. 138 ff. Kohut, *Jüdische Angelologie und Dämonologie*, pp. 75 ff. J. H. Moulton, "The Iranian Background of Tobit," in *Expository Times*, xi, pp. 258 ff.

especial duty of fighting him and annihilating him at the end of time.

In addition to the Divs, a group of maleficent beings is formed by the Druj and its acolytes, which have the same name. Druj is the lie, the incarnation or manifestation of the bad spirit. From this word comes the term Darvant,[1] which, in the *Gathas*, designated the wicked, the atheists, as opposed to the righteous, the servants of God. In the late portions of the Avesta they are demons, embodied in the inhabitants of the marshes of Gilan, south of the Caspian.[2] Among the Drujes is the Nasu, a female demon, who is the corruption of corpses, the most impure of all works. To introduce herself she takes on the form of a fly, and she can be driven from the dead body by the gaze of a dog, a rite called Sagdid, or from the living body by the ceremony of the Barashnum, a nine days' purification. Another Druj is Azhi-Dahaka, whom the Arabian historians, and the *Shah-Namah* after them, made into a king hostile to the Persians, Dahak surnamed Biverasp, ' of the ten thousand horses ', while the Persians gave his name to a fabulous serpent, the dragon (*azhdeha*). The Avesta speaks of him as a monster with three heads, six eyes, and three mouths ; in the *Shah-Namah* he appears with a serpent rising out of either shoulder, which was fed daily on human brains. This king has his capital in Babylon ; in this mythical type there is probably a memory of some oppression of the Persian nation by Babylonia in the days when that kingdom ruled Susiana and the mountains of Fars, which earned the king the diabolical character which distinguishes him.[3] It is he who is overthrown and chained under Mount Damavand by Thraetaona (Feridun), the hero of the revival of Iran. The Yatus are magicians, the Peris are fairies, whose evil influence communicates itself to the earth, water, fire, cattle, and plants ; they bewitch the stars to prevent rain, and make them fall as meteors.

The present world will last twelve thousand years in all.[4]

---

[1] *Dregvant* in the *Gathas* ; *drvant* in the later Avesta ; this derivation is supported by the authority of Bartholomæ.

[2] **CXXXVII**, vol. ii, p. 373, n. 3.

[3] West, *Sacred Books of the East*, x, p. 131 n. 6 ; **CXXXVII**, vol. ii, p. 375 n. 39, and vol. iii, Introd., p. lxix.

[4] With this round figure compare the twelve thousand oxhides (i.e., parchment) on which, according to Parsee traditions, the complete text of the Avesta was written, which was burned at Persepolis by Alexander.

This long period is divided into ages of three thousand years each. The first three thousand years are the age of the spiritual creation. Ahriman proceeds from the darkness, and is dazzled by the light ; Ormuzd offers him peace, and, since he refuses it, proposes a war of nine thousand years, knowing well that the evil spirit will be destroyed in the end. The second age is that of the material creation. Ormuzd creates the Amshaspands, the sky, water, the earth, plants, animals, and man ; at the same time, Ahriman creates the Divs and spirits of evil. The third age shows us, in humanity, the war of good and evil ; it extends from the first man, Gayomard, to the sending of Zoroaster and the adoption of his reform by King Vishtaspa. The fourth age extends from the appearance of Zoroaster to the day of the Last Judgment. The Resurrection of the Dead takes place ; Ormuzd triumphs over Ahriman ; good rules unchallenged.

The Zoroastrians believe in the immortality of the soul. For three days after death the soul still hovers about the body, and feels joy and pain in it as when it was alive. Then it is borne away by the wind, and presents itself at Chinvat Bridge (*chinvato peretu*), where it encounters a tribunal of three judges, the Yazatas Mithra, Sraosha, and Rashnu, like the three judges of the Greek underworld, Minos, Æacos, and Rhadamanthos. These three weigh in the balance the acts done by the man in his life, and their decision depends on the turn of the beam.[1] Then comes the awful crossing of Chinvat Bridge, which reaches over Hell from the Alburz to Mount Daitya. It is broad and easy for the soul of the righteous man, but when it is crossed by the soul of the sinner it grows narrower and narrower, until at last he totters and falls into the depths of the gulf, where the darkness is so thick that it can be held in the hands.

After traversing the abodes of the Good Thought, the Good Word, and the Good Deed, the righteous soul reaches eternal light, the house of hymns, the fair dwelling, Garonmana, which is the ' better world ' (*anhu vahishta*, Persian *bihisht*). So, too, the damned go down in stages to the abode of pain reserved for them. Between Paradise and Hell is a purgatory for the souls of those whose good and evil actions counterbalance each

---

[1] An Egyptian idea, which was extremely popular in the eschatology of several religions.

other, Hamestakan, the Abode of Equal Weights ; there **they** will abide the Resurrection.

The last days will be announced by the coming of a saving and delivering Messiah, Saoshyant, who will renew the world after the Resurrection, and will precede the Last Judgment. A flood of molten metal will cover the earth and purify it. Then there will be the last battle of Ormuzd and Ahriman, of good and evil, of light and darkness, ending in the complete and irreparable defeat of the second.

DISSIDENT SECTS

Zoroastrianism was the State religion of the Persian Empire under the Sassanian dynasty. By the side of this ruling, orthodox religion, dissident, heterodox sects sprang up. The very first chapter of the *Vendidad* admits that the use of the *Dakhmas* or Towers of Silence was not universal in Persia. An Arabian writer of the beginning of the XIIth century, Shahrastani, mentions three principal sects. The first, the Zoroastrians properly so called, followed the teaching of Zoroaster ; the second, the Zervanites, believed that both Ormuzd and Ahriman proceeded from a being more ancient and higher than themselves, Zervan, Infinite Time (*zrvan akarana*) ; the third, the Gayomarthians, held that Ahriman was born of a doubt of Ormuzd.

Two heresies were of considerable political importance— that of Mani, the founder of Manichæism, who at one time had followers all over Europe and Asia, and that of Mazdak, whose projects of social renovation on a communistic basis were within an ace of ruining the Persian Empire.

MANICHÆISM

Recent discoveries in Central Asia have brought to light Manichæan manuscripts, some in Pahlavi and others in Turkish. The excitement of the learned world on the announcement of these finds may be imagined. For Manichæism was hardly known except by the writings of its opponents, Christian or Moslem. It was only quite recently that M. Monceaux succeeded in reconstructing the Latin text of Faustus of Mileve, by means of St. Augustine's refutation of it. The lost Manichæan literature is reconstructed in this way from fragments.

The sands of the Desert of Gobi, in Central Asia, have invaded whole cities, compelling the inhabitants to flee and burying their dwellings. At the end of the XIXth century travellers had observed that old papers came out of this accumulated sand, and some had been used by the natives as window-panes. Systematic excavations were set afoot by the St. Petersburg Geographical Society, from 1893 to 1895 ; three years later Dr. Klementz, the representative of the Academy of Sciences of the same city, resumed the work, which was after-wards continued by other Russian scholars. The locality which they explored lies north of Turfan, on the site of the city which was called Kushan, Khocho, or Kaochang.

Germany sent three missions to the country—that of Grünwedel, subsidized by the Munich Academy of Sciences, in 1902, that of von Le Coq, under the auspices of the Berlin Academy, in 1904, and Grünwedel and von Le Coq together in 1905. Finally, the subsequent fruitful mission of M. Paul Pelliot made its famous discovery of a cache in the caves of Tung-hwang, and enriched the Bibliothèque Nationale with a precious collection of rolls of manuscript.

Among the documents brought to light are Manichæan texts, the decipherment of which has been undertaken by Salemann in Russia and F. W. K. Müller in Germany for the Pahlavi, and by Radlov in Russia and von Le Coq in Germany for the Turkish. Among these last is a Manichæan form of confession, brought back by Sir Aurel Stein, which has been studied by Radlov and von Le Coq in succession ; it is known by the name of *Khwastuanift*. Lastly, among the rolls which were left at Tung-hwang by the European explorers and later transferred to Peking by order of the Chinese Government, which has formed a special library of them, there is a bulky and almost complete roll, in which Chavannes and Pelliot have recognized a Manichæan treatise, which they have translated with a commentary, in the *Journal Asiatique*.

These various documents make it possible to check and complete the information of the Christian and Moslem writers, and also that found in the Chinese historians.

Mani himself related that he was born in a village named Mardinu in the district of the Nahr-Kutha in Babylonia, in 215, that at the age of thirteen he received a first revelation of the divine truth, in 228, that this revelation was repeated when he was twenty-five, in 240, and that he was given the mission of preaching the true religion. It was at this last date, on the day of the accession of Sapor I, that, according to the reports of his followers, echoed in the *Fihrist*, he appeared upon the scene. It was about a hundred years after Marcion and seventy after Bardesanes, and Mani was the heir of these two Gnostic schools. Babylonia was the land chosen by these innovators ; there the population was very mixed, practised a broad syncretism, and was inclined towards the doctrines of Basileides, Valentinus, and their emulators. It was on the banks of the lower Euphrates that the Sabians or Christians of St. John the Baptist had settled, whom the Arabs called *Mughtasila*, 'Ablutionists', because they were always washing in the river ; not only were they still living there in the time of Muhammad, but they are there to this day, under the name of Subau. At the time with which we are dealing there were various Gnostic sects in these parts—Cainites, Nicolaites, Sethites. Hippolytus represented them as followers of a false wisdom, who were led by the alternation of day and night to deify light and darkness, and were given to astrology and magic.

The father of Mani, whom the *Fihrist* calls Fatak Babak, son of Abu Barzam, of the Chascanid family, was bidden by an angel to abstain from meat and wine and women. He entered the community of the Sabians, and brought his son up in the same principles, but Mani, in consequence of the two revelations mentioned above, which were brought to him by an angel named at-Tawam (supposed to be Babylonian for 'companion'), resolved to preach a more rigid and systematic dualism than that of the Sabians. He regarded evil as having existed from all eternity. He doubled the elements, air, earth, and fire, ascribing to each two natures, one good and one bad. He saw no irreducible opposition save between light and darkness. He preserved ritual ablutions, but attached no real importance to anything but the knowledge of the true gnosis. He rejected all the Old Testament, but accepted the Gospels and the Epistles of St. Paul. He was the Paraclete, the Comforter promised by Jesus, the last apostle of Christ, the organ by which the divine truths were transmitted.

Mani wrote much. One of his books, the oldest, was written in Pahlavi, because it was dedicated to Sapor I, but for the others he used Syriac, which Marcion and Bardesanes had used before him. He invented a script (derived from an Aramaic alphabet) of which I have given specimens above. His works, like those of the Mandæans (a name which the Sabians gave themselves), the Ophites, the Sionians, and the Carpocratians, were adorned with paintings and have become proverbial, since the reputation of Mani as a painter survived in Persia all through the Middle Ages and to our own time. According to the refutation which St. Ephrem wrote against him, these illuminations depicted the luminous virtues and the powers of darkness " in the features the most calculated to cause the former to be loved and the latter hated, in order to complement his written teaching for educated people and to supplement it for others ".[1]

The Arabian historians, who are among our chief sources for the history of Mani, relate that Sapor I at first embraced the precepts uttered by the innovator, remained faithful to them for ten years, and then returned to Mazdaism ; that Mani then left Persia as an exile, and went to Kashmir, and from there to Turkestan and China ; and that as he crossed Tibet he kept the faith of his proselytes alive by means of frequent letters. His converts must have been faithful, especially in Turkestan, for we know that the Turks were at that time divided between two religions, Buddhism and Manichæism, and the finds in Central Asia, which have yielded texts in the Turkish language associated with both these doctrines, confirm the accuracy of the Arabian writers.

The supporters of Mani thought that on the death of Sapor in 272 and his son Hormazd in 273, and the accession of Bahram I, they could ask the Master to return to his native land. But the Mobeds were watching. After two years he was arrested, convicted of heresy, flayed alive, and beheaded, and his skin was stuffed with straw and hung to a gallows at a gate of Jundi Shapur (March, 275).

The Manichæan church had been organized by its founder in the following way. At its head were twelve Apostles or Masters, then seventy-two Disciples or bishops, priests and deacons, monks or Elect, and lastly laymen, called Hearers (nigoshak, a Pahlavi word, in the Turkish texts). Mani had designated his successor ; it is probable that the various dignitaries of the hierarchy themselves designated those who

[1] CXXIVa, p. 23.

should replace them, except perhaps the Elect, who may have been chosen by the Hearers. These last met every Sunday to recite prayers, sing hymns, and hear the sacred books read, for they had a peculiarly profound veneration for the works of the Master, and were at pains to multiply manuscript copies. St. Augustine saw in the hands of the Elect a great number of manuscripts, decorated with inks of different colours and sumptuously bound.

The basis of the teaching of Mani was the most thorough-going dualism. As foundation of the universe he adopted the existence of two contrary principles, both eternal, and wholly irreconcilable—good and evil, light and darkness. God is the lord of the former, the Devil of the latter. Their kingdoms extend to infinity, that of God upwards and downwards, north east, and west, and that of the Devil downwards and south-wards only.

The Devil resolved to conquer the countries of light. The Father of Greatness, who is God, could not turn for his defence to the five Æons whom he had begotten for peace, Under-standing, Reason, Thought, Reflection, and Will, for this was war, and the Æons were frightened by the sudden onslaught of the shades. He then created the Mother of Life, who gave birth to the first man. This man was at first laid low by the Devil, and indescribable confusion followed ; good was mixed with evil ; but the mixture broke the impetus of the invader. The Father of Greatness called up the Friend of Light, the latter called up the Great Ban, and this last called up the Living Spirit, who entered into relations with captive man and succeeded in delivering him. So the world was created.

The same dualism exists in man, in whom there are two conflicting souls, one good and the other bad. Luminous thought, sentiment, and intellect are counterbalanced by dark thought, sentiment, and intellect ; the former produce pity, good faith, patience, and wisdom, the latter hatred, self-indulgence, anger and folly. Morality became strict asceticism for the Elect, who were advised to take no animal food or fermented drink, to kill no living being, animal or vegetable, and to abstain from women. The Hearers were not subjected to such severe rules, and could content themselves with avoiding idolatry, lying, avarice, murder, adultery, and heterodoxy.

The world will end in a cataclysm, falling into the gulf of
Hell, where its elements will be burned as in a furnace, and then
covered by a stone as large as the earth, to which sinful souls
will be bound. The Elect go to Heaven ; the Hearers, who
observe the divine precepts only in part, pass into other bodies
until the final catastrophe ; and impenitent sinners fall into
Hell, as we have seen. Good and evil, returning to their
former condition, will remain separated for ever by an impassable
barrier.[1]

It is interesting to follow step by step the propagation of
this teaching over the world. The writings of Mani spread the
more easily in Babylonia because, as we have seen, the country
swarmed with heterodox sects, and the works of Marcion and
Bardesanes were very popular there. From there they reached
Syria, Palestine, and the north of Arabia, the country of the
Nabatæans ; now, the inhabitants of all these regions spoke
Aramaic, the language in which these documents were written.
But they soon crossed linguistic frontiers and made their way
into Egypt, where Gnosticism was in favour ; there Manichæism spread chiefly among the monks, who collected large
crowds about them by their preaching.

It was from Egypt, no doubt, that Manichæan literature
entered Northern Africa and Carthage, where we find it
mentioned as early as the end of the IIIrd century. St.
Augustine, who had commenced his career as an initiate of the
sect, saw in the hands of the Elect at Carthage many
magnificent copies, which were read publicly at meetings and
then explained to the Hearers ; so these books had been
translated into Latin. In spite of the attacks of the illustrious
Bishop of Hippo, Manichæism survived long in this region, for
we find members of the sect under the Vandal kings, Genseric
and Hunneric, and even at the end of the VIth century, in the
pontificate of Gregory the Great.

In Spain, at the end of the IVth century, there were many
Manichees, and St. Jerome knew that in Lusitania many women
read Mani's *Treasure* and other Gnostic works. It was not long
before southern Gaul and Italy were likewise invaded. In
Rome the sect had a large following, and there is evidence of
their presence and activity at intervals from 372 to 523. The
doctrine seems to have been taken there from Africa. When

---

[1] CXXIVa, pp. 32-46.

St. Augustine arrived in Rome he lodged with a Manichee, with whom he often discussed points of doctrine.

The Manichæan scriptures found readers in Asia Minor and in the upper classes of Byzantine society. The Christian authors have devoted a great number of works to the refutation of the principles which they set forth. In Babylonia, the land of their origin, they kept their adherents long into the early Middle Ages ; the Arabian authors knew of them in the reign of the first Abbasid Caliphs, and called the members of the sect *Zandiqs*, that is ' heretics '.

THE RELIGION OF MAZDAK

Mazdak, the son of Bamdad, was born at Nishapur in Khurasan. We have seen above what disorders his preaching created in the Empire, and how Kavadh paid with his liberty for the protection which he had rashly given him. His teaching was derived from that of Mani. Like Mani, he declared that two principles existed, light and darkness, but light acted freely, being sentient and intelligent, whereas darkness acted by chance, being ignorant and blind. The mixture of the two was the result of chance, without preconceived plan, and so was their separation. The universe proceeded from three elements, water, fire, and earth ; from the mixture of these three came the organization of good and that of evil, the former being produced by their pure parts and the latter by their turbid parts.

Mazdak considered that the spiritual world was organized like this world. The Lord of Heaven sits on his throne like a king, and before him stand four forces—Discernment, Intelligence, Memory, and Joy. These four powers direct the affairs of the world through seven ministers, six of whom are enumerated—the Salar (General), the Pishkar (President), the Balvan or Barvan (meaning uncertain), the Kardan (Experienced One), the Dastur (Minister), and the Kudak (Boy). These seven ministers move within twelve spiritual beings, named Khwananda (Caller), Dihanda (Giver), Sitananda (Taker), Baranda (Bearer), Khoranda (Eater), Dawanda (Runner), Khezanda (Riser), Kushanda (Killer), Zananda (Striker) Kananda (Digger), Ayanda (Comer), and Shawanda (Becomer) ; our only source, the Arabian historian Shahrastani, mentions a thirteenth, Payanda (Stander). Every man who combines in his person the four forces, the seven ministers, and the twelve powers becomes a divine being in our world here below, and all responsibility disappears for him.

To put down contradiction, hate, and war, which are evil things, clearly emanating from darkness, Mazdak attacked their principle, which he found in the love of women and of possessions ; in order to dispose of this obstacle, he preached community of wives and goods, which all men should share equally, as they do water, fire, and the wind.[1]

In the world above, the King governs by means of letters which, taken together, form the ineffable name of God. The man who can imagine something of these letters sees the great mystery open before him ; he who cannot, remains in the blindness of ignorance, forgetfulness, stupidity, and distraction, as opposed to the four spiritual forces.

The Mazdakites were divided into four sects. At the time of the Caliphs of Badgad these were the Kudhakites, who lived in Susiana, in Fars, and at Shahrizur in the mountains of Kurdistan, the followers of Abu Muslim, the Mahanites, and the Ispidjamakites, whose name shows that they wore white ; the three last were to be found in Sogdiana and Turkestan.

All socialist and communist innovators lay down rules which could only be put into practice by societies of saints ; but all the world over there are vicious men, idlers, and born criminals. Persia was no exception and the usual thing happened : the dregs of the people took to these theories of equality with ardour, and such disorders ensued that the political authorities had to step in and extirpate the new sect. Nevertheless, as we have seen, it was not until the beginning of the reign of Chosroes I that the monarchy felt strong enough to fight communism.

Mazdak had a book, which no longer exists ; it was known to the Arabs, for two translations are mentioned, one by Ibn al-Muqaffa and the other by Aban al-Lahiqi.[2]

---

[1] Shahrastani, *Book of Religious aud Philosophical Sects*, Cureton's ed., London, 1842-6, pp. 192 ff. ; Haarbrücker's translation, Halle, 1850-1, vol. i, pp. 292 ff. Cf. *Zeitschr. d. deutschen Morgenl. Ges.*, xxiii, pp. 531 ff., and **CV**, vol. ii, pp. 232 ff., where Haarbrücker's translation is reproduced, but incompletely.

[2] Ibn an-Nadim al-Warraq, *Fihrist*, Flügel's ed., Leipzig, 1872, vol.i, pp. 118, 163 ; cf. vol. ii, p. 342.

BIHAFRID

In the time of Abu Muslim, the champion of the Abbasid dynasty, one Bihafrid, son of Mahfurudhin, born at Zuzan, appeared at a place named Saravand in the district of Khwaf, in the province of Nishapur. After living in China for seven years, he brought back curiosities, among which was a silk shirt which was so fine and soft that when rolled up it could be held in the hollow of the hand. Having gone up into a temple one night, he came down next morning and was seen by a peasant who was ploughing his field, and told this man that he had risen to Heaven, that he had been shown Heaven and Hell, and that God had inspired him, had clad him in the shirt, and had sent him back to earth. The peasant believed him, and told others that he had been witness of his descent from Heaven. He found adherents among the Mazdeans.

He accepted the doctrine of Zoroaster, but some of his rites were different. He declared that he received celestial revelations, and instituted seven prayers, the first in praise of a single God, the second about the creation of Heaven and earth, the third about the creation and feeding of the beasts, the fourth about death, the fifth about the Resurrection and Last Judgment, the sixth about the chosen and the damned, and the seventh in honour of the dwellers in Paradise. He wrote a book in Persian, and ordered his followers to worship the substance of the sun, placing one knee to the ground, to turn always towards that star, in whatever quarter it might be, to let their hair grow, to give up muttering prayers (*zamzama*) during meals, not to sacrifice small cattle unless it was already decrepit, to drink no wine, not to eat the flesh of animals which had died suddenly, to avoid *Khwetuk-das* or marriage between near kin, and not to give their women dowries exceeding 400 *dirhems*. He bade them consecrate one-seventh of their property and the earnings of their labour to the upkeep of roads and bridges.

When Abu Muslim came to Nishapur, the heads of the Zoroastrian community denounced the reformer to him, and he sent one of his officers against him ; Bihafrid was taken in the mountains of Badghis, and conducted before Abu Muslim, who had him put to death, with such of his supporters as could be captured. However, some of these survived, and related that their prophet had gone up to Heaven on a dark bay horse, and would one day descend in the same way and take vengeance on his enemies.

In the course of this Sassanian period Christianity and Buddhism were introduced into Persia.

Christianity.—The evangelization of the valley of the Euphrates and Tigris started from Edessa. For long the Sassanids had felt no danger to their power in the presence of Christians within the frontiers of the Empire. Eusebius refers to a letter in which the Emperor Constantine congratulated Sapor I on his benevolence towards them, and rejoiced at the prosperity and continual increase of the churches. The situation changed with the accession of Sapor II, who demanded the restoration of the five provinces which had been ceded to Galerius. He wanted money, and decided to get it from the Christians, who were not liable to military service, and were beginning to be accused of plotting with the enemy and acting as spies. A persecution ensued, lasting from 339-340 to the death of Sapor II in 379. Two decrees were published, one demanding the payment of a double poll-tax, and the other ordering that worship should cease in the churches, and that in case of resistance they should be destroyed. The Bishop of Seleuceia, Simon Bar-Saboe, after long detention, refused to raise a new tax or to renounce his faith, and was condemned to death.

Delation was rampant, and even a Bishop's nephew informed against his uncle, but the officials and Mobeds, or Mazdean priests, chiefly distinguished themselves in the persecution. Procedure was governed by no rules, and men were held against trial for months. The dignitaries and the king himself questioned the prisoners when it suited them. Torture was the means by which confessions were elicited. Punishments were cruel, but were no new invention ; it had always been so in the East.

As happens in such cases, there were misunderstandings ; one of the king's favourite eunuchs, named Azad, was confused with other victims and perished with them. Sapor felt that they had gone too far, and ordered that all except bishops and priests should be spared.

Yazdigird I refused to treat his Christian subjects as enemies, and so incurred the enmity of the Mazdean priesthood, who dubbed him the Sinner. Christian sources praise his goodness, gentleness, and munificence. He was a wary statesman, who favoured peaceful solutions, and at the same time as capricious a despot as the other sovereigns of his line. Towards the end of his life he did not hesitate to resume the persecutions when he thought that the influence of the Christians was growing too great. Proselytism had been conducted freely, and higher officials, some belonging to the great families, had become converts to Christianity. Moreover, there had been imprudent acts on the part of rash priests. A fire-temple near the church of a town in Khuzistan, which offended the Christians, was destroyed by them. The complaint of the Mobeds was taken to court, and the king condemned the bishop to rebuild the temple ; the bishop refused and was sentenced to death. Other prosecutions of the same kind had the same result. Yazdigird would perhaps have issued a decree of persecution, if he had not died in the autumn of 420. At the end of the reigns of Bahram and of Yazdigird II there were still many persecutions of this kind, but one cannot say that there was a general persecution.

However the second of these kings seems to have had a touch of religious fanaticism, for he even forbade the Jews to celebrate the Sabbath. Many Christian bishops and distinguished laymen perished in the storm. In 447 Pethion, who had preached the Gospel in the mountains of Kurdistan, was beheaded.

The Christians felt the repercussion of the wars of Chosroes I against Justinian and of the devastation of Syria which accompanied them. Churches, and above all monasteries, were destroyed ; Persian nobles who had embraced Christianity were thrown into prison and massacred ; but the authorities did not venture to take the life of the Catholicus or Patriarch Maraba, who was confined to the mountains. He was restored to liberty because he contributed by his exhortations to the suppression of the revolt of Anushazad, the son of Chosroes I and a Christian woman (551). In 567 the king concluded with Justinian a treaty which should ensure peace for fifty years; one article in this treaty provided that the Christian religion should be tolerated among the Persians, on condition that the Christians abstained from all propaganda.

Chosroes II observed towards his Christian subjects a fairly malevolent neutrality, so long as his armies were victorious ; but when his dominions were invaded by the troops of Heraclius he showed open hostility. Monophysites and Nestorians alike fell victim to his persecutions. His tragic end was a deliverance for them, for Siroes gave them complete liberty. Fear of Constantinople may have had something to do with this.

The Persian church, as the result of various synods, had become as elaborately organized as that in the Roman Empire. The ecclesiastical provinces corresponded to the territorial divisions ; in 410, in addition to the Patriarchal diocese, there were five Metropoles, all cities in the Tigris valley. Later Marv in Khurasan, Persis, and the islands of the Persian Gulf were added. Other bishoprics must have existed in India, Socotra, and Bactriana. The seat of the Patriarch was naturally in the capital, Seleuceia-Ctesiphon. The Bishop of this city assumed the title of Catholicus and, from 424, that of Patriarch.[1]

Buddhism. Under the Sassanids the eastern parts of Persia were Buddhist. Afghanistan, which has so long been closed to all foreign intrusion, is at last being explored, thanks to the enlightened support of the Ameer, Aman Ullah Khan, and a French archæological mission, directed by M. Foucher, has already discovered monuments revealing Buddhist influence, such as stupas. It should be added that the building at Balkh, the ancient Bactra, which the Arab conquerors regarded as a fire-temple, was called Naw-Bahar, which is evidently a transcription of *nava-vihara*, ' new monastery ', and that the name of the illustrious family of Barmak, which supplied the first Abbasid Caliphs with statesmen, and ended so tragically, represents the title *paramaka*, which designates the Superior of a Buddhist monastery. Moreover, the narratives of the Chinese pilgrims leave no doubt of the existence of centres of this religion on the road which ran from the western parts of China over the Hindu Kush to India, the cradle of the religious reform to which Gautama Buddha has given his name.

[1] **CLVIII,** *passim.*

The first day of the month of Farvardin was the beginning
of the Persian year ; it was called Nau-ruz, ' New Day,' and
was a very great festival. The Sogdians called it Nau-sard,
that is, ' New Year '. It was the custom for everyone to
present his friends with sweetstuffs ; this practice has been
preserved in modern Persia, and the Ottoman Turks have
adopted it for the feast which ends the fast, which is called the
Feast of Sugar (*Sheker-bairami*). This feast was originally
held at the summer solstice, on the 21st June, but gradually,
in consequence of the difficulty of correcting the calendar (the
Persian year had only 365 days), it was shifted towards the
spring equinox, and the reform of Jalal ad-Din Malik Shah
fixed it definitely on the 21st March, the date which the Nauruz-
i-sultani has kept to the present.

On the sixth day of this same month, consecrated to the
Amshaspand Haurvatat (Khordadh), the great Nauruz took
place. It was called the Day of Hope, because it was believed
that the portions of happiness were distributed by fate on that
day. People threw water at one another, because, some said,
the day was consecrated to the guardian angel of water ; others
said that it was in memory of the happy times when the
mythical king Jamshid had caused canals to be dug to make
up for the lack of water and absence of rain ; a third explanation was that it was a memory of the purification by water
prescribed by that king.

It is said that King Hormazd, the son of Sapor I, combined
the two festivals, ordering that the intermediate days should
also be holidays, and commanded that great fires should be
lit on high places, regarding this practice as being of good
omen : a rationalist explanation adds that it was also to purify
the air.

On the 16th of the month of Mihr there was the feast of
Mihragan, which simply means the Feast of Mithra, the
Mithrakana which we found in the religion of Mithra. A fair
was held, and the king, it was said, wore a tiara bearing the
images of the sun (*mihr*) and the celestial wheel on which it
turns. It was said that this feast perpetuated the happy
memory of Feridun's victory over the Babylonian king Dahak.
The angels had come to the aid of the national hero ; therefore
a herald, standing in the court of the palace, used to cry out

" Angels, come down to this world and drive away the demons and maleficent beings ! " This festival, which was originally at the winter solstice, gradually came to fall on the autumn equinox.

The first day of the month of Adhar, which formerly fell at the beginning of spring, was consecrated to the feast Bahar-chashn, the Spring Festival, the occasion of the popular ceremony of the *Kausaj*, when a man with a scanty beard rode on a mule, fanning himself to express joy at the end of the cold weather and the arrival of the hot season. For several days people ate nuts, garlic, fat meat, and other heating food, and took drinks good for driving out the cold. When the man with the scanty beard, who personified the enemy of cold, appeared, they threw cold water over him ; this did not produce a disagreeable sensation, but he shouted in Persian *Germa, germa !*—' Hot, hot ! '

The 10th of the month of Bahman was the feast of the Sadhaq (modern Persian, Sadha), when houses were fumigated to drive out misfortune. The kings caused fires to be lit, over which wild beasts were driven while they drank and amused themselves near by. This custom was supposed to have originated in the fires which people lit on their house-tops to celebrate their deliverance from Dahak by the victory of Feridun.

On the 30th of the same month the people of Isfahan celebrated the feast of Afrejagan, the Pouring of Water (Persian, *abriz*) ; in other cities it was held on the day of the first rain, but at Isfahan it was always on the 30th. Its origin was ascribed to Peroz, the grandfather of Chosroes I. In his time the rain failed, and Persia suffered from drought. The king let the people off taxes for several years, opened the State granaries, obtained money by selling the goods of the fire-temples, and finally went in person to the fire-temple of Adhar-Khura in Fars and implored the god to put an end to the calamity. His prayers were heard ; hardly had he reached a desert plain in those parts when a cloud rose over the horizon and rain fell copiously. In gratitude for this blessing, Peroz built a village in the neighbourhood and gave it the name of Kamfiruz, ' the Desire of Peroz (has been satisfied) '. People joyfully threw water at each other, and this act of spontaneous gaiety became the characteristic rite of the feast of Afrejagan.

On the fifth day of the month of Isfandarmadh, which bore the same name as the month, there used once to be a festival called Muzhjiran, the Receiving of Gifts of Good News, which was preserved, in the early days of Islam, in the cities of Isfahan and Ray and in other parts of the Fahla country which has given its name to the Parthians and to the Pahlavi language, Fahla being the Arabized form of *pahlav* (*parthava*). It was the festival of the women, to whom the men gave generous presents. On this day charms against the bite of scorpions were written on square bits of papyrus ; these were placed on three walls of the house, the back wall being left bare.

THE MAZDEAN RELIGION AT THE PRESENT DAY

Persia to-day is overwhelmingly Muhammadan. The only Christians are the Armenians and the Aramæans of the Urmiyah region. There are a few Jews. The Mazdeans are reduced to small communities established at Yazd and in Kirman, from where a few colonies have gone out to the big towns, Tihran, Isfahan, and Shiraz, and to Baku, to the petroleum wells. They number only between eight and nine thousand. They are called Ghebers, or Gabars, from the Persian *gabr*, infidel, itself derived from the Arabic *kafir*, which has the same meaning ; but they themselves reject the insulting name, and call themselves Bihdin, ' Men of the Good Religion '. Since the Persian revolution the official name of the community has been Zardushti, ' Zoroastrian '.

A colony which left Persia at the beginning of the VIIIth century after Christ to seek a little more liberty than they enjoyed on the soil occupied by the Moslems settled in India and throve there. These are the Parsees, so called from their country of origin (*Parsa*, Persia). It was among them that Anquetil-Duperron found the Zend text of the Avesta and the Pahlavi text of the commentaries, and persuaded a kindly *dastur* to teach him the language. They embarked at Hurmuz on the Persian Gulf, after having stayed there fifteen years, and landed on the island of Diu, near the coast of Kathiawar. There they remained nineteen years, and then circumstances took them to Gujarat, where they disembarked at Sanjan in 716 A.D., and settled permanently with the permission of the native rulers. The Moslem invasion of 1315 compelled them to flee into the mountains of Bharhut, but, when the power of the conquerors weakened, they returned and founded settlements at Surat, Nausari, and Bombay.[1] It was during the domination of the Portuguese that they established themselves in this last town, which has remained the centre of their activity (1530-1666).

RITES AND CEREMONIES

The Persians give the Mazdeans the epithet of *atish-parast*, or fire-worshipper. For the adoration of fire is what strikes the stranger most, of all the rites which constitute the outward part of the Zoroastrian religion. Fire is the symbol of Ahura-Mazda ; it is possible that we have here remnants of nature worship on which a faith from outside has been superimposed. Fire burns on the altar before which Darius stands, and the supreme god hovers in the air above. The *baresma*, a kind of Lictor's bundle, made of sticks of wood, which the officiating person holds in his hand, is known to Strabo,[2] and so is the small veil (*paitidana, panom*) tied round the priest's mouth, to prevent his breath from polluting the fire.

The preparation and consecration of the sacred drink made of the *haoma* from the central point of Mazdean worship. In addition there are holy water (*zaothra*), the sacrifice of milk and butter, the distribution of gifts (*myazda*), and the offering of sacrificial bread (*draonah*). The ceremony of the *nirang* consists in the consecration of cow's stale (*gao maeza*), which is employed in all purifications. The blood-sacrifices mentioned by Herodotos and by local traditions have entirely disappeared from Mazdean ritual.

Careful purifications are enjoined upon the faithful. Every vessel, every utensil, every garment which is the least bit soiled is at once laid aside and thoroughly cleaned and purified by rubbing with earth and water mixed with cow's stale, or by burial in the ground for a fixed time. Something of this practice survives in the custom of the Shiite Moslems, who are careful to break immediately every vessel which has been touched by an

---

[1] On the history of this emigration we have a rhymed chronicle in Persian, entitled *Qissa-i-Sanjan*, which is translated into English in the *Journal of the Bombay Branch of the Asiatic Society*, vol. i, pp. 167-91. Cf. also Dosabhai Cramji Kareka, *History of the Parsis*, 2 vols., London, 1884 ; Seervai and Patel, *Gujarat Parsis*, Bombay, 1898 ; D. Menant, *Les Pasris*, Paris, 1898.

[2] xv.15, p. 733.

impure being, that is, not belonging to their faith. In consequence travellers have difficulty in obtaining food in certain Shiite villages, since the poor peasants hesitate to sacrifice their last crockery in hospitality to the passing infidel.

The *dakhma*, which European travellers call a Tower of Silence, is a building of a special character—a round enclosure with high walls, divided into compartments in which the bodies of the dead are exposed, soon to be torn to pieces by the vultures. When nothing is left but dry bones, these are collected in an ossuary. This is the Zoroastrian cemetery. They are generally built far away from the towns, in the hills.

CHAPTER IV

THE ARTS UNDER THE SASSANIDS

THE new dynasty, which tried to restore the ancient empire of Cyrus and Darius I, and succeeded at least in collecting into a single body the parts which tended to break away under the semi-feudal government of the Arsacids, and in extending the frontiers almost to where they had been before, did not have the architects which it deserved ; at least, methods of construction had changed, and the buildings made of inferior materials, have not resisted weather and all the other causes of destruction. The monuments which the Sassanids have left are in a wretched condition. They are of no interest save to architects, and archæologists are happy if they can find, here and there, a carved capital or details of ornament which add to their knowledge of the stage of development reached by the arts in this period.

In general, the north of Persia is very poor in remains. It is in Persis (Fars) and on the borders of Mesopotamia that the most imposing ruins are found. The district in which Darius I had set on the rock the great triplicate inscription recording the manner in which he had reconquered the country, the neighbourhood of Behistun, affords interesting remains of this later epoch. At Taq-i-Bustan, the ' Arch of the Garden ', near Kirmanshah, a site remarkable for the artificial lake which washes the foot of the mountain, we find capitals in which Græco-Byzantine and Roman influence is apparent. Here, too, is a relief representing three figures, two standing and trampling a captive on the ground ; there is no inscription to tell us what victory is thus recorded, but there can be no doubt about the period—types, costumes, and attributes are those of the coins left by the Sassanian kings.

But the most interesting monument is the vaulted chamber, cut in the rock, from which the site takes its name. In the spandrels of the arch outside are winged Victories, holding a libation cup in the left hand and a triumphal chaplet in the right. At the inner end of the vault, which is 20 feet wide, there is a relief of standing figures, with an inscription of Sapor I, and underneath it is a second relief, representing a mounted warrior ; he is supposed to be Chosroes II Parviz, but since there is no inscription, this attribution is purely hypothetical. This sculpture is striking, and when one examines it in detail one cannot help feeling some emotion ; here is one of the Persian horsemen (if it is the king, he is dressed like his

Fig. 28. CAPITAL AT TAQ-I-BUSTAN.

soldiers, only more richly) who so often defeated the Romans, and, under Chosroes II, conquered Syria, Jerusalem, and Egypt, and besieged the suburbs of Constantinople. Man and horse are armour-clad ; the warrior, in addition to his pointed helmet with its banderoles, is completely covered with a coat of mail, and his charger is likewise covered in armour. The warrior's arms are the lance and arrows, but one cannot see if he has the *kamand*, the lasso with a slip-knot with which the horseman sought to bring down his mounted opponent, in the manner familiar to readers of Firdusi's *Book of the Kings*.

Excavations in South Russia have enabled us to add some details to the above information.   The equipment of the kings varies little ; we have examples showing how they carried the

Fig. 29.   TAKHT-I-JIRRAH.

long sword on the left and the dagger on the right.   On the dish of King Sapor II, recently found at Pereshchepina near Poltava, we see a belt which is always double, and the sword drags on the ground.   In China, in the time of the Han dynasty, a curious influence of Persia is to be noted, as early as the period of the Parthians ; the cuirass of scales and of rings is introduced in the Chinese cavalry, cavalry tactics change, and the equipment is altered in accordance with Iranian models— bow and arrows, short lance, sword, dagger and horse-armour.[1]

Inside the great arch at Taq-i-Bustan, the side-walls are adorned with reliefs which have long attracted the attention of travellers and archæologists.   In these two pictures we see the great pastime of the lords of Iran, then and now—the

Fig. 30.   QASR-I-SHIRIN.

hunting of wild beasts in a walled enclosure by numbers of men on foot.   One picture represents a stag-hunt ; the other, which is still more remarkable, shows us a boar-hunt in a marsh, with female harpists following the party in boats.

The sumptuous garments worn by the figures in these reliefs make it possible to restore the ornament of valuable stuffs, and are irrefutable evidence of the art of the weaver in the early Middle Ages in the East.   The king's costume is made of

[1] Rostovtzeff, " Une trouvaille de l'epoque gréco-sarmate de Kertch," in *Mon. Piot*, vol. xxvi, pp. 133, 136.

a material adorned with winged dragons surrounded by a crown ; on another piece of stuff we see the crescent inside a crown ; and there are yet other motives.

The vault of the building is highly decorated, with coffers adorned with fanciful plants. Here we clearly see the influence of Byzantine art on survivals of the Hellenistic art preserved from the days of Alexander ; but the artists who executed the work were manifestly unskilful. Marcel Dieulafoy has established the identity of origin of the foliage of the capitals with the palmettes on the Susian friezes.

Fig. 31. HAUSH-KHURI.

Takht-i-Jirrah is at the top of the slope rising to the pass in the Zagros, on the road from Bagdad to Kirmanshah ; this always was and still is the chief way of communication between the plains of Mesopotamia and the high table-land of Iran. The Sassanids therefore took the greatest pains to keep this road in good condition, and it has been preserved and can be followed for several miles. At the top of the ascent there are a semicircular arch and some ruins. Was it a dedicatory chapel, announcing the completion of the road ?

As one goes down this road, one comes to Qasr-i-Shirin, the Castle of Shirin (the 'Sweet One'), the well-beloved of Chosroes II, whose name became legendary and has produced a whole cycle of poems in modern Persia. This, then, was the palace which the monarch built. It was surrounded by an immense park of about 300 acres, of which fragments of the surrounding wall have been found ; it comprised isolated villas ; and the remains of a stronghold which was occupied by the garrison can still be seen. The rooms of the palace are vaulted, but it is probable that the upper part was covered with wooden ceilings, as in the time of the Achæmenids.

One may here note the processes employed by the builders. All these edifices are made of rubble, round stones from the neighbouring silt, embedded in plaster. These rough walls were coated with a thick surface of plaster ; this coating has remained in places, and can be examined. The columns were of shaped bricks and plaster. All these were poor materials, and explain the speedy dilapidation of the buildings.

At this point one is quite near the old frontier of what was the Ottoman Empire. About half a mile away one sees a group of ruins, which the people of the country call Haush-Khuri in Kurdish, which means 'Farm of the Stable'. For the natives supposed that these were the stables of the palace, but it is a popular error. An examination of the plan shows that this building formed a complete palace.

The valley of the Sain-Mirrah is full of the ruins of cities. Zaich was once a city, of which a bridge of shaped stones survives. Qal'ah-i-Sam, the 'Fort of Sam ',[1] stands in the mountains ; its fortifications consist of round and square towers. At Shirvan only a heap of ruins remains.

A Sassanian monument which is still standing in great part is the Taq-i-Kisra, the 'Dome of Chosroes ', not far from the Tigris, below Bagdad. The place is marked by a Moslem shrine, that of Salman of Fars, known to-day as Salman-i-Pak, 'Salman the Pure '. It consists at present of a façade wall, broken by a vaulted hall (aywan). The vault is elliptical ; it collapsed only a few years ago, as a result of an earthquake. The building is of large white bricks. There were eight smaller halls, four on each side of the great audience-hall ; they

---

[1] A hero in the *Book of the Kings*, son of Neriman and grandfather of Rustam.

communicated with one another, but only the two first opened
on to the throne-room. The arches are semi-circular, but one
also finds pointed arches over internal spaces.

A new method of construction for Persia was the use of
courses of hard timber, laid in the masonry and connected at
the ends by collars, to resist the sagging of the walls. This
process, which was unknown to the ancient Persians, must
have been borrowed from the Romans; the Byzantines
used it frequently.

On the banks of the Karkha, sixteen miles north-west of Susa,
stands a building called the Taq-Aywan, or Kut Gapan. It has

Fig. 32. BRIDGE AT DIZFUL.

the appearance of a ruined Gothic cathedral, and consists of a
gallery some sixty feet long, in the middle of which was a dome.
It looks like a reduced copy of a royal edifice, for the use of a
provincial governor.

Another building classed among the Sassanian monuments
is the palace of Mashita, east of the Dead Sea. The style
of its decoration connects it with Byzantine influence. The
equilateral triangle is one of the most characteristic elements of
Susian-Achæmenian ornament.

Two bridges must certainly belong to this period—those at
Dizful and Shushtar, now ruined. The former is 415 yards

long and was originally 25 feet wide, but was later reduced, when the bridge was rebuilt, to 19 feet. The construction shows the use of Roman methods. The bridge at Shushtar runs across a dam. It was built by Roman engineers, as, indeed, tradition tells.

At Sarvistan, a fortified village on the road from Shiraz to Darabjird and Bandar Abbas, there are the ruins of a building crowned by an egg-shaped dome of brick, which Dieulafoy ascribed to the Achæmenian period, but without obtaining many adherents to his opinion. Firuzabad is the ancient Gur,

Fig. 33. Customs Gate in the Bakhtiyari Mountains.

to which the Buyid Adud ad-Dawla gave its present name, because *gur* was Persian for ' tomb '. According to the Arabian geographers Ibn al-Faqih and Istakhri, this city was founded by Ardashir, son of Babek ; it is therefore useless to look for the remains of an Achæmenian building in the ruins which it contains.

Dieulafoy has made a careful enumeration of the various sculptures which are to be seen at Naqsh-i-Rustam, the ' Sculptures of Rustam '. They are as follows : (i.) Two horsemen in royal costume, passing a crown from one to the other. One still holds the crown ; the other has his hand open.

The former carries a staff of command ; the latter is fanned by an attendant. (ii.) Three figures. The two men on the right correspond to the horsemen in the first relief ; the fan-bearer is replaced by a deity armed with a staff, which may be the *baresma* of Zoroastrian worship, mounted on a flower ; furthermore, the deity, who has a halo about his head, wears the same costume as the figure on the right. (iii.) On the right of No. i. The triumph of Sapor I over Valerian, with inscriptions in the Pahlavi language and script, commemorating the victory over the Romans at Edessa. (iv.) The king appears to be addressing his high officers, who stand behind a balustrade ; his head-dress

Fig. 34. RELIEF AT SHIKUFT-I-SALMAN.

is that of Bahram II. (v.) Warriors fighting on horseback. (vi.) A king, a queen wearing a mural crown, a child, and an officer ; the king and queen hold a crown over the child. (vii.) Sapor on a horse. Another relief, much defaced, represents a transmission of authority. These two last sculptures are in a small circular space opposite Naqsh-i-Rustam.

Lastly, on the road from Shiraz to the sea, some other monuments have been found, in various states of preservation, representing the defeat of the Emperor Valerian (a much defaced relief), the presentation of the Emperor Cyriades to the Romans, on whom he was imposed, Valerian compelled to do homage to Cyriades (nine compartments showing the king's escort and the Roman army), the triumph of Sapor (four compartments showing spoil-bearers), Bahram II and the submission of the Sijistanis, and the triumph of Chosroes I, who is shown seated and in full face, not in profile—a unique arrangement.

The architectural monuments afford no traces of painting, but this art must have been cultivated in Persia. The traditions of Persia attach to the name of the heresiarch Mani the memory of a book or album adorned with miniatures, which was called Arzheng. This is not a pure literary fancy,

Fig. 35. Relief at Naqsh-i-Bahram.

nor a fictitious tradition born of the desire of the people to have an artistic pedigree. We must go to Central Asia for evidence of it. Excommunicated and anathematized by Christians and Mazdeans alike, the followers of Mani, the Manichees, transported themselves to the regions bordering on the Desert of Gobi, the sands of which afterwards covered up flourishing cities, which have lately been brought to light. Several scientific missions have explored these regions, one British, led by Sir Aurel Stein, one German, led by Messrs. Grünwedel and von Le Coq, and one French, led by M. Pelliot. The second has brought back, among other things, frescoes which are now deposited in the basement of the Kaiser Friedrich Museum in Berlin, and have not yet been exhibited to the public. These frescoes represent Manichæan dignitaries, in their costume. They are Iranians; their white skins and abundant black beards leave no doubt of that. But it seems probable that these wall-paintings were done by Chinese artists, and we can hardly infer anything from them regarding the existence of Persian artists in Persia. It seems certain, however, that if these emigrant Persians had no objection to being represented on the walls of a distant country, they must have been acquainted with portraits of the kind at home, and been desirous that this mode of decoration should accompany them to the new country which persecution had driven them to make for themselves.

It is possible, too, to determine an Iranian influence, creeping in between the Indian and Chinese currents which accompanied the diffusion of Buddhism in eastern Turkestan when it once more became Chinese, after some years of independence. Not only do the Turfan frescoes show us Iranian lords, but even the picture of the Bodhisattva Vajrapani at Dandan Uiliq, near Khutan, shows us a Buddhist deity in the guise of a Sassanian king, with tiara, black beard, long green coat, Persian trousers, and gorgeous riding-boots.

At Bamiyan, on the edge of the Pamir, right in the Hindu-Kush, the discovery was made in 1923 of frescoes showing the same mixture of artistic influences. By the side of Buddhist motives there are figures of Iranian princes carrying a sword or a standard, and even a bearded personage, wearing the Sassanian tiara of globe and crescent combined, showing profound analogies with the portrait of Sapor I. preserved for us in sculpture. Those of these frescoes which date from the VIth century are contemporary with the time when Chosroes I annexed Bactriana to his dominions, about 560. So we seem to have irrefutable evidence of the existence of Sassanian painting.

CHAPTER V

The Origins of the Iranian Epic

BY the side of its real history, which we can only reconstruct by means of the information left us by the Greek and Latin authors, Persia has a mythical history in which, by unconscious euhemerism, ancient abstractions and deities have been transformed into princes of this real world. This history found magnificent expression, in the Xth century of our era, in the *Shah-Namah*, the 'Book of Kings', a poem of about 60,000 lines due to the the genius of Firdusi, a poet of Tus in Khurasan. In dealing with the reign of the Sassanids, we have to disentangle in this poem the contributions of the Avesta, its commentaries, and the Pahlavi literature of the period.

At the beginning two beings were created, Gayomaretan, the first man, and the primal Bull. For the first six thousand years of the world, they lived in joy and happiness, and then, by the mixture of the evil principle with the good, the present world came into being. Gayomaretan lived another thirty years, and the primal Bull died at the same time as he. The soul of the Bull became the guardian angel of cattle; fifty-five kinds of wheat and twelve kinds of useful plant were created from his body. As for Gayomaretan, his seed remained forty years buried in the earth, and then there sprang from it the first human pair, Mashya and Mashyana. These two were created pure, but the evil spirit soon took hold of them and clouded their thought; they began to lie and blaspheme, and so fell utterly into his power. It was to them that the heavenly spirits brought fire and taught the use of it; they made themselves axes of iron, cut down trees, and built a hut.

Seven couples were born of Mashya and Mashyana; Siyamek and Siyameki were one of these couples, and from them sprang Fravak and Fravakain, and from them fifteen couples who are the ancestors of the fifteen races of men.

205

The oldest mythical dynasty is that of the Paradhata or
Pishdadians (these two words have almost the same meaning,
' They of the Old Law '), and the first king of this line was
Haoshyangha or Hushang, who had power over the demons.
He was followed by Takhmo-urupa, or Tahmurath, who is
supposed to be descended from him.   His surname of Dev-band,
' Div-binder ', shows that his power, like his predecessor's,
extended to the supernatural world.   In his reign civilization
began to advance ; he taught men to weave wool, to feed the
domestic animals with grain and straw, to train the snow-
leopard or the cheetah, and various kinds of falcon, for
hunting, and to bring up cocks and hens.

He was greatly helped by his minister Shedasp, a pious
person who introduced the custom of morning and evening
prayers.   So Tahmurath made himself master of the demons
and was able to force Ahriman to act as his steed, and to run
all over the universe.   In his reign, so the *Bundahish* says,
men distributed themselves among the different climes of the
earth, and began to worship fire.   Great buildings were ascribed
to him, such as the old palace at Marv and a castle near Isfahan
where he placed the important books which he wished to save
from the Deluge.

Then came Jamshid, whose true name is Jam, for *shid* is an
adjective meaning ' shining ' ; he is the same as Yima, the
Indian Yama, the first man.   He is the happy ruler, in whose
reign there was no sickness or death or envy or wickedness or
hunger or thirst ; men multiplied so that the earth had to be
increased to three times its former size.   He dominated the
demons and drove them all into Hell, where he shut them in
with bolts and locks, so that in his reign they could not come
out.   It is also said that he was offered the task of proclaiming
the law, but refused because of the circumstances of the time ;
this part was reserved for Zoroaster.   In those days Jam was
continually in touch with Ahura-Mazda, and had frequent
conversations with him.   Jam taught men to eat meat in pieces,
for before him they did not eat it at all, and the custom seems
to have been general in his time.

About the end of Jam's reign there are two stories reproduced
in the Avesta, one in the *Vendidad* and the other in the *Yashts*.
At the end of the long and happy time during which Jam
reigned, Ahura-Mazda announced to him the approach of a

terrible winter ; heavy falls of snow would bring floods which
would cover the plains where the cattle used to feed.   He
therefore advised him to make a square enclosure called Vara,
' Garden ', and there to preserve a lighted fire, the seed of
cattle, draught-animals, and men, the seeds of the fairest trees,
and all kinds of food.   He was to stay there, according to the
Mainyo-i-Khirad, until the rain Malkosan should lay waste the
earth ; and afterwards he should repeople the earth with his
faithful folk.   According to the second version, which Firdusi
has followed, Jam's good fortune made him proud ; he thought
that he was God, and demanded to be paid divine honours.
When he declared this blasphemous belief, the glory which
surrounds kings and is the symbol of their majesty left him,
in the shape of a bird ; he was no longer worthy to rule, and
his kingdom presently fell into the hands of Dahak (*Azhi-
Dahaka*, ' the deadly snake ').

This Dahak, who bore the surname of Baevare-aspa, ' of the
ten thousand horses ', came from Babylonia, and his mother
was a direct descendant of Ahriman.   He was a snake with
three heads, three mouths, and six eyes.   He reigned for a
thousand years over Persia, which he conquered from Jam
without the latter being able to attempt resistance.   The end
of Jam is told in the *Garshasp-Namah* of As'adi the Younger of
Tus, Firdusi's nephew, whose epic, which preserves legends
of the Ghaznah region, is hardly fifty years later than the great
poet's masterpiece.   Dahak promised rewards to any who
should bring his enemy captive to him, and Jam had to wander
about the countryside and the desert.   After long wanderings,
he went to Kureng, the King of Zabul, that is, the district of
Ghaznah, and married his daughter.   From this marriage
sprang the line which afterwards gave the hero Rustam to
legend.   Being compelled, by the pursuit of his enemy, to
take once more to his adventurous wanderings, Jam made his
way at last to China, where he was seized by Dahak's men and
sawn in two.

In order to reign, Dahak needed the royal majesty, but it
could not belong to a wicked man ; he made efforts to obtain
it, but failed, and he remained a usurper.   But human brains
were required to feed the snake, or, according to the later
legend, the snakes which the kiss of Ahriman caused to grow
on the king's shoulders.   At Isfahan there was a smith named

Kava, all of whose sons save one had been taken to feed the serpent. When they tried to take his last son, he raised a rebellion, and fixed on the end of a spear the leather apron which he wore at his work. This was the banner of Iranian independence, and under the name of Dirafsh-i-Kaviyani, ' Banner of Kava ', it remained the national standard until the Arab conquest. A king was wanted ; one was found in the person of Thraetaona (Feridun), a descendant of Jam, who had been brought up in the hills by a herdsman. The new king did not let the service done to himself and his country by the smith go unrewarded ; he gave him the command of part of the army which he was raising to overthrow the tyrant, and the descendants of Kava at Isfahan were one of the first families of the Empire. Dahak was captured in Babylon and chained under Mount Damavand.

Thraetaona had three sons, Selm, Tur, and Iraj, among whom he divided the kingdom. Selm had for his share the cities of the West, Tur had Turkestan and China (from his name comes the term Turan which designates the country north of the Oxus), and Iraj got Iran. Selm and Tur were not content with their portions, and envied their brother, who had been given the land of their birth. They resolved to make away with him and he was killed by Tur. Their father was plunged in grief, and the only tie which bound him to life was the hope of seeing the death of his favourite son avenged. After the death of Iraj one of his wives gave birth to a daughter, who, when she grew up, was married to Pesheng, of royal race, and of this union Minuchihr (Manus-Chithra) was born.

This scion of an illustrious house was carefully brought up by his father, and surrounded by the heroes of the time. Selm and Tur tried in vain to make their father give him up to them. Having failed, they invaded the country. Tur was slain after a three days' battle. Efforts were made to prevent Selm from taking refuge in the forts of the Alans, that is, in the Caucasus ; in spite of the support of a son of Dahak, he was obliged to flee, and was captured and put to death. So Iraj was avenged, and Thraetaona could die in peace, after bequeathing his power to Minuchihr.

The successor of Thraetaona did great works. According to the legend, he caused the Indus and the Euphrates to be dug, and all the canals connecting the Tigris with the latter river ;

he is said to have made the first gardens, both for vegetables and for fruit. In his reign appears the great vassal family from which the hero Rustam sprang. Their ancestral domain was Sacastene, the present Sijistan ; they were the born defenders of Iran. One of the descendants of Jam and the King of Zabul's daughter was Garshasp, the father of Neriman, whose son was Sam ; Sam had a son Zal, who was the father of Rustam. This Zal was born with white hair, and at first nobody dared to announce his birth to his father. Sam took his son for a creature of Ahriman, and caused him to be exposed in the Alburz Mountains, where he was reared by the fabulous bird Simurgh (*Saena meregho*) a kind of vulture. The report of a young hero brought up in this extraordinary way reached the ears of Sam, who remembered that his son had been exposed in those parts. He wished to see him, and did so with the aid of the bird Simurgh, which gave him one of its feathers, telling him to throw it into the fire in case of danger, for it would come to his help. Minuchihr desired to see the wonderful youth, and was pleased with him ; he gave him the command of the South and sent him home to his country with his father.

While Sam was at the wars, Zal took to roaming about the country entrusted to his keeping. The king of Kabul, Mihrab, received him very kindly and invited him into his palace ; but Zal preferred to dwell in his tent, refusing to enter the house of an idolater (i.e., a Buddhist, as Spiegel ingeniously suggests). During this stay the young prince fell in love with Rudabeh, Mihrab's daughter. There were difficulties about concluding a marriage on account of the difference of religion and Minuchihr's fear that a child would be born of it who would one day be an enemy of Persia, for Mihrab was descended from Dahak ; but an astrologer removed all doubts, declaring that the stars were favourable and told that the child would be the defender of Iran. This child was Rustam, a kind of Hercules or Gargantua, a hero of marvellous strength, who, while still quite young, fought a raging elephant. His name is a relatively modern form of Rostahm and Rotastahm, in which it is easy to distinguish the adjective *takhma*, which means ' strong '.

The last years of Minuchihr's reign were unhappy, being marked by a war against Afrasyab (Franrasyan), King of Turan, who compelled the King of Persia to take refuge in the

swamps of Tabaristan, on the shores of the Caspian ; to him
the local traditions of that province ascribe ancient canals and
forts. Finally peace was concluded, and Minuchihr was
allowed to reign over the country, as far as he could shoot an
arrow. He shot from Mount Damavand, and the arrow fell
at Marv, or even, according to the Arabian historian Tabari,
on the banks of the Oxus.

Naudhar, whose name probably means ' the Young ' (*naotar*),
reigned eight months according to the author of the *Mujmal*,
and four years according to Firdusi, the only writers who
mention him. He remained shut up in his apartments,
amassing treasures and eating and drinking, and neglected to
render justice to his people. Disorders ensued, which were
only put down by the intervention of his great vassal, Sam, who
succeeded in convincing the king of the necessity of performing
his duties better. Naudhar was taken prisoner by Afrasyab,
who had invaded Persia, and was put to death by order of that
hereditary enemy of Iran.

He was succeeded by a grandson of Minuchihr, Uzava (Zav),
the son of Tumaspa (in the *Bundahish*, Takhmaspa, ' of the
strong horses ', in Persian, Tahmasp). This king made peace
with Turan, the Oxus becoming the frontier of the two kingdoms
and repaired the losses caused by the faults of his predecessor.

Then Rustam placed on the throne the founder of a new
dynasty, that of the Kaianids, so called because every king's
name is preceded by Kai. They correspond roughly to the
historical line of the Achæmenids, for they end with the
conquest of Alexander, but the incidents of the legend are
quite different from the history of the Achæmenids as we know
it. The first of the line was Kai Kobad (Kavi Kavata), who
reigned gloriously, the Turanian hordes having been vanquished
by Rustam. His capital was Persepolis, and he held the throne
for fifteen years. With his son and successor Kai Kaus (Kava
Usa), Persia once more entered upon a succession of perpetual
wars. In a campaign against Mazandaran, at that time
inhabited by demons, the king was taken prisoner with his
army and rescued by Rustam, who found him after seven
adventures related in the epic ; the seventh was that in which
the hero vanquished the White Demon, Div-i-Sipid. There
was an expedition by sea against Hamaveran, the name of
which very remotely recalls that of the Himyarite country,

Yemen. The king of the country was defeated, and gave his daughter Sudabeh in marriage to Kai Kaus, whom he invited to come and see him ; but on the way back the Berbers ambushed and captured Kai Kaus with all his retinue ; again he was delivered by Rustam. The wars were now ended, for the king ruled not only over men but over the demons ; believers and unbelievers obeyed him alike. With the aid of the demons, be built mighty fortresses in the Alburz ; but the demons, raging at being forcibly constrained, set a trap for him. One of them, disguised as a slave, caused him to believe that his empire should not be confined to the earth, but that he should seek how the sun ended its course. The king caused young eagles to be brought up, chose four, which he harnessed to his throne, and so soared into the air ; but when the eagles grew tired they came down, and left him at Amul in Mazandaran. Losing heart, the king did not wish to leave the forest in which he had fallen, but the great lords of the Empire, after long search, found him and set him on the throne again, where he once more enjoyed the favour of heaven and reigned in peace.

One episode of his reign was the story of Siyavush (Siyavaksh, Syavarshana), who was accused by Sudabeh, his father's wife, of seducing her, and proved his innocence by riding his horse down a narrow passage between two great fires. Afrasyab having once more set out to war, the young prince asked leave to fight him, and with the aid of Rustam defeated the Turanians before Bactra. Their king asked for peace, but Kai Kaus refused to ratify the treaty, whereupon Siyavush returned the hostages and went over to the enemy's camp, since he would not allow the breach of a pact solemnly concluded. He married Firingis, the daughter of Afrasyab, and their son was Kai Khosrau, who later ruled over Persia. Having been falsely accused of rebellion by a traitor, Siyavush was defeated, captured, and put to death.

His son had been brought up among the Turanians, but, since he was the lawful king, he had to be brought to Iran. This task fell on Giv, the son of Gudarz, who set forth alone and wandered seven years before he found the man he sought. At the end of that time he saw him hunting, and knew him by the majesty which stamped his whole person ; a black mark on his arm, which all the Kaianids had had since Kai Kobad, confirmed his birth. The history of Kai Khosrau is taken

up with long wars against Afrasyab, in which the Iranians are
sometimes victors and sometimes beaten ; however, in the end
the King of the Turanians was obliged to flee, and was taken
prisoner and slain near Lake Chaechast, that is, the Lake of
Urmiyah. Only at the end of these interminable battles, in
which the intervention of Rustam gave Persia the victory, did
Kai Khosrau ascend the throne as his grandfather's successor.
His reign was happy, for the hereditary enemy was gone, and
there was nothing left for him to do but to slay a dragon which
had taken up its quarters in the mountains between Fars and
Isfahan.

Kai Khosrau had only daughters, four in number ; it is
true that the Avesta gives him a son named Akhrura, but it
must be supposed that legend made him die before his father.
The king announced to his people that he had chosen for his
successor Lohrasp (Aurvat-Aspa), who is supposed to have been
of a collateral line. Then, wishing to be taken up into Heaven,
he set forth, climbing high mountains, and so came to a spring,
where he washed, and disappeared from before the eyes of some
comrades who had refused to leave him. They looked for him
in vain, and then all perished in a snowstorm and rejoined their
lord in the celestial regions.

Lohrasp had his capital at Bactra, where he set up a fire-
temple. This is not the only change which we find in his reign.
Hitherto, the Turanians have been represented in the legend as
being of the same religion as the Iranians ; now they are
idolaters, that is, probably, Buddhists. Their king is of the
race of Peghu, in which name the Turkish name Baighu can
easily be recognized. Legend here comes close to history ;
it is a projection into the past of the situation which the Arab
conquerors found when they crossed the Oxus for the first time
and came upon Turks, of whom some were Buddhists and
others Manichees. Lohrasp, in whose reign nothing especial
seems to have happened, had two sons, Gushtasp and Zarir.
The legend is devoted to the adventures of the former. Not
being treated by his father in the manner due to his position as
eldest son, he first decided to respond to the invitation of the
King of India, but gave up his plan on the representations of
Zarir, who pointed out how unbecoming it would be for one of
the true religion to accept the hospitality of an idolater. He
then went to the West and sought the humblest employment,

as a scribe, a groom, or a caravan-leader, but the nobility of his bearing prevented anyone from giving him work so unworthy of him. He became apprentice to a smith, but was so strong that he broke both iron and anvil. He was entertained by a *dihqan*, or land-owner of royal race ; that country gentleman persuaded him to present himself among the suitors who thronged about Katayun, the eldest daughter of the Greek Emperor. The princess saw in him the man of her dreams, and they were married, but the Emperor banished the young couple from his court. Having attracted attention by some deeds of prowess, Gushtasp was restored to favour, and finally returned to Persia, having obtained from the Emperor a promise to demand no more tribute. Here again we have a projection into the past of legendary events containing historical details which are not earlier than the time of the Sassanids. It is in the reign of Gushtasp that the legend places the appearance of Zoroaster.

In his life-time, Lohrasp had handed the Empire over to his son and had retired to the fire-temple of the city of Bactra. Arjasp (Arajat-Aspa), who had become King of Turan, resumed the war against Persia ; a bloody battle was fought near the Oxus, and the Iranians were victorious, as the wise minister of the king, Jamaspa, had foreseen, but Zarir, Gushtasp's brother, was killed. Later, Arjasp, learning that Bactra had no garrison, led an expedition against the city and took it. Lohrasp came out of his retirement and took up arms at the head of the townspeople, but fell in the battle. Gushtasp tried to recapture the city, but was beaten, and he and his troops had to take refuge in inaccessible mountains. The minister Jamaspa told the king that only his son, the prince Isfandiyar, could rescue him from his straits.

The wise minister undertook to persuade the king's son, who had been imprisoned on a false charge, to accept the part offered to him, and so to permit Gushtasp to abandon the throne and withdraw from the world. The arrival of Isfandiyar delivered the king and disheartened Arjasp, who had not expected to find a champion of such strength against him. Isfandiyar still had to release two princesses who had been carried off from Balkh by the Turanians, and in going to their rescue he had to go through seven adventures. Coming to the Castle of Bronze, he took it by a ruse and slew the enemy king.

Rustam, in his principality of Sijistan, had not adopted the new faith brought by Zoroaster. Isfandiyar was sent to fight him, but was killed by an arrow ; Simurgh, the fabulous bird which protected the race of the great vassal, had brought from the China Sea the branch from which the fatal shaft was cut. Rustam himself perished soon after by the treachery of Sheghad, his half-brother, the son of another mother, who caused him to fall, while hunting, into a pit filled with spears and swords.

Isfandiyar on his death was succeeded by Bahman, another son of Gushtasp. The first care of Bahman was to avenge the death of his brother, and he drove Feramorz, Rustam's son, out of Sijistan. Then came the reign of Queen Humai, Bahman's wife or daughter, of whom legend tells nothing, save that she was the mother of Darab, and abdicated in his favour. Darab made war on Philip of Macedon, and compelled him to give him his daughter in marriage, but repudiated her before she gave birth to the son with whom she was confined. This son was Alexander. So legend meets history ; the Persians would not own that they had been conquered by a foreigner, and they made the son of Philip into the son of one of their kings. Darab had a son of the same name as himself, who is known as Darab II ; he is Darius Codomannus. His cruelty and avarice made him hated. He sent to Alexander to demand the tribute promised by his father Philip, and the Macedonian seized the pretext to invade Persia. Here the purely Iranian legend stops ; the rest belongs to the legend of Alexander, which was composed at Alexandria into the romance known as that of the Pseudo-Callisthenes.

CONCLUSION

PERSIA still lives ; it has behind it twenty-five centuries of existence. It is a long and fine history. I know well that the introduction of Islam has transformed the manners of the people, the rules of their conduct, the principles of their legislation ; but profound observers, such as the Comte de Gobineau, will tell you that these modifications are superficial, and have not changed the old Persian soul, which still lives in the Persians of our own day. The Persians, who in the early Middle Ages had a profound influence on the evolution of the Moslem religion, have adopted a heresy more in conformity with their national aspirations ; they are Shiites, the followers of Ali and his successors, and have been so especially since an Iranian dynasty, that of the Safavids, tried, in the XVIth century, to restore the old empire of the Achæmenids and Sassanids, at least in the eastern parts of the State. These dervishes of Ardabil claimed descent from Muhammad's cousin and son-in-law, Ali ibn Abu Talib ; being adherents of Sufism, they found a chosen land in Persia ; moreover, Shah Ismail I, who conquered the country, was careful to put down all who maintained a contrary opinion.

The phenomenon which will always be a source of wonder is the establishment, in the VIth century B.C., of an immense monarchy which not only overthrew and succeeded the empires of Lydia and Babylonia (Nineveh, the capital of Assyria, had been destroyed fifty years before by the Medes), but also brought together a great number of peoples of different and, indeed, unknown origin, which had previously lived in barbarism and anarchy, and subjected to a single authority the vast tracts extending from the Indus valley in the east to the Dardanelles in the west. The conquest was the work of Cyrus, the organization was that of Darius I. Hellenic ideas, and above all the arts of Greece, would never have penetrated to the heart of Asia (we see in Herodotos in what a state of savagery the world was plunged outside the great monarchies !), if Alexander had had to deal, not with an empire already organized, but with thousands of tribes in a condition of anarchy. In this respect the heavy rule of the Satraps prepared the way for an advance of humanity, for a development of the peoples of Asia. The centralization was by no means perfect, for, in spite of all precautions, the Satraps still had too much independence ; there were not *Préfets* or Governors-General, but viceroys. Nevertheless, decisions affecting the whole State were taken at the court of the king, the true centre of these immense territories.

This huge body was held together by a strong administrative organization. The only really solid part of the army was formed by the King's Guard, the Immortals, and the other paid troops ; the rest consisted of native levies with their primitive armament, and later of Greek mercenaries. It was a military state ; science and art could not be born there. The former was represented solely by the Greek physician, trained in the schools of the Mediterranean, and the artists were likewise foreigners, Greeks, Lydians, or Egyptians. The scribes in the offices were Chaldeans or Aramæans, certainly Semites. The Achæmenids were able to combine all these forces, and in the dark night of the Middle Ages, when Persia no longer remembered her ancient kings, mythical figures out of the Avesta came and took the place of the real men who for two hundred years had borne the banner of civilization in the heart of Asia.

These princes saw things on a large scale. In their two capitals, Persepolis and Susa, they wanted gigantic palaces as the setting for magnificent ceremonies, the love of which is not lost in Iran to-day. To perpetuate their memory, they wrote the story of their great deeds on the sides of high mountains ; even if the inscriptions were never read by the passer-by, as is very likely, the sculptured scenes spoke to the eye, and in the XIXth century of our era the kings of the Turkoman dynasty of the Qajars tried to revive this proud custom, causing reliefs to be carved on the mountains near Tihran.

For a long time, it is true, the Achæmenian Empire pressed with all its weight upon Greece, but the Greeks, by the energy of their resistance and by their command of the sea, where they had hardly any opponents in the Persian fleet but the Phœnicians, were victorious. They checked the expansion of the Iranians westward, and ended, thanks to the Macedonians, by conquering their enemy. The history of ancient Persia well illustrates the intellectual energy which was latent in the Greeks and gradually revealed itself.

There is still much to be done for the scientific exploration of Persia. Before Marcel Dieulafoy, travellers, not being allowed to excavate, had had to content themselves with observing the monuments which existed in a ruinous condition above ground, and it must be acknowledged that they accomplished this hard task successfully. Dieulafoy did more ; he obtained from the Persian Government sole rights of excavation for France, and at once started to clear the ruins of Susa. After him, the work was carried on by Jacques de Morgan. The discoveries are of the first order, and have aroused the greatest interest all over the world ; but what the archæologists found did not take us one step forward in our knowledge of ancient Persia, for it was the earlier life of the city of Susa which was thus brought to light. Inscriptions and monuments revealed to us the long wars of the capital of Anshan, also called Elam or Elymais, with Babylonia. Father Scheil deciphered and translated the texts in the Anshanite language, and centuries of history, completely unknown, were disclosed in the light of modern knowledge. On the whole it is most fortunate that the ancients, all of them, used to build new cities on the ruins of the old cities destroyed in war, without clearing the ground or using the materials. So Troy has come to us, and excavation is bringing to light the sites of Babylonia and Assyria.

Outside Susa, Persia has not been excavated. An attempt has been made at Hamadan, the ancient Ecbatana, but, since the ancient city lies beneath the present one, which cannot be demolished, the enterprise was unsuccessful. It is unlikely that great cuneiform inscriptions will be found, for the Achæmenids were not great writers. M. Foucher's exploration of Afghanistan, recently opened to Europeans, has so far only reported Buddhist monuments and some of the Moslem period. In the neighbourhood of Damghan, on the road to Khurasan, there are ruins which probably belong to the Arsacid period, and it is generally agreed that Hecatompylos, one of the Parthian capitals, was here. Lastly, the plain over which the shapeless remains of Ray, the Rhages of the Book of Tobit, are scattered is the most accessible of the fields of excavation, for it is at the gates of Tihran. It is incessantly scoured by seekers of glazed pottery, which finds a profitable sale, and it is time to explore it scientifically, with soundings and trenches. The site is ancient and may have important surprises in store.

CHRONOLOGICAL TABLE

B.C.	PERSIAN HISTORY.	CONTEMPORARY EVENTS.
837	Parsua and Amadai mentioned in cuneiform inscriptions.	KINGS OF ASSYRIA Shalmaneser III.
824–812	Campaigns of the Assyrians.	Shamshi-Adad IV.
810	—	Adad-nirari III.
745		Tiglath-Pileser III.
722	Israelites transported to Media.	
715	Dayaukku taken prisoner.	
	MEDIAN EMPIRE	
708	Deioces founds the Empire of the Medes.	
655	Phraortes.	
633	Cyaxares. Scythian invasion.	
625	—	Death of Assurbanipal.
615	End of the Scythian invasion.	
585	Peace between Medes and Lydians.	
584	Death of Cyaxares.	
		GREEK HISTORY.
561	—	Peisistratos seizes the Acropolis of Athens.
550	Defeat of Astyages. End of the Median Empire.	
	THE ACHAEMENIDS	
558	Cyrus succeeds his father Kambujiya, King of Anshan.	
553	Cyrus rebels against Astyages.	
550	Defeat of Astyages. Fall of Ecbatana.	
546	Cyrus takes the title of King of Persia. He attacks Croesus.	
545–539	Wars in the East.	
539	Fall of Babylon.	
538	Cyrus enthroned as King of Babylon.	Return of Peisistratos.
536	Rebuilding of the Temple of Jerusalem.	
528	Cambyses.	Death of Peisistratos.
525	Conquest of Egypt.	
522	Revolt of Gaumata the Magus. Death of Cambyses.	
521	Murder of Gaumata. Darius I. Fall of Babylon.	
519	Oroetes, Satrap of Lydia, disappears.	
517	Darius in Egypt.	
514	Scythian campaign.	
510	—	Hippias driven out of Athens.
508	First Athenian Embassy.	
506	Second Athenian Embassy.	
499–494	Ionian Revolt.	
498	Sardes taken by the rebels.	

B.C.	PERSIAN HISTORY.	CONTEMPORARY EVENTS.
494	Naval battle at Lade.	
493	Thrace recovered.	
492	Mardonius recalled.	
490	Battle of Marathon.	
486	Xerxes I.	
484	Defeat of Khabbisha in Egypt.	
481	Campaign in Greece, Battle of Salamis.	
479	Battle of Platæa.	
465	Xerxes assassinated. Artaxerxes I.	
462	Revolt of Hystaspes.	
455	Revolt of Egypt.	
449	Peace of Cimon.	
424	Xerxes II. Darius II.	431–404. Peloponnesian War.
405	Revolt of Egypt.	
404	Artaxerxes II. Mnemon.	
403	—	Expulsion of the Thirty Tyrants.
401	Battle of Cunaxa. Retreat of the Ten Thousand.	
387	Peace of Antalcidas.	
380	Campaign in Cyprus.	
358	Artaxerxes III.	
356	Flight of the Satrap Artabazus.	
353	First Egyptian campaign.	355–338. Sacred War.
348	Second Egyptian campaign.	
345	Conquest of Egypt.	
340	—	Philip of Macedon besieges Perinthus.
338	—	Battle of Chæroneia.
336	Death of Artaxerxes III.	
335	Darius III Codomannus.	Alexander.
334	Battle of the Granicus.	
331	Battle of Gaugamela.	
330	Murder of Darius III.	
327	Alexander in India.	
325	Nearchus brings the Greek fleet back from India.	
323	Death of Alexander.	
	THE PARTHIAN ARSACIDS	
322	—	Lamiac War.
319	Death of Antipater.	
312	The Seleucids.	
279	—	Delphi pillaged by the Gauls.
261	Bactriana makes itself independent.	
250	Arsaces founds the Parthian dynasty.	
247	The Parthian age.	
223	—	Victory of Antigonos Doson, King of Macedon, at Sellasia.
220	Bagakert I, Priest-king of Persepolis.	
214–196	Artabanus.	

B.C.	PERSIAN HISTORY.	CONTEMPORARY EVENTS.
174–136	Mithradates.	146. Mummius takes Corinth.
76	Sanatroices.	123–63. Mithradates VII, King of Pontus.
69	Phraates III.	
60	Mithradates III.	
56	Orodes.	ROMAN HISTORY.
53	Battle of Carrhæ. Death of Crassus.	
52–48	—	Rivalry of Cæsar and Pompey. Battle of Pharsalos.
51	Attack on Antioch.	
42	—	Battle of Philippi.
39–33	Wars in Parthiene and Armenia.	
38	Battle of Gindarus.	
37	Phraates IV.	
31	—	Battle of Actium.
29	—	Augustus.
A.D.		
14	—	Tiberius.
37	Artabenus.	Caligula.
41	—	Claudius.
51–75	Vologeses I.	54–117. Nero, Galba, Vespasian, Titus, Domitian, Nerva, Trajan.
123	Peace with Hadrian.	117–192. Hadrian, Antoninus, Marcus Aurelius, Commodus.
148–191	Vologeses III.	
199	Pillage of Ctesiphon under Septimius Severus.	
211	—	Death of Septimius Severus.
217	—	Death of Caracalla.
	THE SASSANIDS	
224	Revolt of Ardashir I.	
225	Tiridates, Priest-king of Persepolis.	
226	Ardashir I enters Ctesiphon.	
237	Capture of Nisibis and Harran.	
241	Sapor I.	236–244. Gordian III.
244–270	—	Philip the Arabian, Decius, Valerian, Gallienus, Claudius II.
270–275	—	Aurelian.
271	—	Fall of Palmyra.
272	Hormazd I.	
273	Bahram I.	
276	Bahram II.	276–282. Probus.
283	—	Death of Carus.
293	Bahram III, Narses.	284–305. Diocletian.
297	Loss of Armenia.	
303	Hormazd II, Adhernarses.	
310	Sapor II.	306–337. Constantine I.
340	Siege of Nisibis.	337–340. Constantine II.

A.D.	PERSIAN HISTORY.	CONTEMPORARY EVENTS.
345	Battle of Singara.	337–353. Constans I, Constantius.
359	Fall of Amida.	
361–363	—	Julian the Apostate.
379	Ardashir II.	363–383. Jovian, Valentinian I, Gratian.
383	Sapor III, Bahram IV.	378–395. Theodosius I.
399	Yazdigird I.	395–408. Arcadius, Theodosius II.
420	Bahram V Gur.	
421	Peace with the Romans.	
438	Yazdigird II.	
451	Battle of Avarair.	
453	—	453. Marcian.
457	Hormazd III.	Leo I.
459	Death of Hormazd III.	
474	—	Leo II.
479	Peroz, Balash.	474–491. Zeno the Isaurian.
488	Kavadh.	
491	—	Anastasius I.
497	Jamasp, Kavadh again.	
503	Fall of Erzerum and Amida.	
518	—	Justin I.
527	War with Romans.	527–565. Justinian I.
531	Battle of Callinicon. Chosroes I.	
540	Capture of Antioch.	
553	Battle of the Phasis.	
570	Conquest of Yemen.	
579	Hormazd IV.	
582	—	Maurice.
590	Chosroes II.	
602	—	Phocas.
614	Capture of Jerusalem.	610-641. Heraclius.
624	The Romans recover Asia Minor and Armenia.	
628	Siroes, Ardashir III, Puran, Azarmidukht, Hormazd V.	
632	Yazdigird III.	
638	Embassy to China.	
642	Battle of Nahavand.	
651	Murder of Yazdigird III.	
661	Peroz given the government of Persia by the Chinese.	
668	—	Constantine IV Pogonatus.
674	Peroz goes to the Emperor of China.	
677	Mazdean temple built in China.	
685	—	Justinian II.
707	Narses, son of Peroz, returns to China.	
711	—	Philippicus.
722	Pu-shan-hwo, King of Persia.	717–741. Leo. III, the Isaurian.
728–729	Khosrau, King of Persia.	
732	A Nestorian monk sent to China as ambassador of the King of Persia.	

BIBLIOGRAPHY

NOTE.—Certain English editions are quoted in square brackets; but the references in the footnotes do not refer to these editions.

CLASSICAL AUTHORS

HERODOTOS   I

CTESIAS, *Persica*, Gilmore's ed., London and New York, 1888   II

XENOPHON, *Anabasis*   III

XENOPHON, *Cyropædia*   IV

STRABO   V

DIODORUS SICULUS, *Bibliotheca Historica*   VI

GENERAL WORKS

CHAMPOLLION-FIGEAC, *Histoire de la Perse*, 1859   VII

Encyclopædia Britannica, art. " Persia "   VIII

GEIGER (Wilhelm) and KUHN (Ernst), *Grundriss der iranischen Philologie*, vol. ii, Strasburg, 1896-1904. (Geography, pp. 373 ff.; Achæmenids, by F. JUSTI, pp. 395 ff.; Parthians, by JUSTI, pp. 477 ff.; Sassanids, by JUSTI, pp. 512 ff.)   IX

Grande Encyclopédie, art. " Perse," by C. HUART   X

GROUSSET (René), *Histoire de l'Asie*, vol. i, pp. 305 ff., Paris, 1921–2   XI

GUTSCHMID (Alfred von), *Geschichte Irans und seiner Nachbarländer*, Tübingen, 1888   XII

HALL (H.R.), *The Ancient History of the Near East*, London, 1913   [5th ed., 1920]   XIII

HOMMEL, *Grundriss der Geographie und Geschichte des alten Orients*, 1889, 2nd ed., 1904   XIV

LENORMANT (François), *Histoire ancienne de l'Orient*, 9th ed., revised by E. BABELON, vols. v, vi, 1881–8   XV

MARQUART (J.), *Researches into the History of Iran*, 1905 (an English translation of *Untersuchungen über die Geschichte von Eran*, 1896–1905)   XVI

MASPERO (Sir Gaston), *Histoire ancienne des peuples de l'Orient classique*, 8th ed., Paris, 1909. [*The Dawn of Civilization*, 5th ed., London, 1910; *The Struggle of the Nations*, 2nd ed., London, 1910; *The Passing of the Empires*, London, 1900]   XVII

MASPERO (Sir Gaston), *Les Empires*, Paris, 1899. [*The Passing of the Empires*, London, 1900]   XVIII

MEYER (Eduard), *Geschichte des Altertums*, 2nd ed., vol. i, Heft 2, Stuttgart and Berlin, 1909   XIX

MORGAN (Jacques de), *Mission scientifique en Perse*, vol. iv, Paris, 1896   XX

NOELDEKE (Th.), *Aufsätze zur persischen Geschichte*, Leipzig, 1887, translated by O. Wirth : *Études historiques*, 1896   **XXI**

PERROT (Georges) and CHIPIEZ (Charles), *Histoire de l'art dans l'antiquité*, Paris, 1881-1911. [The volumes quoted are translated as : *A History of Art in Chaldaea and Assyria*, London, 1884 ; *History of Art in Phrygia*, etc., London, 1892 ; *History of Art in Persia*, London, 1892]   **XXII**

PRÁŠEK (Justin V.), *Geschichte der Meder und Perser bis zur makedonischen Eroberung* (in *Handbücher der alten Geschichte*, 1st series, 5, Abt. 1), Gotha, 1906, 1910   **XXIII**

PRÁŠEK (Justin V.), *Forschungen zur Geschichte des Alterthums*, Leipzig, 1897-1900   **XXIV**

RAWLINSON (George), *The Five Great Monarchies of the Ancient Eastern World*, vol. iii, London, 1871-6   **XXV**

SYKES (Sir Percy M.), *A History of Persia*, London, 1915. [2nd ed., 1921]   **XXVI**

ACHÆMENIAN PERIOD

ABBOT (Jacob), *Life of Cyrus*, 1900   **XXVII**

Academy, no. 17, 1880, *Conquest of Media and Babylonia by Cyrus*, by A. H. SAYCE   **XXVIII**

Academy, no. 18, 1880, *The Medic Origin of Zoroastrianism*   **XXIX**

Academy, no. 18, *Rise of the Persian Empire*, by A. H. SAYCE   **XXX**

AHL (A. W.), *Outlines of Persian History, based on the Cuneiform Inscriptions*, London, 1923   **XXXa**

BABELON (Ernest), *Les Perses achéménides, les satrapes, et les dynastes tributaires de leur empire, Chypre et Phénicie.* (*Catalogue des monnaies grecques de la Bibliothèque Nationale*), Paris, 1893   **XXXI**

BANG (Willy), *Zur Erklärung der Achœmeniden-Inschriften*, 1899   **XXXII**

BARTHOLOMÆ (Christian), *Altiranisches Wörterbuch*, Strasburg, 1904   **XXXIII**

BARTHOLOMÆ (Christian), *Zum altiranischen Wörterbuch. Nacharbeiten und Vorarbeiten*, Strasburg, 1906   **XXXIV**

BERTIN, "Herodotus on the Magians," in *Journal of the Royal Asiatic Society*, vol. xxii   **XXXV**

BEZOLD (Carl), *Die grosse Darius-Inschrift auf den Felsen von Behistun : Transscription des babylonischen Textes mit Übersetzung und Commentar*, 1881   **XXXVI**

BEZOLD (Carl), *Die Achœmenideninschriften : Transscription des babylonischen Textes, nebst Übersetzung, textkritischen Anmerkungen, und einem Wörter- und Eigennamenverzeichnisse . . . mit dem Keilschrifttexte der kleineren Achœmenideninschriften*, autographiert von P. HAUPT, Leipzig, 1882   **XXXVII**

BOOTH (Arthur J.), *The Discovery and Decipherment of the Trilingual Cuneiform Inscriptions*, London, 1902   **XXXVIII**

BUEDINGER (M.), *Die neuentdeckten Inschriften über Cyrus*, 1881   **XXXIX**

CASARTELLI (L. C.), "La Religion des rois achéménides d'après leurs inscriptions," in *Comptes rendus du IIIe Congrès scientifique international des Catholiques*, 1894, Brussels, 1895   **XL**

CLEMEN (Carl), *Fontes historiæ religionis Persicæ* (Greek and Latin texts), Bonn, 1920 — XLI

CLEMEN (Carl), *Die griechischen und lateinischen Nachrichten über die persische Religion* (in *Religionsgeschichtliche Versuche und Vorarbeiten*, vol. xvii, Heft 1), Giessen, 1920 — XLII

CLAY (A. T.), "Gobryas, Governor of Babylonia : brief notes," in *Journal of the American Oriental Society*, vol. xli, no. 5, Newhaven, Conn., 1922 — XLIIa

CLERMONT-GANNEAU (Charles), *Origine perse des monuments araméens d'Égypte*, no date. (Only part i has appeared) — XLIII

COWLEY (Arthur E.), *Jewish Documents of the Time of Ezra* (translated from the Aramaic version of the Behistun inscription), London, 1919 — XLIV

COWLEY (Arthur E.), *Aramaic Papyri of the Fifth Century* B.C., Oxford, 1923 — XLV

COX (Sir George W.), *The Greeks and the Persians*, London, 1876 — XLVI

DADACHANJI (Ervad Jamaspi), "On the Cyropedia," in *Journal of the Bombay Branch of the Royal Asiatic Society* — XLVII

DALTON (Ormonde M.), *The Treasure of the Oxus, with other objects from ancient Persia and India* (Franks Bequest, British Museum) (Treasure of the Oxus : vessels, gold plaques, rings, armlets and torques, etc. ; objects from ancient Persia : silver vessels from Armenia, silver vessels of the Sassanian period), London, 1905. [2nd ed., 1926] — XLVIII

DHORME, "La Fin de l'empire assyrien d'après un nouveau document," in *Revue Biblique*, vol. xxxiii (1924), pp. 218 ff. — XLIX

DHORME, "Les Aryens avant Cyrus," in *Conférences de St.-Étienne*, 1910-11, pp. 98 ff. — L

DIEULAFOY (Marcel), *L'Acropole de Suse*, Paris, 1890 — LI

DIEULAFOY (Marcel), *L'Art antique de la Perse*, Paris, 1884-9 — LIa

FLANDIN (Eugene) and COSTE (P.), *Voyage en Perse pendant les années* 1840 *et* 1841, Paris, 1843-54 — LII

FLUEGEL, *Cyrus und Herodotus*, Leipzig, 1881 — LIII

FOY (W.), *Zur altpersischen Inschrift NRd.*, 1908 — LIV

GADD (Cyril J.), *The Fall of Nineveh : the newly discovered Babylonian Chronicle*, no. 21,901 *in the British Museum*, edited with transliteration, etc., London, 1923 — LV

GARDNER (Percy), *The Gold Coinage of Asia before Alexander the Great*, London, 1908 — LVI

GEIGER (W.), *Ostiranische Kultur im Alterthum*, Erlangen, 1882 — LVII

GEIGER (W.), *Civilization of the Eastern Iranians in Ancient Times* (an English translation of the above), London, 1885-6 — LVIII

GEIGER (W.) and SPIEGEL (Friedrich), *The Age of the Avestà and Zoroaster* (English translation), London, 1886 — LIX

GODSPEED (G. S.), "The Persian Empire from Darius to Artaxerxes," in *Biblical World*, Oct., 1889 — LX

GRAY (Louis H.), "The Religion of the Achæmenian Kings according to the Non-Iranian Inscriptions," in *Journal of the American Oriental Society*. (See LXXII below) — LXI

GUNE (P. D.), " The Indo-Iranian Migrations in the Light of the Mitani Records," in *Journal of the Iranian Association*, vol. x (1921), no. 3, p. 81   **LXII**

HALÉVY (J.), " Cyrus et le retour de l'exil," in *Revue des Études juives*, 1880, p. 171   **LXIII**

HARLEZ (C. de), " La Religion persane sous les Achéménides," in *Revue de l'Instruction publique en Belgique*, xxxvii   **LXIV**

HEAD (Barclay V.), *The Coinage of Lydia and Persia, from the earliest times to the fall of the dynasty of the Achæmenidæ*, London, 1877   **LXV**

HERZFELD (E.), *Pasargadæ : Untersuchungen zur persischen Archæologie* (topography, archæology), 1908   **LXVI**

HERZFELD (E.), *Am Tor von Asien : Felsdenkmale aus Irans Heldenzeit*, 1920. (Cf. Sir T. W. ARNOLD, in *Bulletin of the School of Oriental Studies*, ii (1921-2), p. 161)   **LXVIa**

HIRSCHY (N. C.), *Artaxerxes III Ochus and his Reign, with special consideration of the Old Testament sources bearing upon the period* (Berne Dissertation), Chicago, 1909   **LXVII**

HIRTH, *Die Indo-Germanen*, p. 108 (Indian names in the Tell el-Amarna Letters)   **LXVIII**

HOFFMANN-KUTSCHKE (A.), *Die altpersischen Keilschriften des Grosskönigs Dārajawausch des Ersten bei Behistun*, Stuttgart and Berlin, 1909   **LXIX**

HOFFMANN-KUTSCHKE (A.), *Die Wahrheit über Kyros, Darius, und Zarathuschtra*, 1910   **LXX**

HOWART (H. H.), " The Beginning of Persian History," in *Academy*, 1892   **LXXI**

JACKSON (Abraham V. Williams), " The Religion of the Achæmenian Kings. First series : The Religion according to the Inscriptions," with an Appendix by L. H. GRAY on the non-Iranian inscriptions, in *Journal of the American Oriental Society*, vol. xxi, pp. 160-84, and vol. xxiv, pp. 91-2. Summarized in GEIGER and KUHN, **IX** above, vol. ii, pp. 687 ff.   **LXXII**

JACKSON (Abraham V. Williams), " Textual Notes on the Old Persian Inscriptions," in the same journal, vol. xxvii (1906)   **LXXIII**

JACKSON (Abraham V. Williams), *Persia Past and Present : a book of travel and research*, New York, 1906   **LXXIV**

JUSTI (F.), *Geschichte des alten Persiens*, Berlin, 1879   **LXXV**

JUSTI (F.), *Iranisches Namenbuch*, Marburg, 1895   **LXXVI**

JUSTI (F.), *Ein Tag aus dem Leben des Königs Darius*   **LXXVII**

KERSHASP (Pirozeshah), *Studies in Ancient Persian History*, London, 1905   **LXXVIII**

KING (Leonard W.) and THOMPSON (R. C.), *The Sculptures and Inscription of Darius the Great on the Rock of Behistûn in Persia : a new collation of the Persian, Susian, and Babylonian texts, with English translations, etc.*, London, 1907   **LXXIX**

LAGRANGE, " Religion des Perses," in *Revue Biblique*, 1904, pp. 40, 188   **LXXIXa**

LINDL (Ernst), *Entstehung und Blüte der alt-orientalischen Kulturwelt : Cyrus*, Munich, 1903   **LXXIXb**

MEILLET (Antoine), *Grammaire du vieux perse*, Paris, 1915   **LXXIXc**

MENANT (J.), *Les Achéménides et les inscriptions de la Perse*, 1872 — LXXX

MEYER (Eduard), "Das erste Auftreten der Arier in der Geschichte," in *Sitzungsberichte der preussischen Akademie* Cf. OLDENBERG, in *Journal of the Royal Asiatic Society*, 1909, p. 1096, and 1910, p. 849 — LXXXI

MORGAN (Jacques de), *Mission scientifique au Caucase : études archéologiques et historiques*. Vol. i, *Les Premiers Âges des métaux dans l'Arménie russe* ; vol. ii, *Recherches sur les origines des peuples du Caucase*, 1889 — LXXXII

MORGAN (Jacques de), " Histoire de l'Élam " (Susa excavations, 1897-1902), in *Revue Archéologique*, vol. xl (1902) — LXXXIII

MORGAN (Jacques de), " Le Plateau iranien pendant l'époque pléistocène," in *Revue de l'École d'Anthropologie*, 19th year, vol. vi (1907), pp. 189-203 — LXXXIV

MORGAN (Jacques de), *Les Premiéres Civilisations : étude sur la préhistoire et l'histoire jusqu'à la fin de l'empire macédonien*, 1909 — LXXXV

MORGAN (Jacques de), *Manuel de numismatique orientale*, Paris, 1923. (Only no. 1 has appeared) — LXXXVI

MORGAN (Jacques de), *Mémoires de la Délégation en Perse* : vol. viii, *Recherches archéologiques*, 3rd series ; article on pottery, Paris, 1905 — LXXXVII

OBST (Ernst), *Der Feldzug des Xerxes* (Klio, Beiheft xii), Leipzig, 1913 — LXXXVIIa

OPPERT (J.), *Commentaire historique et philologique du Livre d'Esther d'après la lecture des inscriptions perses*, 1864 — LXXXVIII

OPPERT (J.), *Der Kalender der alten Perser*, 1898 — LXXXIX

PERR (A.), *Cyrus, the Lord's Anointed*, 1901 — XC

PILLET (E.), *Le Palais de Darius à Suse* — XCI

PINCHES, " On a Cuneiform Inscription relating to the Capture of Babylon by Cyrus " (fragment of the Annals of Nabonidus), in *Transactions of the Society of Biblical Archœology*, vol. vii (1882), pp. 139, 176 — XCII

POTTIER (E.), MORGAN (J. de), and MECQUENEM, *Mémoires de la Délégation en Perse* : vol. xiii, *Céramique peinte de Suse et petits monuments de l'époque archaïque* — XCIII

PRÁŠEK (Justin V.), *Kyros der Grosse*, Leipzig, 1912. *Dareios*, Leipzig, 1914 — XCIV

PRÁŠEK (Justin V.), *Geschichte der Meder und Perser*, Gotha, 1906-10 — XCIVa

PRÁŠEK (Justin V.), *Forschungen zur Geschichte des Alterthums*, Leipzig, 1897-1900 — XCIVb

RADET (G.), " La Première Incorporation de l'Égypte à l'empire perse," in *Revue des Études anciennes*, July-Sept., 1909, pp. 201-11 — XCV

RAMKRISHNA GOPAL BANDHARKAR (Sir), " The Aryans in the Land of the Asurs," in *Journal of the Bombay Branch of the Royal Asiatic Society*, 1918, p. 768 — XCVI

RAWLINSON (Sir Henry C.), *The Persian Cuneiform Inscription at Behistun, decyphered and translated, with a memoir on Persian cuneiform inscriptions in general and on that of Behistun in particular*, London, 1847 — XCVII

RAWLINSON (Sir Henry C.), "Proclamation de Cyrus aux
Babyloniens," in *Journal of the Royal Asiatic Society*,
vol. xii, pp. 70 ff.   XCVIII

RAWLINSON (George), *The Five Great Monarchies of the
Ancient Eastern World*, vol. iii, London, 1871-6   XCVIIIa

RIDGEWAY (Sir William), *The Origin and Influence of the
Thoroughbred Horse*, Cambridge, 1905   XCIX

ROSEN (Friedrich), "Der Einfluss geistiger Strömungen auf
die politische Geschichte Persiens," in *Zeitschrift der
deutsch. morgenl. Gesellschaft*, Heft i, 1922   XCIXa

ROSTOVTZEFF (Mikhail I.), *Iranians and Greeks in South
Russia*, Oxford, 1922   C

ROZIÈRE (de), *Notice sur les ruines d'un monument persépolitain
découvert dans l'isthme de Suez*, no date   CI

SARRE (Friedrich E.) and HERZFELD (E.), *Iranische Felsreliefs:
Aufnahmen und Untersuchungen von Denkmälern aus
alt- und mittelpersischer Zeit*, Berlin, 1910   CII

SCHRADER, *Chronique de Cyrus (Keilinschriftliche Bibliothek*,
iii, part ii, pp. 130 ff.). *Beiträge zur Assyriologie*, vol. ii,
pp. 214, 235 ff.   CIII

SCHUKOVSKIJ (W. A.), *Die Alterthümer von Transkaukasien :
Die Ruinen der alten Merv (Materialien zur Archæologie
Russlands*, no. 16), St. Petersburg, 1894 (in Russian)   CIV

SPIEGEL (F.), *Eranische Alterthumskunde*, Leipzig, 1871-8.
[*Iranian Art*, London, 1886]   CV

SPIERS (Richard P.), *Architecture East and West : a collection
of essays written at various times . . . now first
brought together and issued with further illustrations*,
London, 1904   CVI

STOLZE (Franz), *Persepolis : die achæmenidischen und sasanidischen Denkmäler und Inschriften . . . zum ersten
Male photographisch aufgenommen von F.S. Mit einer
Besprechung der Inschriften von* T. NÖLDEKE, Berlin,
1882   CVII

THUREAU-DANGIN (François), *Une Relation de la huitième
campagne de Sargon*, Paris, 1912   CVIII

TOLMAN (Herbert C.), *The Behistan Inscription of King Darius :
translation and critical notes. The Persian text with
special references to recent re-examination of the rock
(Vanderbilt Univ. Studies*, no. 1), Nashville, Tenn., 1908   CIX

TOLMAN (Herbert C.), *Ancient Persian Lexicon and the Texts
of the Achæmenid Inscriptions, transliterated and translated with special reference to their recent re-examination
(Vanderbilt Univ. Studies*, nos. 2-3), 1908   CX

TOLMAN (Herbert C.), *Cuneiform Supplement (autographed)
to the author's Ancient Persian Lexicon and Texts, with
brief historical synopsis of the language (Vanderbilt Univ.
Studies)*, 1910   CXI

WEISSBACH (Franz H.), *Uber einige neuere Arbeiten zur
babylonisch-persischen Chronologie*, 1901   CXII

WEISSBACH (Franz H.), *Die Keilinschriften der Achæmeniden*,
critical edition, in transcription, with translation, introduction, notes, and index, Leipzig, 1911   CXIII

WILHELM (Eugen), *Konigtum und Priestertum im alten Eran*,
1886. [*Kingship and Priesthood in Ancient Erân*,
Bombay, 1892]   CXIV

WINCKLER (Hugo), "Boghaz-Keui," in *Mitteilungen der
Deutschen Orient-Gesellschaft*   CXV

WINCKLER (Hugo), "Die Arier in den Urkunden von Boghaz-
Köi," in *Orientalistische Literaturzeitung*, 1910, p. 289   CXVI

PARTHIAN PERIOD

ALLOTTE DE LA FUYE, *Étude sur la numismatique de la Perside*,
1906   CXVII

ALLOTTE DE LA FUYE, "Observations sur la numismatique de
la Perside," in *Journal Asiatique*, Nov.-Dec., 1906,
pp. 517 ff.   CXVIIa

GARDNER (Percy), *The Parthian Coinage*, London, 1877   CXVIII

GAUTHIOT (R.), "Iranica," in *Mémoires de la Société de
Linguistique*, vol. xix (1915), pp. 125 ff.   CXIX

LACOUPERIE (Albert E. J. B. Terrien de), *L'Ère des Arsacides
en 248 av. J.-C. selon les inscriptions cunéiformes*,
Louvain, 1891   CXX

MARKOFF (A. de), *Les Monnaies des rois parthes*, 1877.   Supplement to *Prokesh-Osten* under same title, 1875   CXXI

MEILLET (A.), "Emprunts faits par l'arménien," in *Mémoires
de la Société de Linguistique*, vol. xvii, pp. 242 ff. ; vol.
xviii, pp. 110, 248   CXXIa

MEILLET (A.), "De l'influence parthe sur la littérature
arménienne," in *Revue des Études arméniennes*, vol. i, no. 1   CXXIb

PETROWICZ (A. von), *Arsaciden-Münzen-Katalog*, 1904   CXXII

WILHELM (E.), "Die Parther," in *Avesta, Pahlavi, and Ancient
Persian Studies in honour of Peshotanji Behramji Samjana*
1st series, Strasburg, 1904   CXXIIa

WROTH (Warwick W.), *Catalogue of the Coins of Parthia*, etc.
(*Catalogue of the Greek Coins in the British Museum*),
London, 1903   CXXIII

SASSANIAN PERIOD

PROSPER (Alfaric), "Zoroastre avant l'Avesta," in *Revue
d'histoire et de littérature religieuses*, no. 1, Paris, March,
1921   CXXIV

PROSPER (Alfaric), *Les Ecritures manichéennes : leur constitution, leur histoire*, Paris, 1918-19   CXXIVa

ALLOTTE DE LA FUYE, "Observations sur la numismatique
de la Perside" (see **CXVIIa** above)   CXXV

AVERY (J.), "The Place and Times of the Rise of Zoroaster,"
in *American Antiquarian and Oriental*, vol. ix   CXXVI

BARKER, Sidelights on the Sassanians   CXXVII

BARTHOLOMÆ (Christian), "Zum sasanidischen Recht," in
Sitzungsberichte der Akad. der Wiss. of Heidelberg, 1922   CXXVIIa

BARTHOLOMÆI (J. de), *Collection de monnaies sassanides de feu
. . . J. de B. . . . publiée par* B. DORN,
St. Petersburg, 1873   CXXVIII

BLOCHET (Edgard), *Catalogue des manuscripts mazdéens (zends, pehlvis, parsis, et persans), de la Bibliothèque Nationale,* Paris, 1900   **CXXIX**

BLOCHET (Edgard), *Textes pehlevis inédits relatifs à la religion mazdéenne,* 1895   **CXXX**

BLOCHET (Edgard), *Études sur l'histoire religieuse de l'Iran,* 1898-9   **CXXXa**

BODE (Clement A. G. P. L. de), Baron, *Travels in Lauristán and Arabistán,* London, 1845   **CXXXI**

BURNOUF (Eugène), *Études sur la langue et sur les textes zends* (extract from the *Journal Asiatique*), Paris, 1840-50 (only vol. i has appeared)   **CXXXII**

CHRISTENSEN (Arthur), *L'Empire des Sassanides : le peuple, l'État, la cour* (Memoirs of the Danish Royal Academy, 7th series, Literature section, vol. i, no. 1), Copenhagen, 1907   **CXXXIII**

COURET (Alphonse) Count, *La Prise de Jérusalem par les Perses en 614 : trois documents nouveaux,* Paris, 1897   **CXXXIV**

CUMONT (Franz), *Textes et monuments figurés relatifs aux mystères de Mithra, publiés avec une introduction critique,* Brussels, 1896-9. [*The Mysteries of Mithra,* London, 1903]   **CXXXV**

CUMONT (Franz), *Sur un passage de Diodore relatif à Zoroastre,* 1900   **CXXXVI**

DARMESTETER (James), *Le Zend-Avesta ; traduction nouvelle avec commentaire historique et philologique,* Paris, 1892-3   **CXXXVII**

DARMESTETER (James) and MILLS (L. H.), *Zend-Avesta Translated* (*Sacred Books of the East*), London, 1883-95   **CXXXVIII**

DARMESTETER (James), " Lettre de Tansar au roi de Tabaristan," in *Journal Asiatique,* 1894, vol. i, pp. 236 and 521   **CXXXIX**

DHALLA (Maneckji Nusservanji), *Zoroastrian Theology, from the earliest times to the present day,* New York, 1914   **CXL**

DROUIN (Edme A.), *Observations sur les monnaies à légendes en pehlvi et pehlvi-arabe,* Paris, 1886   **CXLI**

DROUIN (Edme A.), *L'Ère de Yezdeguerd et le calendrier perse,* 1889   **CXLII**

DROUIN (Edme A.), *Notice sur quelques monnaies bilingues sassanides,* 1890   **CXLIII**

DROUIN (Edme A.), *Une Médaille d'or de Kobad,* 1893   **CXLIV**

DROUIN (Edme A.), *Monnaies de la reine sassanide Boran ou Pourandokht,* 1893   **CXLV**

DROUIN (Edme A.), *Les Légendes des monnaies sassanides,* Paris, 1898   **CXLVI**

DROUIN (Edme A.), *Histoire de l'épigraphie sassanide,* Louvain 1898   **CXLVII**

FLUEGEL (Gustav L.), *Mani, seine Lehre und seine Schriften : ein Beitrag zur Geschichte des Manichäismus, aus dem Fihrist des Abu'l faradsch Muḥammad ben Isḥak al-Warrâk . . . im Text nebst Übersetzung,* Leipsig, 1862   **CXLVIII**

GAUTHIOT (Robert), *Essai de grammaire sogdienne ; Part i, Phonétique,* Paris, 1914-23 (Only pt. i has appeared)   **CXLVIIIa**

GOTTHEIL (Richard), *References to Zoroaster in Syriac and Arabic Literature* (*Classical Studies in Honour of Henry Drisler*), New York, 1894   **CXLIX**

GUETERBOCK (Carl), *Byzanz und Persien in ihren diplomatisch-völkerrechtlichen Beziehungen im Zeitalter Justinians*, Berlin, 1906   **CXLIXa**

HARLEZ (Charles de), *Avesta, livre sacré des sectateurs de Zoroastre*, translated from the Zend text, 1876   **CL**

HARLEZ (Charles de), *Der avestische Kalender und die Heimath der Avesta-Religion*, 1882   **CLI**

HENRY (Victor), *Le Parsisme* (Zoroaster, morality, legislation, funerary code, etc.), 1905   **CLII**

HERZFELD (Ernst), *Die Aufnahme des sasanidischen Denkmals von Paikuli* (*Abhandl. der preuss. Akad. d. Wiss.*, no. 1), Berlin, 1914. (Analysed in *Zeitschr. d. deutsch. morgenl. Ges.*, vol. lxviii (1914), p. 465)   **CLIIa**

JACKSON (Abraham V. Williams), *Zoroaster, the Prophet of Ancient Iran*, New York, 1899   **CLIII**

JACKSON (Abraham V. Williams), " On the Date of Zoroaster," in *Journal of the American Oriental Society*, vol. xvii, Newhaven, Conn., 1896   **CLIV**

JACKSON (Abraham V. Williams), "The So-called Injunction of Mani, translated from the Pahlavi of Denkart," in *J.R.A.S.*, April, 1924, pp. 213 ff.   **CLIVa**

JACKSON (Abraham V. Williams), " Studies in Manichæism," in *Journal of the American Oriental Society*, vol. xliii, 1923   **CLIVb**

INOSTRANTSEV (Konstanty A.), *Études sassanides*, St. Petersburg, 1909. (In Russian, with a résumé in French)   **CLV**

JOHANNAN (A.), "Another Old Syriac Reference to Zoroaster," in *Journal of the American Oriental Society*, vol. xliii (1923)   **CLVa**

JUSTI (F.), *Der Bundehesh, zum ersten Male herausgegeben, transscribiert, übersetzt, und mit Glossar versehen*, 1861   **CLVI**

KAPADIA (S. P.), *The Teaching of Zoroaster and the Philosophy of the Parsee Religion*, London, 1913   **CLVII**

LABOURT (Jérôme), *Le Christianisme dans l'empire perse* (*Bibliothèque de l'enseignement de l'histoire ecclésiastique*), Paris, 1904   **CLVIII**

LE COQ (Albert von), *Ein manichäisch-uigurisches Fragment aus Idikut-Schähri*, 1908   **CLIX**

LE COQ (Albert von), *Ein christliches und ein manichäisches Manuskriptfragment in türkischer Sprache aus Turfan* (*Chinesisch-Turkistan*), 1909   **CLX**

LE COQ (Albert von), *Die buddhistische Spätantike in Mittel-asien:* Part ii, *Die manichäische Miniaturen*, Berlin, 1923   **CLXa**

LE STRANGE (Guy), *The Lands of the Eastern Caliphate* (Cambridge Geographical Series), Cambridge, 1905   **CLXI**

LONGPÈRIER (H. A. P. de), " Explication d'une coupe sassa-nide," in *Ann. de l'Institut Archéologique*, 1848   **CLXII**

LONGPÈRIER (H. A. P. de), *Observations sur les coupes sassanides*, 1868   **CLXIII**

MAÇOUDI (MAS'UDI), *Les Prairies d'or*, text and translation by C. BARBIER DE MEYNARD, vol. iv, Paris, 1865   **CLXIV**

MARTIN (Fredrik R.), *A History of Oriental Carpets*, Vienna, 1906-13. (See pt. i, *Sassanidian and Susandschird Carpets*)   CLXV

MEILLET (A.), "Zoroastre," in *Journal Asiatique*, 1916, i, p. 128   CLXVI

MENANT (D.), art. "Gabars", regarding the Zoroastrians who remained in Persia, in HASTINGS (James), *Encylopædia of Religion and Ethics*, Edinburgh, 1908 etc.   CLXVII

MILLS (L. H.), "Origin of the Religion of the Avesta," in *Journal of the Royal Asiatic Society*, 1888, and 1889, p. 273   CLXVIII

MODI (Jivanji Jamshedji), *The Religious System of the Parsis*, 2nd ed., Bombay, 1908   CLXIX

MODI (Jivanji Jamshedji), *Marriage Customs among the Parsees ; their comparison with similar customs of other nations : a paper read before the Anthropological Society of Bombay*, Bombay, 1900   CLXX

MODI (Jivanji Jamshedji), *The Funeral Ceremonies of the Parsees, their Origin and Explanation*, 2nd ed., Bombay, 1905   CLXXI

MODI (Jivanji Jamshedji), *Memorial Papers :* no. 8, pp. 113-126 (on Mazdak, reprinted from the *Memorial Volume in honour of Dastur Hoshang Jamasp of Poona*, Bombay, 1918), Bombay, no date (1922)   CLXXIa

MOULTON (James H.), *Early Zoroastrianism*, London, 1913   CLXXII

MUELLER (F. W. K.), *Handschriftenreste*, pt. ii, 1904. (Cf. ANDREAS in *Sitzungsberichte* of the Berlin Academy, 1910, pp. 307 ff.)   CLXXIIa

NOELDEKE (A.), *Keramik von Raqqa, Rhages, und Sultân-âbâd*   CLXXIII

PUMPELLY (R.), *Explorations in Turkestan (Publications of Carnegie Institution, Washington)* : i, *Expedition of 1903* (no. 26, 1905) ; ii, *Expedition of 1904* (No. 73, 1908)   CLXXIV

SILVESTRE DE SACY (Antoine Isaac), *Mémoires sur diverses antiquités de la Perse, et sur les médailles des rois de la dynastie des Sassanides*, Paris, 1793   CLXXV

SALEMANN (C.), *Manichäische Studien*, i, *Die mittelpers. Texte in revidierter Transscription, mit glossar und grammatischen Bemerkungen*, St. Petersburg Acad., 1908   CLXXVI

SMITH (Vincent A.), "Invasion of the Panjab by Ardashîr Pâpakân (226-240)," in *J.R.A.S.*, 1920, p. 221   CLXXVII

SPIEGEL (F.)., *Avesta, die heilige Schrift der Parsen, aus seinem Grundtext übersetzt mit Rücksicht auf die Tradition*, 1852-63   CLXXVIII

WILHELM (E.), *Königtum und Priestertum im alten Eran* (see CXIV above)   CLXXVIIIa

WOLFF (F.), *Avesta-Ubersetzung auf der Grundlage von Chr. Bartholomæ's Wörterbuch*, Strasburg, 1910. (Reprinted, Berlin, 1924)   CLXXIX

INDEX

233